The IRA 1956–69

MANCHESTER
1824

Manchester University Press

The IRA 1956–69

Rethinking the Republic

Matt Treacy

Manchester University Press

Manchester and New York

distributed in the United States exclusively by Palgrave Macmillan

Published by Manchester University Press
Oxford Road, Manchester M13 9NR, UK
and Room 400, 175 Fifth Avenue, New York, NY 10010, USA
www.manchesteruniversitypress.co.uk

Distributed exclusively in the USA by
Palgrave, 175 Fifth Avenue, New York NY 10010, USA

Distributed exclusively in Canada by
UBC Press, University of British Columbia, 2029 West Mall,
Vancouver, BC, Canada V6T 1Z2

British Library Cataloguing-in-Publication Data
A catalogue record for this book is available from the British Library

Library of Congress Cataloging-in-Publication Data
A catalog record for this book is available from the Library of Congress

ISBN 978 0 7190 8472 0 *hardback*
ISBN 978 0 7190 9120 9 *paperback*

First published by Manchester University Press 2011

First digital paperback edition published 2014

Printed by Lightning Source

Contents

Acknowledgements	*page* vi	
List of abbreviations	vii	
Introduction	1	
1	The 1956–62 armed campaign and the reorganisation of the IRA	9
2	The ideology of traditional republicanism	27
3	Abstentionism and the growth of internal divisions	45
4	The Wolfe Tone Society and the Communists	63
5	The year 1966 and the revival of the IRA 'threat'	88
6	Towards the National Liberation Front	120
7	The Northern crisis and the split	152
Epilogue	189	
Glossary	195	
Select bibliography	196	
Index	205	

Acknowledgements

I would like to thank foremost Professor Eunan O'Halpin for his assistance and patience on waiting for me to complete the thesis on which this book is based, and invaluable advice along the way. I would also like to thank my late mother Patricia, and my father Jimmy who on several occasions insisted that I should continue despite competing pressures.

A number of people have been extremely generous in the giving of their time to be interviewed, allowing me to read documents in their possession and to engage in written correspondence. They include Ruairí Ó Brádaigh, Seán Garland, Tom Mitchell, Seán Ó Brádaigh, Seán Dunne, Shay Courtney, Tony Meade, Anthony Coughlan, Roy Johnston, Seán Bermingham, Martin Casey, Jim Lane, Jim Monaghan, Cathal Mac Liam, Eoin O Murchú and others who prefer to remain anonymous. I would also like to thank Brian Hanley for sharing his views, and the occasional document, pertaining to the subject under review.

I would like to thank the staff of the National Library of Ireland, of Trinity College Library, of the Public Records Office of Northern Ireland, the Public Records Office London and the National Archives of Ireland for their assistance.

And finally, I wish to dedicate it to my daughter Ciara who showed me the virtue of never giving up in overcoming meningitis.

Abbreviations

AKEL	Progressive Party of Working People Cypriot Communist Party
ATGWU	Amalgamated Transport and General Workers Union
BCP	British Communist Party
CIA	Central Intelligence Agency
CPGB	Communist Party of Great Britain
CPI	Communist Party of Ireland
CPNI	Communist Party of Northern Ireland
CYM	Connolly Youth Movement
DFA	Department of Foreign Affairs
DUP	Democratic Unionist Party
EEC	European Economic Community
EOKA	Ethniki Organosis Kyprion Agoniston (National Organisation of Cypriot Fighters)
ESB	Electricity Supply Board
ETA	Euskadi Ta Askatasuna Basque Homeland and Freedom
FBI	Federal Bureau of Investigation
FCO	Foreign and Commonwealth Office
FTA	Free Trade Agreement
GAA	Gaelic Athletic Association
GHQ	General Headquarters Staff
GOC	General Officer Commanding
GPO	General Post Office
HA	Home Affairs
ICO	Irish Communist Organisation
ICTU	Irish Congress of Trade Unions
IRA	Irish Republican Army
IRPB	Irish Republican Publicity Bureau
ITA	Irish Telephonists Association
ITGWU	Irish Transport and General Workers Union
IWL	Irish Workers League
IWP	Irish Workers Party

JIC   Joint Intelligence Committee
MI5   Military Intelligence 5
MI6   Military Intelligence 6
MPs   Members of Parliament
NAI   National Archives of Ireland
NATO   North Atlantic Treaty Organisation
NICRA   Northern Ireland Civil Rights Association
NILP   Northern Ireland Labour Party
NLF   National Liberation Front
NLI   National Library of Ireland
ODESSA   Organization Der Ehemaligen SS-Angehörigen (Organisation of
           former SS members)
OIRA   Official Irish Republican Army
PRONI   Public Records Office Northern Ireland
RSF   Republican Sinn Féin
RTE   Radio Telifis Eireann
RUC   Royal Ulster Constabulary
TCD   Trinity College Dublin
TD   Teachtai Dála Members of Irish parliament
UCD   University College Dublin
UVF   Ulster Volunteer Force
WO   War Office
WTS   Wolfe Tone Society

Publisher's note

Mr Anthony Coughlan wishes to state that he has never been a member
either of the British or the Irish Communist Parties and that any statement or
implication to the contrary contained herein is untrue.

Introduction

While several small rainforests have been consumed in the production of books about the Irish republican movement and the conflict in Northern Ireland since 1969, comparatively little has been written about the period that preceded the crisis and the revival of militant and armed republicanism.

This book looks at the IRA and Sinn Féin between the 1956–62 'border campaign' and 1969. The campaign itself is dealt with in the first chapter as the event that brought about the internal debate after 1962. I examine developments within the movement with regard to internal structural and ideological changes, but also in relation to the movement's relationship with Irish society at a time of rapid social and economic change, and the reaction of the two Irish states and the British state towards any potential threat posed by militant republicanism.

It is important I think in looking at this period to treat it in the context of its own time rather than through the prism of the much more dramatic events which took place after 1969. This is something that has, I believe, been a weakness of much of what has been written, with the earlier period seen in connection to the later events almost as a causative factor. That the IRA did consciously plan the conflict is still an article of faith for many Unionists. My contention is that not only was the republican movement not a key factor in bringing about what happened after 1969, much less a conscious instigator of the crisis, but that radical republicanism was a marginal force carried along for a time on the tide of events beyond its control. I also argue that the movement was primarily occupied with politics in the 26 rather than the 'Six Counties'.

Those who have treated of the period have generally done so as a minor chapter in the history of armed republicanism.[1] Indeed, for many, radical republicanism is regarded as barely relevant except in those periods when it is actively involved in armed struggle. There have been some academic research theses partly covering the period[2] and a number of published works based on more extensive treatment of the ideological changes within the republican movement in the 1960s.[3] The most important of these is Hanley and Millar's *The Lost Revolution* which devotes some space to the same period I deal with but which concentrates on what took place within the Official Republican Movement after 1969. Patterson has explored the ideological issues at the heart of the debate in the 1960s in his study of left republicanism but devotes little attention to the ideological motivations of traditionalist republicans.[4] Very little in the way of political science or sociological work[5] has referred to the republican movement in the 1960s but there has been quite a deal of biographical material dealings with the period, in lesser or greater depth.[6] Most deals with the 1960s as a minor prelude to the events which took place after 1969. Roy Johnston's *Century of Endeavour* is a recent exception to that rule. There have been books written by or about people who were involved in the civil rights movement and which have treated in lesser or greater degree of the republican movement's involvement in the Northern Ireland Civil Rights Association. Purdie's book is probably the most comprehensive survey although I would take issue with some of what he says regarding the role played by the republican movement within NICRA.[7] Finally there have been studies of the Irish state's policy toward Northern Ireland and the IRA which have touched on the republican movement in the period under review.[8]

There have been a variety of approaches to the subject, ranging from the traditional historical narrative and the anecdotal and almost folkloristic approach of Bowyer Bell and Coogan to the high journalistic work of Moloney, Bishop and Mallie and others, through the ideological critiques of Patterson, Bew, Walsh and Foley; the political science perspective as represented by McGarry, O'Leary and O'Malley,[9] although with even less attention paid to the pre-1969 period; the recent treatment of the history of ideas within the republican tradition by Richard English; and finally republicanism as a study in revolutionary violence or counter-terrorism as evidenced by the work of Kelley, M. L. R. Smith, Wright,[10] Taylor and others. But again the limited extent to which any of the above have focused on the period and issues which are examined here has to be stressed.

Smith has referred to the difficulty of obtaining reliable evidence on the internal workings of the republican movement.[11] That is something which it shares with other revolutionary and secretive organisations, which means that much documentary evidence on such groups comes from the state, a source that is not always reliable given the fact that much of that information comes from paid informants and may be tainted by the need to present the material in a certain light. None the less such material is valuable and I have used it extensively, particularly where it concerns the British, Northern Irish and Irish authorities' assessment of the security threat posed by the IRA. Some of this, for example the extensive 1966 report on the IRA compiled by Garda Special Branch, has been referred to in other published work. I would place a radically different interpretation on that report to that made by others, including a leading protagonist who was made aware of the report by the author.[12]

It is clear from Garda intelligence and other official sources that the Irish government had an excellent insight into the republican leadership, provided by at least one long-term informant within the upper levels of the IRA and Sinn Féin. That obviously coloured the government's own assessment of the potential threat, which it rated as low for most of the period, and of which they in turn sought to persuade the British. The informants and their relationship to the internal divisions within the movement may also have been crucial in the development of the crisis involving government ministers supplying weapons to the IRA, and to the state's response to the two different factions of the IRA following the split.

By their nature secret organisations tend not to maintain archives. There are however significant documents available from within the IRA and Sinn Féin and the Wolfe Tone Society and I have used any which have become available to me either through official sources, where the Gardaí or RUC captured IRA documents, or from individual republicans who have copies of such material. Such documentation, along with published internal material, has been important in shedding light on the political and ideological developments within the movement. The republican press was also an important source, particularly the *United Irishman* which was published monthly throughout the period, with varying levels of circulation; from over a hundred thousand in 1957 to probably less than five thousand by 1967. In its pages can be traced the changes to the political and ideological direction of the movement and it provided a forum in which the conflicting factions did battle over issues like abstentionism and socialism.

The other main source was a number of interviews with republicans who were active at the time, some of them in leading positions as members of the IRA Army Council and the Sinn Féin Ard Comhairle or in the Wolfe Tone Society. A number of them were key figures in the political developments that took place after 1962 and the split in 1969. Their evidence was extremely useful in elucidating and clarifying what was found in official and internal documents, and in revealing certain events that were unknown to me. There is considerable debate over the use, and reliability, of oral sources. Berkhofer refers to this in the context of whether it is possible to represent divergent views of historical events properly.[13] Others question its validity in comparison to textual sources[14] but there are those who champion it from a (sometimes ideologically informed) perspective on presenting history from the point of view of subordinate groups.[15] Some indeed have privileged oral accounts of the great events of the twentieth century.[16]

I have also looked at the existing British intelligence reports, particularly those from the Joint Intelligence Committee, which illustrate the generally low level of threat which the British security service believed emanated from the IRA between the ending of the 1956–62 campaign and 1969. I assess that material in the light of the response of the Northern Ireland authorities to the crisis after 1968 and the effect which the RUC Special Branch claim of an imminent IRA campaign in 1965/66 may have had on the attitude of London to the Irish republican movement. The fact that the RUC reports were mistaken or greatly exaggerated possibly persuaded the security service to take even less of an interest than it might have done otherwise, and the IRA was rated as only sixth in a list of threats to internal security. Indeed the available Belfast files also paint a less dramatic picture of the level of concern there after 1966 compared to that which the Unionists presented to London. Both the Irish and British records belie the claim made by some historians such as Taylor, Geraghty and English that the 1966 commemorations were the catalyst for the northern crisis.[17] Evidence from contacts between Irish military intelligence (G2), MI5 and the CIA would also suggest that the IRA was of little concern.[18]

I was given access to the minutes and correspondence of the Wolfe Tone Society which provide a valuable parallel to what was going on within Sinn Féin and the IRA given the role played by individuals prominent in or close to the latter. I also gained access to internal documents and other material from the Irish Workers Party / Communist Party of Ireland, although several requests to be given access to its own archive were unanswered. If there are significant lacunae in this survey one relates to the role of the British and Irish Communist Parties and possibly the Soviet Union. That makes it impossible to draw definite conclusions regarding certain issues touched on here which must await hopefully future access to various archives, both official and otherwise.

I also look at the influence of Catholic social teaching on radical republicans, something that has received little attention in comparison to a substantial body of work on the influence of Marxism. Roy Douglas's excellent book on Ailtirí na hAiséirghe illustrates the substantial work that remains to be done on this topic for other periods. There has also been a related tendency I think to oversimplify this issue, with traditional republicanism being portrayed either as an apolitical military tradition or as a right-wing Catholic tendency differing from the Irish state and its legitimising ideology only in relation to its attitude towards force and the institutions of state. Douglas has argued that there was a uniquely Irish variant of radical right-wing ideas and some of this was certainly reflected in the ideology of the republican movement.

In contrast to most treatments, I have examined the content of traditional republican ideology and the influence of Catholic social teaching as interpreted as part of a radical critique of the Irish state. That critique had remained remarkably consistent within traditional republicanism from the 1920s. Indeed, far from republicans having embarked on a radical departure from official state attitudes in the 1960s under the influence of the leftist modernisers, it was more a case of the elite shedding the vestiges of economic nationalism and isolationism which they shared with republicans. Contrary to the left-wing critique of traditional republicanism as little different from Fianna Fáil, in fact it has been the more orthodox left-wing elements within republicanism, both in the 1960s and more recently, which have come to an accommodation with economic and other orthodoxies. Traditionalist republicanism remains outside the mainstream discourse of Irish politics as a separate and coherent trend, albeit a marginal one. That marginalisation has to a great extent been self-imposed, and the motivations of the modernisers in attempting to broaden the appeal of republicanism were understandable. However, as this book and indeed the more recent history of the Provisionals demonstrates, once a revolutionary movement accepts the parameters of constitutionalism and makes a serious attempt to win electoral support it is forced to jettison much of its ideological *raison d'être*, not least its commitment to armed struggle.

The modernisers have often tended to be depicted as having moved, or attempted to move, republicanism towards a more democratic position. Such an interpretation aligned itself with the modernisers' own view of what had taken place within the movement, and with the more favourable attitude taken by most academic and other observers during the northern conflict when the modernising faction, as Official Sinn Féin / The Workers Party / Democratic Left, was regarded, perhaps understandably, as a more benign element than the traditionalist Provisionals.

That however also led to a less critical interrogation of the motivations and roots of the influence of the Marxists, and of the nature of the ideology and the organisations which were the source of their critique of traditional republicanism. Even some who were sympathetic to the Provisionals have depicted the leftist departure of the 1960s as a positive development. I have attempted to balance that with a more critical view of the influence of the Marxist left, which was 'alien' within the context of both republicanism and Irish society, and the role of individuals and organisations from outside the movement of whom many republicans were suspicious. That aspect has been largely overlooked with some commentators like English depicting the Connolly Association as 'socialist republican' and downplaying the actual links between key modernisers and the Communists. Others have questioned whether republicanism and socialism are compatible at all. Although sympathetic to the modernisers' objective of demilitarising republicanism, Patterson describes left republicanism as a 'pathological' expression of real left-wing politics.[19] That view is shared by Walsh, who claims that Johnston and Greaves exaggerated the historical importance of the socialist republican element.[20]

One other minor theme was the influence of events internationally in 1968 on what was happening in Ireland. It is clear, from the testimony of some of those involved,[21] official sources and the actual nature of radical activity in Ireland, that many people were aware of, and in some instances directly influenced by, what was happening in Paris, the United States and elsewhere. This is examined in Simon Prince's book on the more radical student element within the civil rights movement, as is the extent to which whatever provocation may have been present emanated from there rather than the IRA.[22] The year 1968 was also identified as pivotal in the evolution of the republican movement by Bowyer Bell.[23] The seeming openness of Goulding and other modernisers to more militant tactics after 1968 may also have reflected not only the developing situation in the North but also a generalised feeling among radicals that conditions were perhaps more conducive to militancy including the use of arms. Interestingly, the caution of Johnston, Coughlan and Greaves reflected a similar uneasiness about the 'new left' shared by the orthodox Moscow-oriented Communist movement. From the state's perspective, the events in France in particular must have increased anxiety over the influence of radical movements, particularly in the context of their being involved in what was clearly an increasingly popular movement for democratic rights in Northern Ireland. The Irish state was certainly concerned, as can be seen from the official records from 1968 and 1969, over the implications which the Northern crisis might have had for the stability of the southern state.

I use the terms 'modernising' and 'traditionalist' to describe the two factions because they are the most accurate and neutral descriptions of the conflicting wings of the republican movement, and are generally accepted and understood among most historians and commentators on the period. Labelling the two factions left and right, as is sometimes done, is too simplistic and is often based on subjective bias.

I am aware that this book is somewhat 'Dublin-centric'. That reflects the fact that the available internal and official sources mainly concern Dublin and the fact that the IRA and Sinn Féin leadership during the period was mostly Dublin-based. I am conscious that this colours the overall impression especially given the paucity of available material on the republican movement in the north. It might also be regarded as weakening my contention that the movement was a far more minor factor in the civil rights movement and the crisis which developed in reaction to it than is sometimes alleged. However, the impetus for republican involvement came from Dublin-based individuals and the Wolfe Tone Society and that is treated in some depth. The IRA and Sinn Féin did not dominate the Civil Rights Association, and its members were as much taken by surprise and influenced by what happened in 1968 and 1969 as anyone else. This also explains to a large extent the disjunction between the response to the crisis of the northern republican grassroots, many of them influenced by the militant tactics of Peoples Democracy, and the Dublin-based leadership.

My hope then is that in examining the different aspects of the republican movement during this time I have provided some new insights into the history of the period and added to the existing body of work that deals with the IRA and Sinn Féin and their relationship to the broader events of that period.

Notes

1 J. Bowyer Bell, *The Secret Army* (Dublin 1998), P. Bishop and E. Mallie, *The Provisional IRA* (London 1987), Ed Moloney, *A Secret History of the IRA* (London 2002), Peter Taylor, *Provos* (London 1997), Kevin J. Kelley, *The Longest War* (London 1982), Conor Foley, *The Legion of the Rearguard* (London 1992), Richard English, *Armed Struggle* (London 2003), Richard English, *Irish Freedom* (London 2006), Seán Cronin, *Irish Nationalism* (Dublin 1980), Kevin Rafter, *Sinn Féin 1905–2005* (Dublin 2005), Robert W. White, *Provisional Irish Republicans* (Westport 1993).

2 Philip Beresford, *The Official IRA and the Rep Clubs in NI 1968–1974* (Phd. Exeter 1979).

3 Seán Swan, *Official Irish Republicanism, 1962 to 1972* (Belfast 2006), Pat Walsh, *Irish Republicanism and Socialism* (Belfast 1994).

4 Henry Patterson, *The Politics of Illusion* (London 1997).

5 Brendan O'Leary, *The Politics of Antagonism* (London 1993). John McGarry and Brendan O'Leary, *Explaining Northern Ireland* (London 1995), Richard Rose, *Governing Without Consensus* (London 1971), Paul Dixon, *Northern Ireland: The Politics of War and Peace* (Houndsmills 2001), Liam De Paor, *Divided Ulster* (Harmondsworth 1970), Peter Bew, Peter Gibbon and Henry Patterson, *Northern Ireland 1921–1994* (London 1995), Paul Arthur, *Government and Politics of Northern Ireland* (London 1984).

6 R. J. Johnston, *Century of Endeavour* (Dublin 2007), Robert W. White, *Ruairí Ó Brádaigh* (Bloomington 2006), Gerry Adams, *Before the Dawn* (London 1996), Brendan Anderson, *Joe Cahill* (Dublin 2002), Derry Kelleher, *Irish Republicanism* (Greystones 2001), Seán Mac Stíofáin, *Memoirs of a Revolutionary* (London 1975).

7 Bob Purdie, *Politics in the Streets* (Belfast 1990), Eamonn McCann, *War and an Irish Town* (London 1993), Michael McKeown, *The Greening of a Nationalist* (Dublin 1986), Bernadette Devlin, *The Price of My Soul* (London 1969), Michael Farrell, *Northern Ireland, The Orange State* (London 1980), Paul Arthur, *The Peoples Democracy 1968–73* (Belfast 1974), Pat Walsh, *From Civil Rights to National War* (Belfast 1989), Aidan Corrigan, *Eye Witness in Northern Ireland* (Dungannon nd), Paul Routledge, *John Hume* (London 1997), NICRA, *We Shall Overcome* (Belfast 1978), Seán Redmond, *Desmond Greaves and the Origins of the Civil Rights*

Movement in Northern Ireland (London 1999), Raymond Quinn, *A Rebel Voice: A History of Belfast Republicanism 1925–1972* (Belfast 1998).

8 John Bowman, *De Valera and the Ulster Question 1917–1973* (Oxford 1982), Catherine O'Donnell, *Fianna Fáil, Irish Republicanism and the Northern Ireland Troubles 1968–2005* (Dublin 2007), Eunan O'Halpin, *Defending Ireland: The Irish State and Its Enemies Since 1922* (Oxford 1999).

9 Padraig O'Malley, *Uncivil Wars* (Boston 1993).

10 M. L. R. Smith, *Fighting for Ireland* (London 1995), Joanne Wright, *Terrorist Propaganda* (London 1991).

11 Smith (1995), p. 5.

12 Roy Johnston, *Century of Endeavour* (Dublin 2007).

13 Robert F. Berkhofer, *Beyond the Great Story: History as Text and Discourse* (Cambridge 1995).

14 Robert Perks and Alistair Thomson, *The Oral History Reader* (London 2006).

15 Stephen Yeo, 'Whose Story? An Argument from within Current Historical Practice in Britain', *Journal of Contemporary History* Vol. 21, April 1996.

16 Ronald Fraser, *Blood of Spain* (New York 1979), and Howell Raines, *My Soul Is Rested: Movement Days in the Deep South Remembered* (Putnam 1977).

17 Taylor (1997), p. 30, Geraghty (2000), p. 12, English (2006), Mary Daly and Margaret O'Callaghan, *1916 in 1966: Commemorating the Easter Rising* (Dublin 2007).

18 O'Halpin (1999), p. 282.

19 Patterson (1997), pp. 209–10.

20 Walsh (1994), p. 45.

21 See for example Devlin (1969) and McCann (1993).

22 Simon Prince, *Northern Ireland's '68: Civil Rights, Global Revolt and the Origins of the Troubles* (Dublin 2007).

23 Bowyer Bell (1998), p. 345.

1

The 1956–62 armed campaign and the reorganisation of the IRA

The IRA 'border campaign' of 1956 to 1962 occupies a peculiar place in the history of Irish republicanism. It has arguably been romanticised not only by republicans themselves but in books like Coogan's first edition of *The IRA* and in Bowyer Bell's *The Secret Army*. A more recent work, however, by Barry Flynn comes to the conclusion that the campaign itself was both ill-conceived and futile. For republicans during the period under review here it was important in terms of assessing both why the campaign had failed and more importantly what lessons could be drawn from it in order to make the IRA more effective militarily or indeed to move away from militarism and towards popular revolutionary struggle. The tensions which that brought about eventually led to the split in 1969 and 1970.

Operation Harvest began on 11 December 1956 with thirteen attacks on targets within Northern Ireland. When IRA Volunteers Seán South and Fergal O'Hanlon were killed in a raid on the RUC Barracks at Brookeborough, County Fermanagh, on 31 December 1956, for those sympathetic to the republican message it appeared to be an echo of an earlier heroic phase. The campaign had been reasonably well prepared and the IRA claimed to have had 47 trained units prepared for action but the head of Garda Special Branch Chief Superintendent Philip McMahon believed that preparations had been hampered by a lack of funds. British Military Intelligence, well briefed by McMahon, who was described as 'our regular source', was confident that there was little likelihood of IRA actions in Britain.[1]

Sinn Féin, described at the 1956 Army Convention as 'the link between the Army and the people', won four seats and took 5.5 per cent of the votes in the 1957 general election. Ruairí Ó Brádaigh was elected in Longford-Westmeath, John Joe Rice in Kerry South, Eineachain, the brother of Fergal, O'Hanlon in Monaghan and John Joe McGirl in Sligo-Leitrim. All refused to take their seats. The election had been brought about when the three Clann na Poblachta TDs, who supported the Fine Gael-led government, refused to vote for the reintroduction of the Offences against the State Act. Support for the IRA was also indicated by sales of the *United Irishman*, which had a circulation of

120,000 in 1957. Support was fleeting, however, and, according to Seán Garland who was badly wounded at Brookebrough, was largely a result of the wave of sympathy that followed the deaths of South and O'Hanlon.[2]

Unemployment had increased from 71,661 in January 1956 to 94,648 in January 1957, and John Murphy of the Unemployed Movement was elected in Dublin South Central with 3,036 votes compared to 1,734 for the Sinn Féin candidate Tomás O Dubhghaill. Jim Lane, a Cork Volunteer active in Tyrone at the beginning of the campaign, believes that the social unrest of the period was one of the motivating factors in people joining the IRA, but republicans in Cork were hostile to the unemployed movement.[3] The IRA denied that it had any connection with social agitation and its journal *An t-Óglach* made no reference to any social objectives other than to claim that Britain controlled the whole of Ireland economically. In denying involvement in a land dispute in Kerry, the IRA said that: 'The only task of the Irish republican movement is to achieve the sovereignty of the Irish people in a 32 County Republic'.[4] A motion at the 1958 Ard Fheis calling on the party to revise what was described as its 'outdated' social and economic programme was defeated. The IRA was overwhelmingly comprised of young men from working-class and small farming backgrounds, and Seán Cronin, who had been a newspaper sub-editor, was an exotic presence among them. The IRA prisoners held in Belfast Jail were from similar backgrounds.

Although Fianna Fáil benefited from the political uncertainty caused by the IRA campaign, in power the party was no more willing to be tolerant towards militant republicanism than it had been in the 1940s. Internment under the provisions of the Offences against the State Act was introduced on 4 July 1957. By October 1958 there were 141 detainees in the Curragh, where morale was described as 'very low'.[5] In total 206 people were detained under internment orders. On 11 March 1959 the last of the internees were released as the IRA campaign seemed to be disintegrating under the impact of internal splits and a marked falling off in the number and quality of operations. In effect the Irish authorities, which had excellent intelligence from within the IRA, had broken the campaign and, in contrast to the attitude of the Northern Ireland government, appeared content to allow it to peter out.

According to the RUC, which had a highly placed informer codenamed HORSECOPER, in March 1958 there were 455 IRA Volunteers in Dublin and approximately five hundred elsewhere in the Republic. It believed that, despite the pressure which the IRA was under, the campaign would continue and possibly move to Britain. Belfast may have hoped that by raising that prospect they would encourage heightened pressure from London on Dublin to take stronger measures against the IRA. The IRA called a temporary lull in operations in summer 1959 to encourage public pressure to force the Northern Ireland authorities to release internees. The Unionist government refused to yield, and the RUC believed that IRA operations would recommence in autumn.

Barry Flynn's book on the campaign and White's biography of Ruairí Ó Brádaigh highlight the bitter internal divisions that persisted throughout, and the IRA Convention of June 1959 saw the removal of Mac Curtain, McLogan and Magan from the leadership. Seán Cronin resumed as Chief of Staff, replacing Ruairí Ó Brádaigh who remained as his Adjutant. Cathal Goulding, elected as Quartermaster General, and Manus Canning, recently released having been sentenced in 1953 for taking part in the raid on the Felstead Officers Training Corps Academy, won support for the adoption of tactics similar to those employed by EOKA in Cyprus. The emphasis was to shift towards attacks on individual security forces personnel but the IRA was badly equipped to escalate operations. The other Felstead raider, Seán Mac Stíofáin, remained wedded to the strategy which became the basis for the IRA's military plan drafted in 1965. The RUC feared that the new tactics if employed in Belfast would provoke a violent reaction from loyalists. It also felt that the Irish government was more willing to tackle the IRA given Dublin's desire for economic co-operation, but the British Ambassador Sir Alexander Clutterbuck thought that De Valera was 'lukewarm in his desire to suppress the IRA'.

In the June 1960 local elections 16 Sinn Féin candidates were returned to county councils in Kerry, Clare, Cavan, Monaghan, Donegal, Sligo, Tipperary, Galway, Leitrim and Laois and a further 12 were elected as Urban District Councillors compared to six in 1955. Seven wards were contested in Dublin but Sinn Féin only won 3.84 per cent of the overall poll. Seán Bermingham who was a prominent member of Sinn Féin in Dublin recalled that the campaign was poorly organised and that selling the *United Irishman* was regarded as more important than canvassing.[6] British military intelligence believed that there were 'tensions' within the IRA and that 'older and more responsible members' of the IRA favoured prolonging the summer lull in operations but that they were likely to resume in the autumn.[7]

Sinn Féin fought the 1961 general election with 21 candidates and declared that it was committed to bringing about a 'full scale revolution' and the creation of a 'democratic Christian social order as envisaged by Pope Leo XIII'. The cause of Ireland's economic underdevelopment was identified as partition and under-investment. Once the border was removed, and if republicans were successful in winning power, Sinn Féin would introduce credit control and break the link with sterling. Irish assets abroad would be repatriated and foreign investment strictly curtailed. Sinn Féin referred to growing materialism and 'an insidious campaign...to undermine the faith of the people in their traditional concept of Irish freedom'. It also attacked economic growth led by 'foreign interests and speculators', opposed EEC membership and, while protectionist, was critical of the manner in which that policy had been operated under Fianna Fáil. RTE refused to allow Sinn Féin to produce election broadcasts on the grounds that the party did not recognise the authority of the Oireachtas.

Sinn Féin lost all of the seats won in 1957 and its share of votes fell to 3 per cent. The Dublin results were even worse than the 1960 local elections. The three candidates received just over 2,500 votes and, to rub salt into the wound, Joe Christle, a former IRA Volunteer associated with Saor Uladh, took 1,814 votes in Dublin South West compared to 444 for Sinn Féin. The RUC claimed that Christle had given them an 'oral undertaking' when arrested in 1957 that his group would cease military operations.[8]

The Sinn Féin Publicity Committee said, that while the party had suffered a 'reverse', it was not so much a rejection of republican principles on the part of the people, as a tribute to Sinn Féin's refusal to accept partition. Ruairí Ó Brádaigh declared: 'We have lost support but we have lost nothing else. We have not lost our self-respect, nor have we bartered our principles or compromised the full national demand.' For Ó Brádaigh and other traditionalists, one of whom claimed that Sinn Féin had 'triumphed in a deeper, more spiritual manner, than the selfish little materialists who scorn their aims can ever realise', allegiance to the *de jure* Republic was more important than popular support. The Connolly Association, however, was certain that abstentionism had been the main cause of Sinn Féin's decline, and the Irish Workers League claimed that, had Sinn Féin 'pursued the excellent statement which they issued on the Common Market, it would have brought them more in touch with realities'.

Despite the electoral setbacks, the IRA campaign continued. A RUC constable was killed in January 1961 and there were a number of other attacks which led to renewed calls for the Irish government to take stronger measures. In response to the Church of Ireland Bishop of Kilmore, Dr Edward Moore, the Taoiseach Seán Lemass assured him that he deplored the 'futile, evil campaign of violence' but that there were 'formidable difficulties' in the way of sterner action being taken. Lemass pointed out that the annual cost of policing the IRA, almost £400,000, was one 'which our small country can ill afford'. Peter Berry, the Secretary of the Department of Justice, urged that the Taoiseach in his reply should emphasise the government view that the IRA was in a weakened state. Garda reports indicated that the IRA and Sinn Féin were at a low ebb and that the probable collapse of the Sinn Féin vote in the general election would engender further apathy. The government also needed to avoid creating martyrs, and trial by jury for indictable offences had proved to be unworkable.

Condemning the killing of Constable W. T. Hunter at Jonesborough, County Armagh, on 12 November 1961, Lemass hinted at 'some sinister influence' behind the campaign which was designed 'to do maximum damage to the nation's interests'.[9] When he met the British Ambassador to Dublin, Sir Ian MacLennan, Lemass conveyed his concern over 'mischievous' suggestions by Unionist Ministers that the campaign was in some way tolerated by Dublin and suggested that London might contribute to a solution by indicating that it would 'welcome the ending of partition by agreement'. As far as the IRA was concerned, Lemass told MacLennan that it was not thought to present much of a threat in its present state. It had 'lost much of its strength and most of its earlier leaders who had the intelligence to realise that their campaign was futile'.

Special Branch estimated that the IRA had fewer than a thousand Volunteers and was smaller than at any time since 1957. Saor Uladh and Fianna Uladh, the main splinter groups, had ceased to exist, although there was still a potential danger posed by the Dublin dissidents who had access to weapons and were under an 'irresponsible leadership'. Sinn Féin had 336 cumainn with a total of around five thousand members. Most of the IRA's finances came from the United States, a source which the Gardaí had requested the FBI to close down, and was supplemented by collections in Ireland and sales of the *United Irishman*. Sixty thousand copies of the newspaper were printed each month, half of its 1957 circulation, and 'appeals only to the converted'. The IRA leadership had at various times been on small full-time wages but its financial position was believed to be adequate solely for the purpose of supporting the Active Service Units, most of whom were known to the Gardaí. The IRA was well armed but running low on stocks of ammunition and explosives. Cronin, who had been replaced as Chief of Staff by Ruairí Ó Brádaigh in June 1960, was described as a person who 'has never shown marked ability in his ordinary jobs'. The leadership with the exception of Cronin, and Ó Brádaigh who was a teacher, were 'non-descript persons in lower middle class and working class families who make no particular impact on persons outside the organisation'.

While anxious not to be seen to be responding to British pressure, the Minister for Justice, Charles Haughey, placed a number of options before the Cabinet including internment, extradition, reintroducing the Special Criminal Court, controlling the IRA's finance and propaganda, better liaison between the Gardaí and the RUC, and 'creating a climate of opinion amongst local cumainn etc. contemptuous of IRA'.[10] The Cabinet agreed to reconstitute the Special Criminal Court despite opposition from Labour, which was concerned that persons brought before the court would not receive a fair trial,[11] and from Jack McQuillan of the National Progressive Democrats who blamed the campaign on the 'frustration and disillusionment of our youth today at the failure of our Government to take steps to end partition'.

Among the 'formidable difficulties' to which Lemass had referred in his response to Bishop Moore was the legal challenge to the Offences Against the

State Act taken to the European Court by Gery Lawless, a member of Saor Uladh who was interned in July 1957. The Court ruled on 1 July 1961 that the Republic had been in contravention of Article 5 of the Human Rights Convention concerning the liberty and security of the individual but that it could introduce internment under Article 15 of the European Convention on the grounds that an emergency situation existed. Although the IRA called on people to campaign for the closure of the Special Criminal Court, it was already preparing to end the campaign but delayed the announcement until after Christmas.

Garda reports of demoralisation and logistical problems appeared to have been confirmed by the IRA statement of 26 February 1962 stating that operations were being suspended. Among the reasons given were that people's minds had been deliberately distracted from the task of ending partition. The IRA did not, however, rule out a return to armed struggle at some future date. In the meantime it would use the cessation to 'conserve its resources, to augment them, and to prepare a more favourable situation'.[12]

In the conclusion to his book on the campaign, Barry Flynn claims that the later Provisional campaign had its roots in the failure of 'Operation Harvest'. While it is clear that, as White's biography of Ruairí Ó Brádaigh shows, there were people in the IRA leadership who did indeed see the cessation as providing an opportunity for the movement to rebuild and plan for another campaign, the political and military planning of the post-1962 period proves that there was little appetite for simply beginning a similar rurally based guerrilla campaign. As subsequent chapters will also demonstrate, neither was the post-1969 campaign the consequence of deliberate IRA planning and when the North did break down the IRA itself was woefully unprepared to mount any sort of offensive.

Among the 43 republican prisoners in Mountjoy in February 1962, some of whom were serving far longer sentences handed down by the Special Criminal Court, the general feeling was one of boredom and resignation to the fact that the campaign had been defeated. According to Tom Mitchell who was on the Army Council, no one at the meeting that took the decision argued in favour of continuing and there was no vote. He spoke to Mick Ryan in the yard of the farmhouse where the meeting was held about the need for another long process of reorganisation.[13] Ruairí Ó Brádaigh oversaw the cessation, having escaped from the Curragh with Dáithí Ó Conaill in September 1958, and had hoped to take part in reinvigorating the campaign. An understanding of the actual situation persuaded him that this was not possible and that a cessation was the best option.[14]

Differences over the direction of the campaign and the way it ended led to tensions between the IRA and Sinn Féin and a co-ordinating committee was established between the IRA General Headquarters staff and the Ard Comhairle. Ruairí Ó Brádaigh and Mick Ryan were the IRA representatives while McLogan, Seán O'Mahoney and Mick Traynor represented Sinn Féin. Ó Brádaigh refused to allow Sinn Féin to issue a separate statement on the cessation. The real source of tension was the McLogan/Magan faction's unhappiness at being subservient to the new IRA Army Council, and at the 1958 Ard Fheis South Kerry Sinn Féin had proposed that 'visitors' not be given speaking or voting rights, the 'visitors' being IRA officers who were not members of the party. That was overruled by the Chair but a motion from the IRA prisoners' cumann in the Curragh calling for the Sinn Féin constitution to be amended in order to make it subservient to the Army was defeated.[15]

Haughey had welcomed the cessation and his statement contained what might have been construed as a conciliatory element, 'urging those concerned to turn their attention to constructive purpose. The nation can do with the services of all her citizens.'[16] Curiously, a reference in Haughey's original draft to 'wiser counsels' having prevailed within the IRA leadership was excluded from the published version, perhaps to dampen suspicions of government knowledge of the internal workings of the organisation. The Department of Justice view was that the emergency measures implemented had been effective. As he pondered the early release of the IRA prisoners, Peter Berry was almost dismissive of the organisation:

> The prisoners are men of limited education and poor personality who have made no particular mark in their jobs or private lives and, whatever about their ability to use the gun, there is no particular reason to fear their organising ability . . . A general release would scarcely create any immediate problem of law and order but it might be regarded by waverers on the fringe of the organisation and members of the IRA splinter-group as an indication that they could commence reorganising again.[17]

Haughey favoured a general release with the proviso that strict measures be taken to ensure that the IRA did not reorganise. It was also noted that no arms had been surrendered following the February amnesty and that no prisoners had applied for early release. The Garda view was that the IRA was determined to maintain the organisation and they were opposed to early release except where prisoners signed the undertaking. According to Berry 'there was a general understanding both within the IRA and the "S" Branch, that the cessation was temporary and for the purpose of a reassessment and regrouping'. On the other hand, because the IRA itself had recognised that it had little public support, a return to violence was unlikely to be contemplated for some time. The movement was short of money, and proposed new legislation would prevent it from using public collections to redress that situation.

It was believed that many IRA members would now leave the movement but that if prisoners continued to be held they might remain out of loyalty to their comrades.[18]

The Cabinet sanctioned the releases under a 'general amnesty' which began on Good Friday, 20 April 1962. Belfast remained sceptical long after Dublin had accepted the bona fides of the cessation. In response to calls to free the remaining 30 internees in December 1962, the Unionist Minister for Home Affairs Brian Faulkner said: 'It was made very clear that the IRA was keeping its organisation intact' and 'was taking advantage of an interval to reform and that it still looked forward to what it called the successful conclusion of its campaign against this part of Ireland'.[19] It was not until September 1963 that the remaining prisoners in Belfast were released. When the Department of External Affairs made representations to the British Government in February 1963 to have border roads reopened, the British Ambassador relayed RUC concerns that the IRA was holding training camps in the border region. The Gardaí reported that they could find no evidence for IRA activity of this nature.[20] The British government, judging by the absence of discussion at the Joint Intelligence Committee, was more inclined to Dublin's assessment of the likely IRA threat.

Flynn correctly identifies the demoralisation that accompanied the cessation, and for those who had been involved in the campaign there was the question of where to go next. Tom Mitchell, who spent seven years in Crumlin Road, resumed his job with Dublin Corporation but remained on the Army Council and took part in the reorganisation of the IRA. He agreed with those who were advocating involvement in social and economic issues and did not see any prospect of an early return to armed struggle. Unlike Mitchell most of those who had been active in the campaign returned to normal lives with only a small number continuing their involvement. Jim Lane, who had been expelled in 1957 for having gone to Tyrone without the permission of the Cork OC, had his application to rejoin the IRA refused in 1961. He recalls that most republicans were demoralised and had little interest in the movement although the fact that people like Goulding and Garland had moved into the leadership was seen as encouraging. Lane still believed in armed struggle but felt that it needed to be wedded to socialist politics.[21] Seán Ó Brádaigh agreed that the movement was weak and that they needed to rebuild and wait for another opportunity that might present itself when objective conditions were different. He agreed with the need to build public support but was completely opposed to any moves towards constitutionalism which he claims is inevitable once the focus shifts to electoralism.[22] Seán Garland claims to have recognised that the campaign had been a failure from an early stage and that simply reorganising the IRA for a similar effort would be futile. The emphasis had to be on social and economic agitation.[23]

Patterson correctly identifies that move towards social and economic struggle as a recurring theme within republicanism, particularly following one of
its periodic defeats. He sees it as a means whereby the movement can 'exploit'
the relationship between the ongoing failure to resolve the national question
and 'a range of social, economic and communal grievances'.[24] He also believes
that it was the continued emphasis on the former that frustrated the attempts
by the modernisers to engage in genuine socialist politics and which ultimately led to the more radical departure by the modernist faction from
republican orthodoxy in the 1970s. In the early 1960s, however, the modernisers still regarded the new strategy as a means towards the traditional republican objective. That was shared by traditionalists, many of whom, as White
shows in relation to Ó Brádaigh, were equally unhappy with the social and
economic status quo. They were far more suspicious, however, in essaying new
strategies that threatened as they saw it central tenets of revolutionary republicanism, in particular its attitude towards the two Irish states and the role of
the IRA as the vanguard of a military uprising.

For former prisoners there was the problem of finding work. Those convicted in the Special Criminal Court were debarred from publicly paid jobs
and that applied to five released prisoners. Roscommon County Council,
where Ruairí Ó Brádaigh was employed as a teacher, claimed that it was
'wrong to penalise persons for pursuing their political ideals'.[25] The government opposed a Private Member's Bill to repeal the provision but on Haughey's advice decided in June to remit the forfeitures and disqualifications
contained in the Act, and Ó Brádaigh was able to return to his position. Noel
Kavanagh was employed in the Mater Hospital after his release. After a time,
one of the nuns in administration noticed the gap in his CV covering the time
that he had been interned and reported the matter to the Archbishop of
Dublin, John Charles McQuaid, who in turn contacted Special Branch. They
recommended that Kavanagh be sacked but he was retained at the request of
Professors O'Malley and Counihan. Years later Kavanagh discovered that the
two had also paid his wages for three years. He says that Special Branch har-
assed active republicans in their employment in the hope that they would
emigrate. Kavanagh says that the failure of the campaign had convinced him
that another would be futile.[26]

Despite the change in the IRA leadership at the 1959 Convention this was
not fully reflected within Sinn Féin until after the campaign had ended.
McLogan was re-elected party President at the 1961 Ard Fheis and the Ard
Comhairle was a mix of his allies like Tony Magan and younger men like
Tomás Mac Giolla and Seán Ó Brádaigh. In his presidential address, McLogan
said that Sinn Féin's task was to continue to represent the interests of the Irish
people 'irrespective of creed or class'. He dwelt at length on those who had
defected from the movement in the past to pursue the 'murky by-ways of

political party manoeuvring' but there was nothing to indicate that he was referring to anyone currently in the movement. There had been a proposal at the 1960 Ard Fheis from the Sinn Féin cumann in Melbourne, Australia, that Sinn Féin TDs should enter Leinster House under certain conditions, but the motion met with such hostility that it was withdrawn.

In June 1962 Magan tried unsuccessfully to have the Ard Comhairle reject what was known as the 'Three Points' strategy that had been agreed by the IRA leadership and put to the Sinn Féin Ard Comhairle, emphasising the supremacy of the Army Council as the government of the Republic and that while Sinn Féin was an 'autonomous and independent organisation' 'its policy must conform with Army policy'. The third point forbade Sinn Féin from issuing any statement on the ending of the armed campaign. According to Tom Mitchell the 'Three Points' document was written by Goulding and Costello and the dispute was about IRA control over Sinn Féin rather than policy. Although Ruairí Ó Brádaigh and most traditionalists supported this it was also undoubtedly regarded by Goulding and others as a first step in reorientating the movement politically. The sidelining of McLogan and Magan, with the support of Ó Brádaigh, also succeeded in dividing and weakening the traditionalist faction. An article in Irish in the *United Irishman* of May 1962 committed Sinn Féin to taking seats in Leinster House once it had secured an overall majority and stated that the movement needed to form a cohesive unit under one leadership.

The dispute came to a head over McLogan's request that the IRA issue a further statement that would have made it clear that the Sinn Féin leadership had nothing to do with the ceasefire. While not openly challenging the cessation, it would be a public declaration that the McLogan/Magan faction had disapproved. When the Army Council refused to issue a second statement McLogan tried unsuccessfully to win support at the Ard Comhairle and on 30 June 1962 he resigned and was followed by Magan and Seán O'Mahoney. Mac Giolla was then elected President. To reassure the republican faithful, in his first Bodenstown oration that month Mac Giolla attacked any republican who would take part in Leinster House or Stormont as a 'traitor, a liar and a hypocrite'. A conference of Sinn Féin councillors held in Dublin on 1 July unanimously passed a resolution condemning the advocacy of taking seats in reaction to the proposal by Galway County Councillor Pádraig Ó Ceallaigh that Sinn Féin should enter Leinster House.

The resignations were reported in the July 1962 issue of the *United Irishman* but lest there be any suspicions of sinister ideological influences the paper republished a statement on Communism from the 1950s. Referring to rumours of people with Communist connections attempting to join the movement, it called upon republicans not to become involved in organisations controlled by Communists. That was a reference to the Connolly Association and the fact that Roy Johnston and Anthony Coughlan were in contact with people like Goulding and Cronin. The editor Martin Shannon was strongly anti-Communist and soon after was replaced and became extremely critical of Goulding.

Writing in the Connolly Association newspaper the *Irish Democrat*, Anthony Coughlan claimed that while abstentionism had not been an issue in the internal dispute there were members who favoured entering the Dáil 'but this current of opinion is not, certainly as yet, represented on the Ard Comhairle'.[27] More resignations followed and the former leadership issued a circular criticising their replacements. This was countered by another which reiterated the primacy of the Army Council and rejected the demand for a special Ard Fheis. It also stressed that there was no intention of abandoning abstentionism. The Ard Comhairle was now made up of younger IRA members and Sinn Féin was now effectively controlled by the IRA which made it easier to deal with the internal crisis caused by the resignations. All eight Ard Comhairle members who had stepped down were expelled and the expulsions were ratified by 108 votes to 21 at the Sinn Féin Ard Fheis. The affair was reported in the press as having been caused by deviations over policy.

As yet there was no hint of ideological differences within the IRA leadership. Both the modernisers and traditionalists on the Army Council shared an impatience with the McLogan faction whom they regarded as dead wood and who were holding back the development of a more dynamic organisation. Cathal Goulding replaced Ruairí Ó Brádaigh as Chief of Staff at the IRA Convention of September 1962 but the transition was amicable and Ó Brádaigh stood down for personal reasons as he was living and working in Roscommon. He now feels that he missed out on much of the internal debate owing to his absence from Dublin.[28] The Convention did not, however, delve overmuch into the future direction of the movement and is not recalled by Ó Brádaigh as having been the beginning of the radical shift claimed by Goulding in retrospect. The mood was downbeat and the general assessment one of defeat and isolation in which the priority was survival and regrouping.

The McLogan affair resurfaced in July 1964 when he was found shot dead at his home in Dublin. According to the Gardaí there was no suspicion of foul play. There were, however, rumours that the IRA had killed McLogan. One senior figure was even purported later to have said that they had dealt with McLogan, just as they would with anyone else who stood in their way. There was also a rumour that McLogan had been planning to organise another armed campaign, in collusion with Irish American republicans who were critical of the IRA leadership. Clan na Gael and the Irish Republican Veterans of America claimed that the armed campaign had been 'the brainchild of either an idiot or a rogue'[29] and cautioned IRA Volunteers against being led into a similar 'monstrosity' in the future. They accused the leadership of being afraid to confront the 'Free State' and noted that abstentionism was now 'qualified in that it is limited only to that time when Sinn Féin lacks a majority'. Such a majority would only lead to a new party in power in Leinster House. The alternative was a revolution that would destroy every aspect of the British system in Ireland and replace it with one conducive to the 'distinctive economic and social wants' of the Irish people.

Little of the internal power struggle being carried on within the republican movement was reflected in the *United Irishman*. There was a brief denial of the claim in the *Sunday Times* of 9 September 1962 and the *Belfast Telegraph* of 10 September 1962 that Sinn Féin had abandoned abstentionism. According to Ruairí Ó Brádaigh, the report was the creation of an *Irish Independent* journalist who chose to misinterpret the McLogan controversy. The *Belfast Telegraph* feared that the defeated faction in Sinn Féin would initiate another military campaign and saw the change in policy as a victory for the younger element; it quoted a government spokesperson who mischievously welcomed the move as recognition of the Irish Constitution.

Over two hundred delegates attended the 1962 Ard Fheis on 27 and 28 October where elections to the Ard Comhairle consolidated the position of the new leadership. Mac Giolla was elected party President and his address to delegates devoted long sections to opposition to the EEC: 'No economic advantages could compensate for loss of sovereignty and independence of action to become pawns in a nuclear holocaust.' He claimed that between 30,000 and 140,000 jobs would be lost as a result of joining the Community. While rejecting the idea that Ireland should join an anti-Communist military alliance, Mac Giolla made it clear that this was not due to any affinity with the Soviet Union: 'In so far as the Communist menace is a battle for men's minds, we should undoubtedly be playing a leading part in the fight against it, as we should in the fight against materialism of every brand.' Mac Giolla also warned republicans not to view the end of the armed campaign as a break from struggle. An Irish-American lawyer, James C. Heaney, wrote to the *United Irishman* to suggest a different aspect to that struggle, recommending 'discussion of social and political problems' and taking civil rights cases in Northern Ireland. Republicans then were aware of the potential that lay there, separately from any suggestions emanating from Greaves and the Connolly Association.

While the immediate post-ceasefire period had seen little evidence of IRA activity, after 1963 both the IRA and republican dissidents were involved in violent incidents. An IRA training camp in the Knockmaeldown Mountains in County Waterford was raided in July 1963. Among those arrested was Phil

O'Donoghue, the OC of the Dublin Brigade. In a note to Lemass, Haughey claimed that the raid was good news in that it proved that the Gardaí were on top of the situation, and obviously still in receipt of good intelligence, but that 'it creates a bad impression'. With increased IRA activity causing concern in Stormont, Peter Berry met with the Minister for Home Affairs William Craig and his Secretary William Stout in Belfast on 4 October and assured them that the IRA was not conducting arms training along the border. He told Craig that Garda Special Branch had the same information as Scotland Yard, which Craig had cited.[30] Berry said that Craig had not known of a recent meeting between the Garda Chief Superintendent Philip McMahon and Chief Inspector Smith of RUC Special Branch. Berry and Stout agreed to exchange information on the IRA, an arrangement that apparently worked quite efficiently from then on. It did not, however, prevent Belfast continuing to take a very different view of the potential threat posed by the IRA even though it presumably had access to, or shared, the same intelligence. London, meanwhile, remained reliant on information conveyed to it from Belfast and Dublin rather than its own Security Service, something that was to become significant at the end of the decade.

On 17 March 1963 a former IRA prisoner, Desmond Swanton, was killed as he and Jeremiah Madden attempted to blow up a memorial to the 1920s IRA in St Finbarr's Cemetery, Cork, in protest at its reference to their having died to establish the Irish state. The IRA issued a statement on 18 March denying that the organisation had sanctioned the operation although it did admit that the men involved had been members of the IRA.[31] The Army Council had been aware of the plan and had attempted to call it off. Jim Lane and other Cork republicans organised the funeral and established a Commemoration Committee which became the focus for disaffected republicans in Ireland and the United States, and in August 1963 the Cork group, styling itself the Irish Revolutionary Forces, began publishing a newspaper entitled *An Phoblacht*.

Although Goulding by 1963 may already have been intent on weaning the IRA away from violence, or at least another campaign in the North, the organisation was involved in a number of incidents which were approved by the Army Council. Among the sanctioned agitations were protests against the seizure of Easter lily collections under the Street and House to House Collections Act, 1962. This was a major source of scarce income, exacerbated by the sharp fall in sales of the *United Irishman*, after 1962.[32] The year 1963 saw the first serious attempt by the Gardaí to enforce the Act, and republicans listed seven incidents where they alleged that Easter lily sellers had been assaulted and contrasted that to the lack of interference in the North. Some of those who were arrested refused to pay fines and several prisoners embarked on hunger strikes which a Cabinet meeting on 22 October decided not to react to and they had all ended the following week.[33] Subsequent short hunger strikes and Dáil protests were handled adroitly by Haughey.

The Easter lily campaign continued in 1964 and the *United Irishman* called on people to wear the lily and defy the state.[34] Nollaig Ó Gadhra, in a letter to the *United Irishman*, claimed that the republican movement was trying to create martyrs by refusing to apply for permits in the same way as every other organisation wishing to make collections. Tom Mitchell saw the legislation and the confrontation over the Easter lily as a sign that the state was determined to ensure that the republican movement did not rebuild itself. He says the Army Council regarded it as an issue which it needed to deal with on that basis rather than as a deliberate attempt to foment confrontation.[35]

Reflecting perhaps their intelligence insight into the organisation, some Government Ministers were openly contemptuous of the IRA. In December 1963 the Minister for External Affairs, Frank Aiken, declared: 'We see no sign of the IRA. There is nothing of any account.'[36] However, that perceived weakness also led to some questioning of the methods used by Special Branch to monitor political subversion, including phone tapping. Haughey dismissed the issue as the 'Loch Ness Monster' of journalism and politics, continuously being dragged up by 'pseudo liberals'. He was however careful to deny that the phones of trade unionists were under similar scrutiny.

While the *United Irishman*'s Mac Dara pondered the debate on phone tapping as 'evidence of solidarity and strength among the common people' public concern was focused not on the civil liberties of radical republicans but on the possibility that the telephones of trade union officials were tapped. While the ICTU was generally supportive of the Programmes for Economic Expansion, unions had opposed the attempt by the government in September 1961 to outlaw strikes in the ESB. Republicans for the most part did not regard such matters as relevant and one prominent Dublin republican informed the organiser of a meeting on the use of the Offences against the State Act against strikers that the issue would be resolved only if people supported the republican movement.

IRA weapons were an intermittent cause of concern most notably when in August 1964 two children were killed while playing with a grenade they had found in Monaghan. The IRA denied that it was left there from the recent campaign. The organisation did make attempts to source new supplies and in October 1964 Berry sent a note to Hugh McCann of External Affairs, warning of IRA efforts to import weapons from the United States.[37] This followed several interceptions of small caches from the US in Dublin after which the Irish authorities were promised increased vigilance by the FBI.[38]

Republicans organised protests against a visit by Princess Margaret in January 1965 which had been leaked by the press. Although Lemass saw the visit as strengthening 'republican self-respect', Seán Garland defends the protests as having reminded people of the British presence in the north.[39] One of Garland's allies, Roy Johnston, however, regarded such actions as in conflict with overall strategy and he does not accept that they had Goulding's approval.[40] Those involved included Richard Behal and his brother Raymond who were sentenced to terms of four months each. Sixteen republicans received jail sentences but were released on 25 February to mark the elevation to the College of Cardinals of Archbishop Charles Conway.

The first public attempt by the IRA to engage in social agitation was in February 1965 when the Cork IRA became involved in a campaign to stop the sale of houses in Midleton from the estate of the Earl of Midleton. The IRA organised protests and, while the IRA Executive did not feel that the agitation had been a success locally, 'on the national scale the movement has benefited from it'.[41] The most striking example of IRA militancy were a series of protests and attacks against visiting British naval vessels. These escalated from peaceful pickets on HMS *Virago* and HMS *Ghurkha* at Waterford in July 1963 and HMS *Malcolm* at Dublin in September 1963 to shots fired at HMS *Relentless* as it left Cork harbour on 20 November 1964. The Cork IRA claimed responsibility for that incident. Though Roy Johnston and others have questioned whether the IRA leadership sanctioned such operations it is clear from contemporary documents that they had. Seán Garland confirms this[42] and GHQ had instructed all Command OCs to prepare plans to attack any visiting vessel and to apply to the Army Council for approval.[43]

That meant that the Gardaí knew, through an informant, of the IRA plan to attack the *Bloodhound* when it visited Cork harbours in August 1965. The IRA claimed that it had abandoned the action because of the presence on board of civilians. They also threatened to attack the *Lofoten* if it called at Cork in October. The threat was taken seriously and McCann of External Affairs informed Berry of Aiken's dislike for such visits if they were undertaken for recruiting purposes. Berry presumed that it was 'not contemplated that External Affairs might suggest to the UK representative that visits of this kind were not welcome'. While Lemass was likewise unenthusiastic, rather than ask for it to be cancelled they ought 'gently' to suggest that they were perhaps not appropriate in the current circumstances of improving relations.[44]

The IRA informant notified Special Branch that the leadership had authorised the attack on the *Lofoten*. They knew of all the weapons to be used, how the attack was to be carried out, that Goulding had visited Cork, and that 'it was agreed by the Council that the loss of IRA personnel by way of arrest or the loss of arms was immaterial provided the object is successful'. Berry assured O Nualláin that the information was completely reliable.[45] Berry also ensured that sensitive Garda intelligence was transmitted only by himself.

Interestingly, Berry believed that those responsible could 'probably' be arrested afterwards, but that it might perhaps be wiser if a request was made to postpone the visit. That may have been to protect the source, and Lemass gave his consent to such a request. On 6 October O Nualláin confirmed that the visit would be cancelled as the *Lofoten* conveniently had to call to Le Havre or some place near by at around the same date. The British Ambassador Sir Geoffrey Troy was unhappy about the cancellation while McCann sought to explain why the visits were 'not on the same footing as courtesy calls to, say, the Scandinavian countries'.[46] Troy was also worried that the IRA had become aware of the *Lofoten*'s proposed call before the British Embassy, and about the arrangements for the planned celebrations of the fiftieth anniversary of the 1916 Rising which McCann assured him would be a 'forward-looking occasion without any attempt to reopen old wounds'.

In Waterford on 10 September 1965 shots were fired from an anti-tank gun at HMS *Brave Borderer*. The ubiquitous Richard Behal, Edward Kelly and Walter Dunphy were arrested in connection with the attack. *An Phoblacht* claimed that certain members of the republican leadership were horrified at the attack and considered Behal to be an 'irresponsible character'.[47] Scuffles broke out as the three men arrived at Waterford Court on 24 September. While the firing of shots at British naval vessels was a worrying development, the Irish government remained confident that such actions were not a prelude to another sustained armed campaign. It had intelligence which suggested that the IRA leadership was not particularly enthusiastic about the attacks, and those directly involved in the Waterford and Cork incidents were increasingly at odds with Goulding supporters. The British response, as conveyed by Ambassador Troy, was one of alarm at the breach of security but mostly a concern that naval visits might be forced to stop. There is no hint that London believed that the actions signalled the beginning of another armed campaign against the North.

From the IRA's perspective it is clear that, while such actions were enthusiastically greeted by many members, other influential voices were persuading Goulding to move away from such adventures. They also highlighted the contradiction between the IRA's role as a military organisation, which included the training of members for another campaign, and the logic of the new political strategy embraced by Goulding which emphasised engagement with broader social and economic forces and a consequent move away from the conception of the IRA as the spearhead of another armed uprising. The two elements coexisted uneasily in the immediate post-campaign period but led to increasing conflict as the contradictions became more apparent and as Goulding clearly sought to discourage the sort of actions which he had approved in 1964 and 1965.

Notes

1 WO 32/17577, Public Records Office, Kew.
2 Interview with Seán Garland, 28 February 2005. Garland himself stood as a candidate, while imprisoned, in a by-election in Dublin North Central in November 1957. He received 13.4 per cent of the vote.
3 Interview with Jim Lane, 14 May 2005.
4 IRPB, 21 February 1960, NLI, Ms. 22,938.
5 WO 32/17577, RUC Review 10 October 1957 – 17 March 1958, PRO, Kew.
6 Interview with Seán Berminghan, 20 April 2005.
7 WO 32/17577, Military Intelligence report, 19 October 1960, PRO.
8 WO 32/17577, RUC Review up to 10 October 1957, PRO.
9 Department of the Taoiseach, 98/6/494, NAI.
10 Department of the Taoiseach, 98/6/494, Appendix, p. 4, NAI.
11 *Dáil Debates*, Vol. 192, col. 841.
12 *United Irishman*, March 1962.
13 Interview with Tom Mitchell, 11 January 2002.
14 Interview with Ruairí Ó Brádaigh, 22 May 2002.
15 HA/32/2/13, PRONI.
16 *Irish Press*, 27 February 1962.
17 Department of the Taoiseach, 98/6/494, memo of 30 March 1962.
18 Taoiseach 2001/61/10, NAI, memo from Berry to Jack Lynch, 8 June 1970.
19 Parliament of Northern Ireland, *Commons Debates*, Vol. 52, col. 1785.
20 Taoiseach, S11575B/94 – 18 February 1963, NAI.
21 Interview with Jim Lane, 14 May 2005.
22 Interview with Seán Ó Brádaigh, 21 May 2005.
23 Interview with Seán Garland, 28 February 2005.
24 Henry Patterson, *The Politics of Illusion* (London 1997), p. 5.
25 Taoiseach, 2001/6/244, NAI.
26 Interview with Noel Kavanagh, 7 March 2005.
27 *Irish Democrat*, September 1962.
28 Interview with Ruairí Ó Brádaigh, 21 May 2002.
29 *Irish Republican Bulletin*, September 1963.
30 *Magill*, May 1980, 'The Berry Diaries', p. 74.
31 *Irish Republican Publicity Bureau Bulletin*, 18 March 1963, NLI Ms. 22,939.
32 *United Irishman*, September 1963.
33 Taoiseach, 98/6/495, NAI.
34 *United Irishman*, March 1964.
35 Interview with Tom Mitchell, 11 January 2002.
36 *Irish Independent*, 4 December 1963.
37 Department of External Affairs, A12/2B, NAI. Berry to McCann, 2 October 1964.
38 DFA A12/2B, NAI. Report by Chief Superintendent W. Davoren, 9 September 1964, and Fay to McCann, 21 November 1964.
39 Interview with Seán Garland, 28 February 2005.
40 Interview with Roy Johnston, 4 April 2001.

41 Minutes of IRA Executive meeting of 30 January 1966, contained in Garda Report 3C/15/66, NAI.
42 Interview with Seán Garland, 28 February 2005.
43 Taoiseach, 98/6/495. Undated IRA directive, contained in Garda report 3C/15/66, NAI.
44 Taoiseach, S1657, NAI.
45 Taoiseach, 98/6/495, NAI. Berry to O Nualláin, 30 September 1965.
46 Taoiseach, 98/6/495, NAI.
47 *An Phoblacht*, Vol. 1, no. 2, November 1965.

2

The ideology of traditional republicanism

The general view of the republican movement in the 1940s and 1950s, including that of former Chief of Staff Seán Cronin, was that it was imbued with a
deeply conservative ideology.[1] It has been argued that the movement was
reactionary, and had more in common with European fascism than it did with
the leftist image of the movement in the 1930s, although the prominence of
socialist ideas projected through *An Phoblacht* under the editorship of Peadar
O'Donnell and Frank Ryan did not necessarily reflect the republican support
base. Others have claimed that the movement was by and large apolitical but
while it is true that republicans during the 1950s tended to concentrate on
the national question Sinn Féin did have a social and economic programme
which stated that unification of the country was not an end in itself but a
means towards creating a socially just society.

The republican view of Irish society was increasingly at odds with the new
thinking among an elite that recognised the failure of the economy in the
Republic and which was willing to attempt new ways of ensuring its survival
and by extension their own political and social position. It is interesting to
look at the extent to which republicans presented a coherent alternative to the
new thinking, and to what extent it might even support the view that Sinn
Féin's opposition to the new economic policy constituted a reactionary rejection of modernisation.

The Sinn Féin social and economic programme was not socialist but it did
set out a radical view of how the Irish economy on a 32-county basis ought
to be developed. Private enterprise was deemed to be preferable to state
control, which would be confined to 'essential industries', but was subordinated to the overall interests of the state and its citizens.[2] It was also held that
private individuals would have more interest in the success of an enterprise
than civil servants. Profit making was not the cause of social ills 'but the abuse
of those profits and the purpose to which they are applied'. It was recognised
that workers might be subject to exploitation and where that was the case Sinn
Féin would bring it to an end. Only where private businesses were not run 'in
conformity with the requirements of a nationally organised economy' would

there be any question of adopting 'the concept of organised society that it is understood operates in Russia'.

The year 1958 saw the publication of two significant documents on the future of the Irish economy. On 11 November the government published its White Paper on Economic Development while two weeks later T. K. Whitaker, who was largely responsible for the White Paper, published his discussion document *Economic Development*. The emphasis was on encouraging sufficient entrepreneurial initiative to ensure economic 'take off'.[3] However, given the extent to which Irish assets were invested abroad, as was recognised by Whitaker, the logical conclusion was that such development required large-scale inward foreign investment. In a speech in early 1959 the Chairman of Aer Lingus, Professor Patrick Lynch, attacked what he termed the 'Sinn Féin myth' which 'assumed that Irish political independence implied economic independence'.[4] Lynch was referring to Arthur Griffith's party but the critique could equally have been applied to Sinn Féin in the 1950s. Economic isolation was impossible and it was time to recognise that development required closer ties, and indeed integration, with the British economy. According to Lynch, emigration was a positive and necessary phenomenon given the restricted size of Irish natural resources.

A *United Irishman* piece by 'Norman' on the White Paper in June 1959 detailed the extent of the economic failure of the Irish state where the labour force had declined by a hundred thousand since 1951. He attributed this to successive governments having attempted to implement the original Sinn Féin policy on a partitionist basis. By abandoning protectionism, the government was embarking on a road that would lead to economic and political dependence. The alternative was a continuation of protectionism on an all-Ireland basis with an expanded agricultural sector as 'the country's salvation'. He rejected Lynch's assertion that the original Sinn Féin economic policy was based on a myth:

> An old fashioned nationalism, to use Mr. Lynch's phrase, holds far greater safe-guards for Irish culture, outlook and way of life than any contemporary 'ism' which Mr Lynch might like to see in its place. His 'defunct economists' had this in mind when they formulated their 'myths' and 'dogmas' – a far more worthy object than the pursuit of a slick materialism and an efficiency which reck not man's longing for liberty and his love of country.

The *United Irishman* highlighted the fact that two hundred thousand had emigrated between 1951 and 1956, and that up to sixty thousand were leaving each year by 1959, a fact confirmed by a later official study. Republican advice was simple: 'Our people should refuse to emigrate. Stay at home! Demand your right as Irish men and women to live and work and settle down in your own land.' The paper bemoaned the 'extraordinary fact that Ireland...is the only country in Europe where no serious attempt has ever been made to develop the mineral resources and fisheries that would provide employment for innumerable thousands of Irish citizens who have no other alternative unless to emigrate'. The dependence of Irish agriculture on live cattle exports to Britain was contrasted with the recent trade deal between Denmark and the UK, and Danish agricultural co-operativism and the Norwegian fishing industry were cited as models. The live cattle trade was described as Ireland's 'historical role in the overall British economic plan' and responsible for most of the social and economic ills that had afflicted the country: 'We are an agricultural country. Where are our giant food-processing industries?' In a letter to the *United Irishman*, Emmet O'Connell, who later became a successful businessman and owner of Eglinton Exploration, claimed that financial dependence on the Bank of England was the main flaw in the Irish economy. The system was robbing people of their sense of industry and self-reliance, prompting them to 'seek state and other aids for many things which their own industry and enterprise could provide'. While the rhetoric was similar to a conservative critique of the 'welfare state', Sinn Féin accepted that it was necessary to provide for those who for whatever reason were unfit for work but the solution to the problem was to provide full employment so that people would become independent of state assistance.

A piece by Tom Doyle, or Tomás O Dubhghaill, in the *United Irishman* of October 1960 explained that the revolution would cause the disruption of 'all those vested interests who are thriving on the injustices of the old system – in our case alien landowners, foreign based banks and industrial concerns' and be based on the 'principles of social justice and charity so firmly enunciated by Leo XIII in his encyclical *Rerum Novarum*'. A review by Seán Ó Brádaigh of an Irish translation of *Rerum Novarum* claimed that, while there were many definitions of socialism, Leo 'teaches us the correct way to address the problems of this century', presumably accepting the Pope's strictures on socialism. Ó Brádaigh cited the encyclical on the merits of co-operation between employers and workers and the papal warning regarding control over the financial system.[5] Ó Brádaigh believes that Catholic social ideas were influential not only because they were an integral part of any Catholic's intellectual background but because their recommendations could be contrasted with the reality of economic and social conditions in Ireland. Their influence on republicans, he feels, ought also to be looked at in the context of the relative paucity of other influences.[6]

While it might have appeared odd that any person claiming to be a revolutionary at the beginning of the 1960s would have placed much importance on a Papal encyclical written in 1891 it shows the extent to which Catholic social thinking still had a major influence especially where there was a suspicion of socialism and its connotations of atheism. That was not unique to republicans. In 1967 the leader of the Labour Party, Brendan Corish, cited Pope John XXIII as having endorsed the principles that underlay his party's socialism, and the ITGWU journal *Liberty* cited Papal encyclicals as occasionally did even the Communist *Irish Socialist*. The icon of the republican left James Connolly, however, had ridiculed Leo's critique of socialism, although he did cite historical and scriptural references where it suited his purpose of blunting the Church's political attacks. Interestingly Patterson refers to Connolly as having been partly responsible for creating the paradigm through which republicans could try and camouflage their social objectives under the rubric of Catholic social teaching. However, he also fails I believe to distinguish between the impulse behind radical republican references to such principles and the motivation behind the Blueshirt / Fine Gael embrace of corporatism.[7] Of course a similar dichotomy existed in other Catholic countries between 'egalitarian' and 'elitist' advocates of Catholic social teaching and fascism.

Rerum Novarum voices the Catholic Church's concern at the 'moral degeneracy' of capitalism, and suggests that, in the absence of the guild system, working men were prey to 'crafty agitators' attempting to exploit legitimate grievances in order to destroy religion, private property and order.[8] Socialism was unjust because it interfered with private property which accords with the Natural Law, and underlay the Christian family, which was under threat from the intrusion of the state. Workers were entitled to proper wages and conditions so as to be able to provide for their family with no need for state welfare, all of which was echoed in the Sinn Féin programme. The Pope referred to distributive justice which again was something regularly found in republican policy in the 1960s and in the early social and economic policy of the Provisionals. However, distributive justice in the sense employed by Leo XIII by no means implied a *re*-distribution of resources by public policy, but was employed in the Thomistic sense of treating all classes equally according to Natural Law. There was, however, the possibility that if a worker received proper wages and was thrifty then in that manner 'property will certainly become more equitably divided'.

Much of the influence that Catholic social teaching had on republicans originated in the redirection of the movement away from socialism in the 1930s, but it had always been greater than leftist ideas, reflecting the influence which those ideas had within the broader society, through the education system and Catholic press. The question is, how could such ostensibly conservative and even reactionary ideas provide the motivation for militant revolutionaries within a society that was dominated by elites who claimed adherence to those self-same principles?

Republicans were sympathetic to the radical Catholic critique of the post-1922 state where the levels of poverty, unemployment and emigration meant it was easy to point out where the new elites were failing in their duty to promote social justice. That may also have fed into a cultural antipathy towards social elites that could at the same time be egalitarian and opposed to what were regarded as malign modernising influences, including socialism, which were perceived as threats to an organic conception of Irish society in which distinctions of class were less important than communal solidarity. Most importantly for republicans influenced by such ideas, the continuing centrality of the national question and the apparent failure to address the issue of Partition meant that there was a recognisable context in which to promote revolution and in which Catholic social teaching could provide ideological justification. Some critics of traditionalist republicanism have recognised the historical identification of popular Catholicism with democratic and even egalitarian impulses in Irish society[9] but others regard traditionalist republicanism as having been an integral part of a conservative Catholic polity.[10]

While republican ideology was influenced by the ideas contained in the encyclicals of Leo XIII and Pius XI, the circumstances in which Catholic teaching was applied to Irish politics after 1922 were very different from those which had motivated the original Papal documents. There had been a Papal ban on Italian Catholics taking any part in the institutions of the state, including elections, and in *Graves De Communi Re* of 1901 Leo had criticised Christian Democracy where it might be seen 'to support popular government' and to favour the interests of the poor.[11] In his 1905 encyclical *Il Fermo Proposito* Pius X was unapologetic in harking back to a period when the basis of civil society was founded upon 'the public recognition of the authority of the Church' and the 'subordination of all the laws of the State to the Divine laws of the Gospel'.[12] That reading of the encyclicals provides a far more prosaic view of the motivations of the Papacy, which can be seen as reactionary in a way that is not apparent from *Rerum Novarum* although a significant number of Irish Catholic radicals did believe in the temporal supremacy of the Church over the state. In the 1930s for example *An Rioghact* advocated a radical egalitarian agrarian-based society similar to that found in the traditionalist republican Comhar na gComharsan policy, but in which the Catholic clergy provided the leadership at parish level.

Rerum Novarum and *Quadragesimo Anno*, promulgated by Pius XI in 1931 on the fortieth anniversary of Leo's encyclical, retained their radical utility for those Catholics who were interested in social and political change but who rejected socialism for religious reasons.[13] *Quadragesimo Anno* was written at a time when the Papacy had come to an accommodation with the Italian fascists in the Lateran Concordat in 1929, and collaborated in the destruction of the Catholic Party which had been the last legal opposition. In it the Pope defined social justice as a medium between unbridled individual ownership and collectivism and approved corporate forms of organisation to bring about the harmonious union of labour and capital. The reference to the concentration of financial power echoed contemporary anti-Semitic theories about international finance. Where socialists confined themselves to seeking to establish public authority over the manner in which ownership was exercised, it was compatible with 'striving to remould human society on the basis of Christian principles' but 'no one can be at the same time a good Catholic and a true socialist'. The extent to which Irish Catholic radicals, including republicans, took the Papal strictures on socialism seriously, while at the same time advocating revolutionary changes in the social and economic system, should not be underestimated.

Other European nationalist movements were similarly influenced. One of the founders of Plaid Cymru, Saunders Lewis, referred to Papal encyclicals in his 1942 book *The Party for Wales*. A Marxist critic has claimed that Lewis's vision of Wales was steeped in 'medievalism',[14] a critique also made of traditional Irish republicanism. Traditional Basque nationalism was also Catholic, rural and in conflict with the centralising and modernising influences of both the Spanish state and the Spanish socialist movement. ETA to a great extent emerged from Catholic youth groups although the experience of repression by Franco gave it a leftist tinge. Similarly to the IRA, however, the influence of Marxism and Marxists within ETA was not uncontested. The Breton nationalist movement of the 1930s, Emsav, was deeply influenced by Catholic social teaching which arguably made it susceptible to fascist ideas and nationalists like Yann Fouere collaborated with the German occupation. Traditional influences persisted after 1945 despite that stigma although younger leftist Bretons, who founded the Union Democratique Bretonne in 1964, self-consciously aligned themselves with international anti-colonial movements and for a time with the Communist Party of France in a pattern similar to that pursued by the republican modernisers.

The radical possibilities of Catholic social teaching were most prominent in the 1920s, 1930s and 1940s but were also tapped into by the Lia Fáil movement. It was founded in Lusmagh, County Offaly, in 1957 by Fr John Fahy who had been involved with the IRA in the 1920s and 1930s before supporting Fianna Fáil and who claimed to have been one of the authors of Sinn Féin social and economic policy in the 1920s.[15] Lia Fáil wanted to expropriate all foreign property owners and holdings of more than 100 acres and distribute the land to smallholders.[16] It styled itself as a 'Land Army' in obvious tribute to the Kenyan Mau Mau and its roots lay in localised disillusionment with government policy towards small farmers at a time when the Minister for Lands, Erskine Childers, had made it clear that the state could not afford the cost of redistributing land to smallholders.

Lia Fáil attacked the Programme for Economic Expansion as a plan to 'replace people with cattle' and was involved in a series of agitations in 1958 and 1959. Brian Murphy describes the *raison d'être* of Lia Fáil in terms that might equally have been applied to republicans of the period, as engaged in a 'revolt against the nation's failure after thirty-five years independence to create a volkisch social order guaranteeing opportunities in their own country for the people who were the nation's soul'.[17] There was also a marked anti-urbanism which was a feature of traditional rural republicanism. Although there were no organisational connections between Lia Fáil and the republican movement, Lia Fáil boasted that it would 'blast the border out of existence' and paid tribute to the 'young men dying on the border' and Seán South was praised as someone who had 'laid down his life for Irish political and economic freedom'. The social revolution which it envisaged would abolish secret societies, close the banks, establish a national currency, set a standard income for all, abolish state companies, place people on the land and create full employment through small farming and agriculturally based small industries. Anti-Semitism was a regular theme of the *Lia Fáil* newspaper. W. H. Milner, a Portarlington farmer who had been involved in the Irish Monetary Reform Association in the 1940s, claimed that capitalism and communism were both means by which the Jews were attempting to establish a world republic.

It is likely that South would not have been uncomfortable with those sentiments. South had canvassed for Clann na Poblachta in Limerick City in 1948 but had then fallen under the influence of Ailtirí na hAiséirghe and Maria Duce.[18] Maria Duce was founded in 1942 by Fr Denis Fahey, whose book alleging Jewish control of world finance, *Money Manipulation and the Social Order*, was still on sale at Sinn Féin headquarters in 1965. A review in the *United Irishman* in March 1964 claimed that Fahey's book was based on *Quadragsimo Anno*. Maria Duce published *Fiat*, which in 1956 railed against the election of Robert Briscoe as the Lord Mayor of Dublin, on the grounds that he was 'a member of the Nation that implacably refuses the Rule of Christ'.[19] Membership records prove that it was small, mainly Dublin middle-class based and unconnected, and like Fahey, unsympathetic, to militant republicanism. South sold *Fiat* and had written letters to the *Limerick Leader* condemning the influence of Communists and Jews in the cinema.[20] South may, however, have outgrown the views of his early youth and Seán Garland, who knew him, claims never to have heard anti-Semitic sentiments from South.[21]

Tom Doyle was one of the key republican ideologists of the 1950s. He had been the IRA Adjutant General in the 1940s, and in common with a considerable number of IRA members had been influenced by Ailtirí na hAiséirghe who echoed many of the ideas of European fascism.[22] Doyle wrote a considerable amount of social and economic policy for Sinn Féin and was a regular contributor to the *United Irishman*. Doyle along with other republican trade union members attended courses at the Jesuit Workers College at Sandford

Lodge in Dublin, which began in February 1951. According to the Reverend Timothy Hamilton, the College's objective was to provide the student with 'a thorough grasp of Catholic Social Principles' so that he would 'respond as the Church confidently expects he will'.[23] Doyle, who was a trade union official, was one of the most influential figures of the late 1950s and early 1960s and was later cited by the Provisionals as one of the first opponents of the modernising faction. The Dublin internee and ITGWU member Noel Kavanagh also attended Sandford. Kavanagh had read *Rerum Novarum* and *Quadragesimo Anno* and felt that they were progressive documents although he was hostile to the historical role of the Catholic Church in Ireland. According to Kavanagh Catholic journals, in particular *Christus Rex*, were widely read among Curragh internees, and there was little in the way of socialist literature available.[24]

Kavanagh claims that only a small number of prisoners were socialists and makes the point that the IRA Volunteers who were interned tended to be young, with little formal education, and had been deliberately kept away from Sinn Féin for security reasons, so that they had little experience of political ideas.[25] Tony Meade, who spent seven years in Crumlin Road, says that most of the long-term prisoners' time was spent in reading, studying and debate. In contrast to the Curragh, among the publications available were the *Communist Manifesto*, *New Statesman* and the writings of James Connolly. Meade says that 'there was quite a lot of discussion on socialism. After all, it was the only -ism to discuss.'[26] However, Eamonn Boyce from Dublin who was also held in Belfast, recalls that while there was discussion about socialism that most prisoners were strongly Catholic and he records having been highly offended at the Catholic hierarchy's seeming equation of the IRA and Communists.[27] Interestingly when Eamon Timoney wrote an article in the prison journal *Saoirse* entitled 'Quo Vadis Hibernia?' advocating a return to the left-wing politics of the 1930s he was strongly criticised by Seán Garland.

Christus Rex was published at Maynooth by the Christus Rex Society. It attacked communism[28] and reiterated Catholic teaching on socialism but capitalism was also condemned and contrasted unfavourably with the medieval guild system. Some writers saw the latter as a third way between capitalism and socialism, a notion dismissed by Seán Garland. The Reverend A.M. Crofts stated that elements in Irish society hostile to the social teachings of the encyclicals had to be eliminated in order to 'break the chains of a foreign liberalist social enslavement'. Unlike the Catholic press of the 1930s there was very little concern expressed about the domestic influence of communism and the lack of support for the Connolly Association and the Irish Workers League was noted. Although republicans may have been influenced by the ideas contained in *Christus Rex*, they would have found little to support their own involvement in, or support for, the armed campaign. The ban on Catholics being members of the IRA was approved, and Sinn Féin's claim that the obligation to sign a declaration to uphold the Constitution was inimical to natural rights was rejected as 'a contradiction in terms; but then logical consistency does not seem to be a key virtue of those who are organising the present series of raids on Northern Ireland'. Bishop William Philbin of Clonfert, in an essay on 'Patriotism' that was published separately as a pamphlet, reminded Catholics of their duty to obey the public authority. While some republicans, like Seán Garland, became hostile to the Church even to the extent that anti-clericalism transformed itself into actual atheism, the majority of republicans managed to balance their politics and religion and remain influenced by Catholic social teaching.

Corporatism, as outlined in *Quadragesimo Anno*, had a significant influence on republicans in the 1930s despite the impression sometimes given that the left was more influential. That was reflected in the *Republican Review* and in the *Wolfe Tone Weekly* which were published after the banning of *An Phoblacht* in 1935. The regular references to the encyclicals and the occasional praise for European fascism and, in the case of the *Wolfe Tone Weekly*, anti-Semitism underline the extent to which the apparent leftism of the 1930s had reflected the individual opinions of Marxists like O'Donnell and Ryan rather than popular republican sentiment, although the latter was supportive of radical social objectives some of which was echoed by Fianna Fáil. The *Catholic Bulletin* of the period, which, under the editorship of J. J. O'Kelly of Sinn Féin, remained sympathetic to republicanism, was another weather vane. Attacks on Freemasonry featured prominently up to 1939 and O'Kelly defended earlier anti Semitic articles. Córas na Poblachta which was established by the IRA in 1940 set out as its objective the establishment of a 'Christian state'[29] and included supporters of the Nazis among its members.

There were journals such as *Studies* which promoted corporatism more broadly, sometimes as practised in fascist Italy, and Catholic writers championed the social encyclicals as the 'charter of the liberties of the working classes' and vocationalism as a voluntary alternative to fascist corporatism. Social justice based on diffuse ownership represented a middle way between capitalism, where only a minority owned property, and communism, which it was claimed took capitalism to its extreme logic by reducing ownership to a single entity, the state.

The Blueshirts and Fine Gael were the main Irish advocates of corporatism and were clearly sympathetic to the Italian model. De Valera commissioned a report on corporatism by a senior civil servant, Thomas Kiernan, in 1933 but did not act on the recommendations which were based on Italian corporatism. A Senate Commission chaired by Bishop Michael Browne of Galway published another report on vocationalism, similarly influenced by European fascism, in 1944 but it was savaged by Lemass who, it has been pointed out, was a member of a government influenced more by Keynes than by the popes. While Keogh and O'Driscoll note the prominence of Catholic social radicalism here even after 1945 owing to the perception that liberalism and capitalism were 'alien', they note that the Church itself had little interest in promoting radical Catholic Action in a situation where they were by and large comfortable with the post 1922 Irish state.[30]

The republican movement re-emerged into semi-legality in 1948 in an environment that was less hostile following the entry of Clann na Poblachta into government. Several of that party's TDs had been in the IRA, and republican dissatisfaction with Fianna Fáil over the suppression of the IRA as well as over social and economic issues was a major element in the Clann's support. It appealed for Christian principles to be applied in social and economic matters and when speaking in favour of the 1950 Social Welfare Bill the Clann TD for Dublin North-East, Peadar Cowan, referred to the failure to apply the precepts of *Rerum Novarum* and *Quadragesimo Anno* to the Irish state.

The *United Irishman* began publication in May 1948 as the first legal republican movement newspaper since the late 1930s. It contained references to the encyclicals and rejected both capitalism and Communism as anti-Christian in their ideas on marriage and the family. The Irish revolutionary tradition was 'Christian, republican, and democratic' and state ownership was rejected on the grounds that 'every man must be an owner to be free'. The republican alternative was based on the 'Old Gaelic system', Comhar na gComharsan, 'an economy of owner workers grouped into co-ops'.[31] The object of distributive ownership was to enable man to achieve 'true freedom', which was the capacity to know, love and to serve God through one's work. There were proposals to divide large holdings, and a Proudhonian one to 'establish the wage-earners of the towns and cities as owner workers of the shops, factories and industries in which they toil'.

In a piece entitled 'The Land for the People', 'Fear Domhainn' outlined a scheme to divide the country into three hundred administrative units within which all the land would be divided to ensure an average of 27½ acres for each family, allowing 2,280,000 people to be settled on the land. Michael Traynor, who remained a prominent member of the movement until he resigned in 1962 in support of McLogan, recommended a system of industrial unionism, similar to the syndicalist idea, as an alternative to parliamentary democracy. Allegations that the IRA was communist were strongly rejected, and state tolerance for Communists was contrasted to the repression meted out to republicans. There were darker influences. Attacks on republicans were contrasted to media silence on the alleged persecution of Catholics in Israel because newspapers were afraid to offend 'the Judaeo-Masonic news agencies' and 'because Jewish influence is rampant in some of those pseudo-Catholic parties and because Jewish finance is a power with which they fear to contend'.[32]

Such overt anti-Semitism, apart from occasional letters from readers, had disappeared by the late 1950s. However, it does indicate that an extreme variant of Catholic radicalism had survived Nazism and the extent to which republicans had been influenced by Ailtirí na hAiséirghe. Indeed Douglas claims that there was a uniquely Irish corpus of radical right-wing ideas, which was based on the stresses of post-colonial modernisation rather than class, which seemed unaffected by events in Europe and was clearly influential among traditionalist republicans.[33]

The liberalisation of Catholic social teaching, signalled by John XXIII's encyclical *Mater et Magistra* of May 1961, coincided with Sinn Féin's greater orientation towards economic and social issues even though John reiterated the stricture that 'no Catholic could subscribe even to moderate Socialism'. Despite that, left-wing ideas did become more acceptable in Ireland to the extent where the Labour Party felt comfortable styling itself as a socialist party and Communists sometimes cited Catholic clerics. Deasún Breathnach, a former member of Ailtirí, claimed that to engage in class struggle was a 'Christian duty'[34] and when the Pope died in 1963 the *United Irishman* said that he had moved the Church 'to the left'. Derry Kelleher, who was a Goulding supporter, sought to demonstrate how Christianity and Marxism could be compatible through an exegesis of the works of Teilhard de Chardin and appealed to traditional Catholic morality as a basis for joining the left in opposing the 'growing tide of hedonism' that was symptomatic of monopoly capitalism.[35]

Republicans were also influenced by anti-colonial movements in Africa and Asia. 'Art O Laoire' praised the Nkrumah regime in Ghana which had threatened to ban the investment of capital abroad, a preoccupation of radical republicans since the 1920s, and contrasted that with the 'ignoble' record of the Irish state that remained 'a provider of cheap agricultural goods' and 'cheap labour'. As an example of the hold that the British financial market had on the Irish economies, O Laoire cited the £350 million from the Republic and £200 million from Northern Ireland that was invested in London. Sinn Féin would establish an independent monetary system under a state reserve or Central Bank and the export of capital would be banned.[36]

In February 1961 the Sinn Féin Publicity Committee issued a statement on foreign investment which it termed 'A New Plantation'. Sinn Féin claimed that foreign companies were attracted only by state grants, and would leave if the climate changed. They were also in unfair competition with Irish firms that were not entitled to the same support and were contributing to the growth in external debt. Another piece rejected the claim by Jack Lynch that the Republic was a friendly environment for British capital and that past animosities were being eliminated: 'In the past at least we didn't have to pay them to rob us.'

The republican critique of economic liberalisation was connected to its rejection of the European Economic Community. The Irish government formally applied to join the EEC on 31 July 1961, on the same day that Harold Macmillan announced that the UK was applying, and this was regarded by republicans as proof that the Irish government was tied to whatever the British did. Lemass admitted to the Dáil that that was the case and that 'if Britain should take this step we should…endeavour to secure terms of membership or association which would satisfactorily take account of our economic circumstances'.[37]

The Sinn Féin Publicity Committee rejected Lemass's claim that joining the EEC would help bring an end to Partition. It might eliminate tariff barriers and there was the danger that closer economic ties with the North would be sold as 'unity'. Once protectionist measures were dropped, Irish industry would be damaged while Irish farmers would be able to compete only through increased productivity or the elimination of smaller holdings. Membership entailed surrender of sovereignty over the economy. 'Ferdia' admitted that in theory a common trading area ought to bring benefits but because of Ireland's weakness the consequence would be depopulation and the destruction of small farms.

Tom Doyle echoed the concern of the Federation of Irish Industries that native businesses would be endangered and rejected the 'mobility of capital and labour' which meant foreign investment and foreign workers. Republicans were also wary of the danger that the Republic would become part of a European military alliance, on the basis of Irish antipathy to Communism. In his address to the Sinn Féin Ard Fheis in December 1961 McLogan said that opposition to the EEC was not based on 'narrow nationalist prejudices' and that if the best interests of the nation lay in entry then they would support it, but that Ireland could have nothing to do with the defence of the colonial interests which would inevitably lead to a military alliance. Joining the EEC would be the equivalent of joining NATO and would increase the malign influence of Freemasonry that was a bigger threat to the religious faith of the Irish people than Russia was.[38] Opposition to NATO did not, however, indicate support for the Soviet Union: 'The vast majority of Irish people reject Communist imperialism and the sources from which it stems. By none among them is it more emphatically rejected than by members of the Republican Movement.' Another argument against joining the EEC was that the Republic would be entering an alliance with Italy and France which had the two strongest Communist parties outside the Soviet bloc and whose members would be free to enter Ireland.[39]

At root, republican opposition to the EEC had little to do with economic factors. Indeed 'economic hardships' outside the EEC would be preferable to abandoning sovereignty. MacDara (the pseudonym of Richard Roche, another former member of Ailtirí) described the application to join the EEC as an example of 'the blind pursuit of materialism',[40] and referred to the need to 'rid ourselves of the false concept of materialistic progress and prosperity'. In a pamphlet entitled *Nation or Province* published in January 1963, Sinn Féin referred to the attempt to have the Irish Christian way of life 'swamped in a flood of European materialism'.

The ideas found in republican policy statements of the late 1950s and early 1960s prove that Sinn Féin had little in common with the ideology of the Communists who were beginning to court them politically. While there were references to looking after people's interests and ending unemployment and emigration, all of this was subsumed under the overriding objective of achieving national sovereignty and independence. The achievement of 'national aims and objectives' was a spiritual quest and Irish freedom was something that was superior to material prosperity. There was also an emphasis on individual and community self-reliance rather than on the state. While this clearly differentiated the republican movement from the orthodox European left and its preoccupations, it is rhetoric that was similar to that of revolutionary movements in some of the former colonial countries and with other European nationalist movements. Myrddin Lloyd of Plaid Cymru asserted: 'Our main task is a spiritual one.'[41] Deasún Breathnach proposed that Ireland 'take the same chances as Egypt, or Israel or Ghana...to accept, if it be necessary, a lower living standard'.[42]

If the influence of Catholic social teaching separated traditionalist republicans from the left, the sharp contrast between the attitude of republicans and the Fianna Fáil leadership with regard to the EEC was reflective of even more profound differences over the future of the country and modernisation and illustrated how far Fianna Fáil had evolved since its radical formative period. Indeed as late as 1955 De Valera had warned of the dangers of Ireland entering a European Federation in which 'you had a European Parliament deciding the economic circumstances, for example, of our life here'.[43] Lemass rejected that ascetic vision of sovereignty and, in his speech to the 1960 Ard Fheis, he denied that a choice had to be made between modernisation and national independence: 'We used to say that we would prefer freedom in the hair shirt to the fleshpots of serfdom but that is not a choice we have to make. We believe in the beneficial force of disciplined nationalism.'[44] Traditional republicans would still have opted for the hair shirt.

It is possible in one sense then to see the republican movement at this period as being representative of a resistance to modernisation. While it did put forward a radical vision of what Ireland might be, Sinn Féin to some extent was also defending the type of policies that Fianna Fáil governments under De Valera had implemented. Although it qualified its support for protectionism by claiming that it had never been properly utilised, for Sinn Féin protectionism's main flaw was that the policy was not implemented on an all-Ireland basis. At some level, republicans were also voicing a concern, which was shared by others such as Lia Fáil, that whatever had remained from the revolutionary era as part of the ethos of the Irish state was being jettisoned. There were also wider concerns regarding the impact of opening up the country to new influences, including socialism. The modernist faction eventually came to reject the traditional republican vision even though their template for economic development and modernisation looked towards the socialist states rather than the West.

While there was continuity within traditional republican ideology, Ruairí Ó Brádaigh has claimed that Sinn Féin had embarked upon a revision of its social and economic programme in 1962 independently of any external influence. He was aware of the kind of thinking that was taking place in the Connolly Association, as the *Irish Democrat* had circulated among the republican prisoners in the Curragh, and had read some of Johnston's articles and had found himself in general agreement with what he was saying. However Ó Brádaigh's attitude was that republicans did not need the advice of the Communists.[45] Seán Garland is of the view that Ó Brádaigh and Mac Stíofáin had no real interest in radical social ideas or political strategy[46] although Tony Meade recalls that neither Ó Brádaigh nor Mac Stíofáin ever demonstrated any overt opposition to socialism,[47] as opposed to Marxism and more importantly members of Marxist organisations.

The public discourse of republicanism did become more left-wing following the end of the armed campaign and the consolidation of the new leadership around Cathal Goulding. Tom Mitchell's oration at the Wolfe Tone commemoration at Bodenstown in June 1963 referred to the existence in Ireland of 'a pseudo-aristocratic group become rich upon the sweat of thousands of their fellow-men', and spoke of the reorganisation of the republican movement. Mitchell considered himself to be a socialist and, coming as he did from a working-class Dublin background, was influenced by Connolly and Larkin but he had no time for Communism.[48]

It is clear from the *United Irishman* that the views expressed after 1962 reflected a wide range of ideological leanings outside of the one common commitment to the traditional republican aim of separation from Britain. A regular contributor like Mac Dara, who in his youth had been a member of Ailtirí na hAiséirghe, was capable of sounding conventionally left- or right-wing depending on the topic. People who had widely divergent social and economic opinions felt a bond of solidarity that outweighed for a time any affinity they might have had to individuals of like mind outside the IRA or Sinn Féin. It is clear too that Marxist ideas were viewed with all the more suspicion by traditionalists because the main promoters of this were regarded as people with no republican background. Traditionalists in the 1930s tended not to have such a jaundiced view of Marxists like Frank Ryan and Peadar

O'Donnell who were well known to them through the IRA, and they defended them against clerical attack.

For Marxists, the type of politics which was put forward by Sinn Féin was evidence of the party's petit-bourgeois roots. While this was a crude definition, it did have some validity. That was most apparent in the type of economic and social issues with which Sinn Féin chose to engage in the early 1960s. The party called upon Irish consumers to boycott foreign-owned chain stores and supermarkets and to replace their products with Irish-made goods bought in Irish-owned shops. The alternative to foreign takeovers was for small traders to form co-operatives and buy in bulk in order to compete. Sinn Féin motions in support of the Buy Irish campaign were passed by several Town Commissions and Urban District Councils. While the movement was too small and dispersed to claim that it had anything approaching what might be termed a social base, some leading republican activists were small business people and so naturally concerned about issues like retail taxes that affected themselves as well as others in their situation.

Republicans had failed, after the split with Fianna Fáil in the 1930s, to retain the support of any substantial section of Irish society. It was the failure to win working-class support that particularly motivated the modernising left within the movement to alter the policy and organisation of the IRA and Sinn Féin. However, as Michael Keating has noted, lack of working-class support tends to be a feature of all similar European nationalist movements, and the industrial working class has little interest in 'peripheral' nationalist movements because its concerns are focused on the central state and are traditionally represented by democratic left-wing parties and trade unions.[49] That has been the case in the Basque region where radical separatists have enjoyed less support than the Spanish left, and in Cyprus the conflict between Cypriot nationalists seeking *enosis* with Greece and the Cypriot Communist Party led to EOKA killing members of the Communist AKEL during the 1955–59 war against the British. For Irish republicans the problem facing them in the 1960s during a period of rapid economic and consequent social change was that neither their emphasis on ending partition, even though it remained a popular if passive 'aspiration', nor their appeal to self-sacrifice in place of a 'materialistic' rise in living standards, struck much of a chord. Indeed it was only the manner in which the Unionists reacted to the democratic demands of northern nationalists which gave them once again any sort of entrée into mainstream southern life.

With the new emphasis on social and economic engagement as early as 1963 there was some disquiet expressed over where the movement might be going politically. Traditional republicans sometimes referred to 'class war' as a distraction from the movement's aims. One letter to the *United Irishman* decried the raising of the issue of class, in relation to reports on strikes and housing, saying that 'while Irishmen fight Irishmen the Communists rub their hands and plan for the day when they can come out in the open posing as the saviour of the workers'. James Connolly was often central to the ideological disputation. Ever since his execution conservatives and radical Catholics had attempted to claim that Connolly had not really been a Marxist, would have rejected Marxism had he seen it in practice, or that his ideas were compatible with Catholicism. Fr Denis Fahey argued that, while Connolly had been a Catholic and had died in the Faith, he had not understood the contradictions between Marxism and Catholicism. Interestingly he also claimed that social-ism as it existed in the Soviet Union was the antithesis of the popular democ-racy and workers control envisaged by Connolly.[50] A biography of Connolly written by Proinsias Mac An Bheatha in 1964 put forward the theory that Connolly's views were compatible with Catholic social doctrine and that Con-nolly would have rejected Communism had he lived to see it being imple-mented.[51] Traditional republicans were certainly closer to that view than the projection of Connolly by the republican left as an international revolutionary socialist.

Despite the critique of its alleged intellectual poverty, however, there were elements in the traditionalist Sinn Féin programme that taken together pre-sented a coherent alternative to the emerging consensus among the political and business elite. It was also clearly rooted in Catholic social teaching and, while there was a commitment to the need for social justice and the rights of workers, equal emphasis was placed on the need for the protection of native businesses against foreign capital. Sinn Féin stressed the potential that lay in the development of natural resources, and highlighted Fianna Fáil's abandon-ing of the promotion of tillage farming in favour of turning Ireland into a 'giant ranch for the supply of cheap beef to Britain'. Sinn Féin warned of the dangers posed by the EEC's policy of eliminating small farms, and claimed that co-operativism was the only viable strategy for Irish agriculture.

While the critique of the new policies initiated by the Programme for Economic Development united the traditionalists and the modernisers within the movement, it also formed a point of contact with the non-republican and Communist left. That became the basis of the alliance between the modernis-ers and the Communists and led to a rift with the traditionalists who while radically opposed to the social and economic status quo based their opposi-tion on a critique rooted in traditional nationalist and Catholic social ideas rather than socialism and its notions of development and modernisation which were perceived to be every bit as alien and malign as capitalist consum-erism. The orthodox left, more importantly, also brought radically different notions on how to implement policies and on engagement with the wider society. That was the basis of the ideological conflict between traditionalist and modernising republicans which led to many of them departing from the movement in the 1960s as the modernising faction came to dominate the leadership and policy development. However, it was the outbreak of the northern conflict in 1969 and disagreements over the role and function of the IRA and over abstentionism that underlay the formal split although there were also references to differences over socialism. The marginalisation of the movement during the 1960s also proves I believe that neither the radical traditionalist critique nor the modernist embrace of Marxism had much resonance in a society in which people could see an improvement in living standards and in which their economic aspirations were catered to by the state and the trade unions rather than any desire for revolutionary change.

Notes

1 Cronin (1980), p. 187.
2 *United Irishman*, March 1959.
3 T. K. Whitaker, *Economic Development* (Dublin 1958), p. 7.
4 Patrick Lynch, 'The Economics of Independence', in Basil Chubb and Patrick Lynch, ed., *Economic Development and Planning* (Dublin 1969), p. 130.
5 *United Irishman*, May 1961.
6 Interview with Seán Ó Brádaigh, 21 May 2005.
7 Patterson (1997), p. 95.
8 www.vatican.va/holy_father/leo_xiii/encyclicals/documents/hf_l-xiii_enc_ 15051891_rerum-novarum_en.html, p. 1–2, viewed 5 August 2006.
9 Foley (1972), p. 17.
10 Moloney (2002), p. 54–5.
11 Leo XIII, *Graves de Communi Re*, www.ewtn.com/library/encyc/l13grcom.htm, viewed 23 August 2006.
12 Pius X, *Il Fermo Proposito*, www.ewtn.com/library/ENCYC/P10FERMO.HTM, viewed 23 August 2006.
13 Tom Buchanan and Martin Conway, *Political Catholicism in Europe 1918–1965* (Oxford 1996).
14 Tom Nairn, *The Breakup of Britain* (London 1977), p. 197.
15 Brian Murphy, 'The Stone of Destiny: Fr. John Fahy (1894–1969), Lia Fáil and Smallholder Radicalism in Modern Irish Society', in Gerard Moran, ed., *Radical Irish Priests 1660–1970* (Dublin 1998), p. 201, note 72.
16 *Lia Fáil*, no. 1, August 1958.
17 Murphy (1998), p. 215.
18 Mainchin Seoighe, *Maraiodh Seán Sabhat Aréir* (Baile Átha Cliath 1964), p. 44.
19 *Fiat*, no. 40.
20 *Limerick Leader*, 24 January 1949.
21 Interview with Seán Garland, 28 February 2005.
22 R. M. Douglas, *Architects of the Resurrection: Ailtirí na hAiséirghe and the Fascist 'New Order' in Ireland* (Manchester 2009), p. 169.

23 *Christus Rex*, Vol. XIV, no. 3, July 1960, p. 195–8.
24 Ruairí Ó Brádaigh, however, recalls that the *Irish Democrat* was available (Interview with Ruairí Ó Brádaigh 22 May 2002).
25 Interview with Noel Kavanagh, 7 March 2005.
26 Email from Tony Meade, 18 April 2005.
27 Eamonn Boyce, *The Insider* (Dublin 2008), p. 37.
28 *Christus Rex*, Vol. XI, no. 1, January 1957, p. 493.
29 *Córas na Poblachta* (Dublin 1940), p. 3.
30 Dermot Keogh and Finín O'Driscoll, 'Ireland', in John Buchanan and Martin Conway, ed., *Political Catholicism in Europe 1918–1965* (Oxford 1996), p. 281.
31 *United Irishman*, May 1948.
32 *United Irishman*, July–August 1949.
33 Douglas (2009), p. 287.
34 *United Irishman*, November 1965.
35 Derry Kelleher, *Republicanism, Christianity and Marxism* (Dublin 1970), p. 9.
36 *United Irishman*, July 1963.
37 *Dáil Debates*, Vol. 189, 16 May 1961.
38 *United Irishman*, March 1962.
39 Sinn Féin, *Nation or Province* (Dublin 1963), p. 10.
40 *United Irishman*, April 1962.
41 D. Myrddin Lloyd, *Plaid Cymru and Its Message* (Cardiff 1949).
42 *United Irishman*, February 1963.
43 *Dáil Debates*, Vol. 152, col. 548.
44 *Irish Press*, 9 November 1960.
45 Interview with Ruairí Ó Brádaigh, 21 May 2002.
46 Interview with Seán Garland, 11 December 2001.
47 Email from Tony Meade, 18 April 2005.
48 Interview with Tom Mitchell, 11 January 2002.
49 Michael Keating, *State and Regional Nationalism* (Hemel Hempstead 1988), p. 73.
50 Fr Denis Fahey, *The Tragedy of James Connolly* (Cork 1947), p. 26.
51 Proinsias Mac an Bheatha, *Tart na Cora* (Baile Átha Cliath 1964).

3

Abstentionism and the growth of internal divisions

For traditionalist republicans, the refusal to recognise the parliaments in Leinster House and Stormont symbolised their allegiance to the *de jure* Republic which they claimed had been illegally overthrown in 1922. For them it still had legitimacy with legal authority having been passed to the IRA Army Council in 1938 by the surviving anti-Treaty Sinn Féin members of the Dáil elected in 1923. Traditionalists, as represented today by Republican Sinn Féin and the Continuity IRA, still adhere to that belief.

A proposal to abandon abstentionism was put to the IRA Convention in November 1964. The strength of the opposition led to a decision to instead hold an extraordinary Convention in 1965. According to Mac Stíofáin the 'Goulding faction' was 'becoming obsessed with parliamentary politics and wished to confine the movement almost entirely to social and economic agitation'. Although he had been friendly with Goulding, Mac Stíofáin came into conflict with the Chief of Staff at an Army Council meeting following the Convention when he proposed that Roy Johnston be expelled on the grounds that IRA Army Orders prohibited members of Communist organisations from becoming members.[1] Goulding implied that if Johnston were expelled then he would also resign and defended Johnston as 'the best thing that had happened to the republican movement'.[2]

The 1964 Ard Fheis, held in the Bricklayers Hall on 5 and 6 December, approved a paper on Economic Resistance written by Roy Johnston. Seamus Costello's cumann in Bray called for a re-examination of electoral policy but this was defeated. There was another motion that proposed expelling any member of the movement who advocated change but that also fell. As with the IRA Convention it was decided to hold an extraordinary Ard Fheis in 1965 to deal with those issues. Although the *United Irishman* had reported that a key aspect of the Ard Fheis would be the presentation of the draft social and economic programme, the document was not completed but the heads of the draft were agreed. Seán Ó Brádaigh claims that it was effectively put aside because Goulding had asked Johnston to work on an alternative programme[3] which had been discussed at the Wolfe Tone Society.

In his Presidential address Mac Giolla referred to the renewed 'onslaught' by foreign capital on the Irish economy. Despite the increase in foreign investment Mac Giolla pointed out that fewer people were working than in 1956. He said that the new land policy would lead to a hundred thousand farmers leaving the land, North and South. Sinn Féin's proposal was to maintain the Land Commission holdings which would be farmed co-operatively.[4] The republican and labour movements needed to revive their common aim of restoring control by the Irish people over natural resources.

Although the modernisers had lost the first battle to radically alter republican policy, they were determined to press ahead. The IRA internal journal *An t-Óglach* of January 1965 said that IRA Volunteers needed to be active within the community and that a 'Republic without equality would not be worth fighting for'. The tone was dismissive of traditional republican attitudes. An interview with Tony Meade, in a special issue of *TCD Miscellany* in February 1965 devoted to the IRA, attempted to set the agenda for the Special IRA Convention and Sinn Féin Ard Fheis. The editorial described the efforts of a young radical 'ginger group' to politicise the republican movement and wean it away from militarism. The group was opposed to abstentionism and might transform Sinn Féin into a 'new radical party which would give welcome new life to the present stale charade of Irish politics'.[5] Elsewhere, however, Sinn Féin was described as a 'dead group' and the *United Irishman* as filled with 'unrealistic fanaticism'. Another article in the *Miscellany* predicted that there would be an internal struggle within the republican movement between 'diehards' and the 'new left-wing (but certainly not Communist) element'.

Despite the debate on abstentionism, when it was announced that Ruairí Ó Brádaigh would contest the next general election for Longford-Westmeath it was made clear that he would not be taking his seat if he repeated the success of 1957.

The decision to contest was described as 'the first move in a new and vigorous campaign of political action by Sinn Féin'. At a local election convention in Louth, Larry Grogan claimed that contesting elections would dispel the notion that Sinn Féin were 'wild and woolly characters' divorced from day-to-day realities. Sinn Féin did not contest the general election held on 7 April owing to lack of finance, but also to the unresolved internal debate over electoral strategy. The party said it would concentrate instead on a campaign of militant agitation for a British withdrawal and opposition to the 'growth of a foreign dominated capitalist society'. The Ard Comhairle announced that Sinn Féin would take part only when it was able to present a sufficiently strong team of candidates to secure an overall majority in Leinster House.

Such optimism had begun to irritate some of those who were impatient for change and in March 1965 the editor of the *United Irishman*, Denis Foley, delivered a devastating critique of the political strategy that had been pursued by the republican movement since the 1920s. Republicans had properly criticised the state but had 'done nothing constructive to alter the position'. Dismissing a Coiste Seasta statement which said that Sinn Féin would enter Leinster House as a majority and then 'proceed to legislate for all Ireland', Foley was scornful of the claim that the republican social and economic programme would be implemented in a 'free Ireland': 'In the meantime do the Irish people have to wait indefinitely for the miracle which republicans promise "in the free Ireland"?' He described this attitude as 'Live horse and you'll eat grass…The Republican Movement, if it is to be of service to the Irish people must put its policy into effect now and forget about waiting for the "free Ireland".' He cited Connolly and Davitt as examples of revolutionaries who 'saw that the improving of the welfare of the people went hand in hand with the "freeing of them," and that every avenue' should be used in the pursuit of freedom.

Foley's editorial gave rise to furious debate. A letter from Eamon Mac Tiomanai said it was an insult to Sinn Féin candidates to suggest that they would be corrupted by taking their seats in Leinster House, and it was inconsistent. After all, why take part in local but not state government and why do so in the Republic but not in Northern Ireland?[6] Mac Tiomanai said that he could not conceive of a situation in which Sinn Féin would win a majority in Leinster House but that even if that did come to pass the party would still have to use the existing constitutional machinery of the state to establish an All Ireland parliament. He attacked the notion that 'Republicanism is some form of a mystique esoteric cult'. The former Dublin Brigade OC Phil O'Donoghue congratulated Foley for his call on republicans to become involved in social struggles and contrasted what he described as the 'trivial' agitation over the Royal visit to a lack of republican commitment to attacking the existing social system. Roderick Corcoran of Dublin wondered how Sinn Féin proposed to win the majority they spoke of being 'given' to the party: 'Majorities are never given – they are worked for and won and to suggest otherwise betrays a complete lack of political sense.'

There were also letters of protest but they did not appear until May. Seán Ó Brádaigh, the Sinn Féin Director of Publicity, refused to distribute the March issue of the *United Irishman* as did other party cumainn and IRA units. Ó Brádaigh wondered 'by what authority this questioning of the official policy of the movement had been allowed' and described the editorial as 'an unwarranted attack' by the 'official organ of the Republican Movement on the political wing of that Movement'. Ó Brádaigh is still not certain whether Foley had official sanction from Goulding to publish the piece[7] but suggests that Foley must have been acting with at least his tacit consent.

It is clear that Foley's view was shared by a number of those on the IRA Army Council. The fact that Foley was to step down from the position later on in the year, however, may also have been indicative that his intervention had been premature and indeed no similar attacks on abstentionism were published prior to the split. A later report claimed that Goulding had read the editorial only while on his way by aeroplane to England and that he was shocked by it. How genuine was his surprise is another matter. At the time, Foley was sharing a house in Rathmines with Roy Johnston, who was believed by others to be behind the initiative.

Seamus Ceitinn supported Foley but attacked the notion that there might be an alliance in the future between Sinn Féin and any of the three main parties. He was particularly wary of the Labour Party and was insistent that republicans could only join forces with those committed to an 'Ireland, United, Christian, Gaelic and Free'.[8] Proof that opposition to abstentionism was not necessarily of a piece with support for left-wing ideas was provided by J. Doherty of London who said that Sinn Féin should enter Leinster House but also that the *United Irishman* should have no articles on Communism 'and the rest of that muck'.

The debate on abstentionism was encouraged by the political education programme that had begun in earnest in early 1965. The IRA leadership emphasised the priority of social agitation and ruled out a new campaign begun in the same manner as 1956. However, only the Dublin and Cork IRA had so far appointed a Political Education Officer. Johnston was Director of Political Education and on 7 March 1965 a series of debates and lectures on political education was held in Howth covering economic resistance, co-ops and trade unions. All Command areas were ordered to organise similar courses and were visited by officers attached to the Political Education Department.[9] While electoral policy was not one of the subjects covered by the lectures, the climate of debate encouraged republican activists to challenge aspects of the movement's policy including abstentionism.

The IRA Easter statement of 1965 expressed satisfaction at the manner in which the 'internal examination of our Movement in all its branches' was proceeding and implicitly encouraged members to look favourably on the proposals to be put before the extraordinary Ard Fheis. The *United Irishman* approved of the content of the orations that had been delivered at Easter and noted a 'minimum of sabre-rattling' and a concentration on social and economic issues. Roy Johnston, writing in the *Irish Democrat*, heralded what was described tentatively as a 'Republican New Departure?' and referred to the role being played by the Wolfe Tone Society which was 'carrying new flexible and diversified republican tactics into other areas'.[10]

There were further clashes over Easter lilies in 1965 and an armed threat made against a Cork Garda. That incident highlighted the contradiction between the IRA's commitment to militant action, and the desire of the modernisers to move away from militarism. Although a resolution passed at the

1964 Army Convention had sanctioned 'counter intimidation' against Gardaí, an Army Council directive in 1965 banned any use of force. Special Branch attributed this to GHQ fears that the 1964 resolution was being misused. The Cork Volunteers involved had acted without the authority of the leadership and so their actions were disowned. A local republican activist of the period, however, believes that they had the approval of the Cork IRA including Mac Stíofáin.

The extraordinary IRA Army Convention was held on 5 June 1965. The modernisers hoped that it would initiate a radical reform of the movement and Goulding had appealed directly to Volunteers to give the proposals their full consideration. However, the proposals on electoral policy and the reorganisation of the movement caused such controversy that they were forced to back down and appoint a committee to draw up a plan that would allegedly embody the general feeling of the Convention. Traditionalists like Ruairí Ó Brádaigh believed that Goulding had underestimated the strength of opposition to the proposals and that the committee was a means to circumvent it. Goulding ensured that the committee was dominated by those close to him and it submitted an initial report to the Special Ard Fheis. Rejection there meant that the committee had to draft another report. It was partly approved by the Army Council in August 1965 and was captured by the Garda Special Branch when they arrested Army Council member Seán Garland at Mountrath, County Laois, in May 1966.

The extraordinary Sinn Féin Ard Fheis was held on 12 and 13 June 1965. According to Ruairí Ó Brádaigh, the proposals presented by the IRA committee included some that had already been rejected by the Army Convention. Ó Brádaigh had been appointed to the committee appointed by the Army Council to draw up the recommendations but did not attend any of its meetings. The proposals were first submitted to the Ard Comhairle but that body did not recommend that all of them should be passed. The fact that most of the Ard Comhairle members and a substantial number of the Ard Fheis delegates were IRA Volunteers familiar with what had transpired at the Convention made their rejection all the more likely. The document that was put before the IRA delegates came to be known as the 'Nine Points' but there were ten proposals in the Ard Fheis document. Point 1 proposed that the movement should develop 'political and agitational activities and the infiltration and direction of other organisations'. That was the object of the 'educational and training programmes in both organisations'. There also needed to be 'closer integration of the executives of both organisations' and closer integration of the IRA and Sinn Féin.[11]

Although the proposal was couched in terms of infiltrating and taking over other organisations it was regarded by traditionalists as opening the door to co-operation and indeed a formal alliance with the Communist parties and the Connolly Association. The Ard Comhairle recommended that the first proposal should be accepted in its entirety but, while the delegates accepted the references to education, they removed the reference to 'infiltration and control', and referred to co-operation with other organisations on 'limited objectives', and turned down the proposal to merge the IRA and Sinn Féin. The Ard Fheis also inserted a clause which made it clear that nothing in the proposal implied altering electoral policy. The second proposal recommended that while '*de jure* recognition' would not be given to the state, members ought to be free to defend themselves in court when charged with 'political and agitationary activities'. Where the charges related to armed IRA operations, 'the decision to defend or not rest with the executives of both organisations'. That was rejected although a proposal to establish a legal panel who could be contacted in the event of any republican being arrested was passed.

Proposal No. 3 upheld the convention that republicans refused to account for their movements as they were required to under Section 54 of the Offences against the State Act. Any prosecution under that section would be contested and a case prepared for the European Court of Human Rights. It was also proposed that some person who was not a member of the movement would bring a constitutional case against the Offences against the State Act. This was one of only two proposals that were accepted by the Ard Comhairle and the delegates and passed without amendment. No. 4 recommended that in general the organisers of parades and commemorations should notify the police. The Ard Comhairle accepted this but the delegates voted it down. Delegates also rejected a proposal that republicans should apply for police permits to hold raffles and collections.

No. 8 (a) recommended that Sinn Féin should register as a political party. The Ard Comhairle had decided to examine the full implications of this before coming to a decision but the Ard Fheis rejected it in any event. The next section proposed that the attitude of republicans to prison be reconsidered. That was passed, as was a proposal that republicans should be permitted to write to government TDs and another that republicans 'acting as members of local organisations' be encouraged to take part in delegations to meet government Ministers. The final section of the proposal, that republicans should co-operate with other organisations in the pursuit of specific objectives and adopt a pragmatic attitude to approaching individual parliamentary representatives, was rejected, again because of the belief that there was a plan for a formal relationship with the Communists.

Recommendation No. 9 was the most controversial, proposing that the movement 'give consideration to action within existing parliaments on a guerrilla basis'. It is clear that the committee that had been appointed by the Army Council was not representative of the Convention, otherwise the proposal would not have been put to the Ard Fheis. As it transpired it was rejected by both the Ard Comhairle and the delegates. The final proposal was the only other recommendation that was accepted as it stood, to organise a conference on 'the foreign take-over of land, industry and trades and the general issue of foreign influence in Ireland'.[12] This conference took place later in 1965, organised by the Wolfe Tone Society.

As an attempt by the modernisers to fundamentally change the tactics and organisation of the republican movement, the Convention and Ard Fheis were failures. Sinn Féin had rejected abandoning abstentionism and while delegates had accepted the proposals for involvement in social agitation and for limited co-operation with other organisations they had rejected any formal alliance. Traditionalists also clung to a curious existential relationship with the southern state which they recognised in all practicalities, even to the extent of allowing that others, not members of the movement, might take legal action against it on their behalf, but insisting on their own purity when it came to any engagement with the state, other than as normal citizens through their contact with the public service and even the Gardaí.

It could be argued that traditionalist opposition to the institutions of the Irish state allowed them to appear as revolutionaries while in other respects they were unprepared to challenge the economic and social status quo and that their reluctance to go down the road advocated by Goulding and Johnston was a reflection of their own conservatism. As White's biography of Ruairí Ó Brádaigh demonstrates, however, many traditionalist republicans were serious about both their desire to overturn the 1922 settlement and their belief in a more radical and egalitarian social system. It is also true to say that they shared most of the mores and attitudes of their Catholic neighbours whereas urban-based republican leftists tended to identify themselves with modern liberal attitudes on sexual issues for example and regarded themselves as part of a wider international movement for radical change as well as Irish republicans. In that sense, some of the divisions within radical republicanism reflected wider divisions within Irish society as it experienced the impact of economic and cultural modernisation.

Roy Johnston maintains that Sinn Féin was an impediment to the new departure in all its aspects and that IRA activists were making the running in whatever involvement the movement had in social agitation.[13] That may have been true of the leadership but most IRA Volunteers clearly shared Sinn Féin's opposition to change and the Ard Fheis refusal to alter electoral policy encouraged the modernisers to sideline traditionalists where they were particularly strong, as in Kerry, and thereby weaken any potential opposition.

The Sinn Féin Vice President Seán Caughey resigned over the failure to change electoral policy. The *United Irishman* made no reference to the extraordinary Ard Fheis although Tony Meade delivered what amounted to a potted version of the new IRA strategy in his oration at the Wolfe

Tone commemoration at Bodenstown on 20 June. He spoke of the need for republicans to engage in popular struggles and while he referred to a future campaign against the British presence as 'inevitable' it ought not be an 'untimely attempt' and the movement had to ensure that they would have behind them an educated people united in their opposition to economic speculators.

Speaking at Drogheda on 15 August Goulding promised that 'there will be a fight' on military, economic, social and cultural fronts with the military struggle having precedence.[14] That reflected the pressure from traditionalists on Goulding following the Convention and, according to Johnston, they had no intention of pursuing such a strategy.[15] Goulding told Patterson that the leadership needed to maintain a military strategy in order to win acceptance for the political changes,[16] an analysis which was echoed by their close observer in the Department of Justice, Peter Berry.[17]

The first issue of *An Phoblacht,* the paper published by the Cork group formed from the Swanton Commemoration Committee, described the differences within the party as a symptom of the 'violent contradiction between the petty bourgeois spirit of Sinn Féin on the one hand, and its decision to abstain from the country's mainstream of petit bourgeois politics on the other'.[18] *An Phoblacht* agreed that abstentionism was a 'farce' and that electoral participation was a logical step for a party that 'stands only for the unification of the prevailing social, political and economic order, and not for its total destruction'. While the group accepted that Irish republicans had been fixated with armed struggle in the past, they dismissed the notion that republican objectives could be achieved without an armed organisation. They ridiculed Goulding's Drogheda speech and claimed that the IRA was incapable of leading any fight as it had become a 'standing joke'.

The report based on the modified 1965 proposals was discussed by the Army Council in August and contained two main components, one of which dealt with policy and organisational changes, the other outlining a plan for a future military offensive. According to the Gardaí the military plan had not, as of November 1966, been approved by the Council. In order to attract 'people of national outlook in the Trade Union movement',[19] the IRA would have to adopt 'a radical social and economic programme'. All of this would take place under the control of the Chief of Staff. It was also proposed that the IRA would 'make the fullest use of experts to lecture to republicans on Trade Union, Economic and other subjects'.

Roy Johnston as Director of Education had responsibility for that aspect of what became known as the 'Garland Plan'. Johnston says that the internal education programme came under the auspices of a Joint Education Centre that included himself, Seán Ó Brádaigh and Anthony Coughlan representing, respectively, the 'Garland Plan' – i.e., the IRA leadership – Sinn Féin and the

Wolfe Tone Society.[20] Seán Ó Brádaigh was unhappy with Coughlan's involvement and, seconded by Mitchell, proposed at the January 1966 Ard Comhairle meeting that Coughlan be excluded from the Education Department because he was a Communist. The motion was passed, reflecting the weakness of the leftist modernisers in the wake of the Special Ard Fheis and Army Convention.[21] Coughlan, however, while never formally joining either the IRA or Sinn Féin, remained a key influence on Goulding.

According to the new strategy, committees needed to be established to work alongside other radical groups but reference to the Labour Party was deleted before the Army Council approved the draft. These would be under overall Army control, which was crucial not only to maintaining the cohesion of the IRA but also because the education programme was adjudged to be successful in the IRA but not in Sinn Féin, whose members were apparently reluctant to embrace the new policies. The IRA would use the committees to further the project of radicalising the movement through a process of re-educating and re-invigorating Sinn Féin and by attracting new members. Sinn Féin would confine itself to publicity and election work.

The IRA would recruit a different type of member with the emphasis on social and economic objectives rather than arms. The IRA would back up and consolidate revolutionary action initiated legally rather than initiate military action. To ensure that the Army would retain its capacity to act in the old way, specialist groups would be trained in military tactics but the eventual aim was to create a movement which would have an open membership and legal existence. In other words the IRA would cease to be a secret military force.

The document referred to 'the transition from the gun to politics' with the movement transformed into an open and legal 'social-revolutionary organisation'. The basic organisational unit would be branches focused on community organisations, trade union branches and youth groups as 'the basic channel for recruitment'. Regional conferences would co-ordinate the overall work and the annual conference would be the ruling body alongside regular regional conferences and a Standing Committee. The IRA would retain a separate structure and 'function within the revolutionary organisation as a backbone' comprised of the 'best and most conscious members of the organisation' and would jettison the 'emotional appeal of arms'.

The IRA Convention would remain the main policy making body until the National Conference of the open organisation began to act 'correctly'. The IRA would no longer exercise its dominance over the organisation as it did with Sinn Féin which was an 'imposition on the many good people in Sinn Féin'. The Army Convention would then become a specialist conference for 'examining technical problems connected to the military aspect of the revolution'. The Constitution of the new revolutionary body would be drafted in a way that would allow the affiliation of the kind of organisations that would contribute to a 'vast and diversified movement under the republican umbrella'. The latter proposal was to lay the basis for a formal alliance with the Communists.

There was a compromise proposal designed to postpone any decision on abstentionism which indicated that the restructuring of the IRA and the building of an alliance with the Communists had greater priority for the modernisers. Elections would not be contested until there was a chance of doing well and the question of taking seats would be considered 'when necessary'. The document then indulges in a flight of fancy to propose that, when there was a Sinn Féin majority, MPs and TDs would meet in some central location like Athlone 'and proceed to legislate for the whole country'. This would establish a dual power situation with the IRA, unions and co-ops confronting the old state. When the two structures came into conflict the situation would be resolved by the intervention of the IRA. It was a meaningless aspiration in the light of the movement's weakness but did serve the purpose of postponing confrontation over abstentionism. It also illustrated that the modernisers were no less attracted to grandiose plans than were the traditionalists, and some of them appeared to assume that the organisational and electoral changes which they wished to implement would quickly place the movement in a position to challenge for power.

The second part of the 'Garland Plan', which was not approved by the Army Council, set out the details of a future military campaign. This was in contradiction to the stated aim in the political strategy of moving from the gun to politics. The military plan was broken down into five stages which were to begin immediately and proceed to the level where they would be combined with the type of revolutionary political actions described above, in a full-scale armed insurrection. The first stage was described as an 'Anti-agent campaign' aimed at the police. It was recommended to be commenced immediately and would be carried out 'quietly' to 'prepare the way for a campaign', and to 'get our people psychologically prepared for future killing'. The next stage would consist of 'large stunt-type operations' but would not commence until the IRA had enough trained personnel to carry them out and 'inflict as many fatal casualties on the British as possible'.

The staging of operations would prove whether the organisation was capable of sustaining a campaign; if not 'we can draw back'. Interestingly, it was noted that while the campaign would be fought in Northern Ireland it was felt that the 'structure, organisation and control of the army in that area is unsound for campaign conditions the nature of which is envisaged'. This would make classic guerrilla tactics worthless and so the IRA would have to 'learn from the Cypriots and engage in terror tactics only'. That would bring police pressure on the organisation including the use of torture and, on the assumption that this would lead to the divulging of information, it was recommended that units consist of no more than four men.

Part of the document deals with issues raised by those who had read it including the possibility of a *coup d'état* scenario either directed against the movement or one organised by the IRA itself through infiltration of the state apparatus. While assassinations of police would be kept quiet, informers could be assassinated openly. Kidnapping would be used to secure hostages where republicans were under threat of execution. If there was a repeat of the 1964 Divis Street riots in Belfast it was agreed that retaliatory actions would be taken. Given the fears expressed by the RUC in late 1965 and early 1966 concerning the alleged plans by the IRA to stage a military uprising, and that the military plan apparently came into the possession of the Garda Special Branch only when Seán Garland was arrested in May 1966, it is clear that the RUC knew of the proposed plan prior to that.

In order to mount the campaign it was estimated that the IRA would require ten tons of plastic explosive, timing devices, 5,000 grenades, 1,000 short arms of 9 mm or .45 calibre automatic, 1,000,000 rounds of short arm ammunition, 200 FN automatic rifles and 100,000 rounds of ammunition, and 300 bazookas with 3,000 shells.[22] Volunteers active at the time were under the impression that there were not many weapons. The plan does not estimate how many IRA Volunteers would be involved in a future campaign. Special Branch believed that the organisation had 923 members at the end of 1965, an increase from 657 at the end of 1962.[23] Again that illustrated the gap between IRA aspirations and the reality of a movement that was stagnating or actually in decline. People like Johnston would argue that they were aware of this and also that Goulding appeared to approve of the military planning only in order to keep as many people on board as possible while they went ahead with the political aspects.

Even if that were the case, most republicans assumed that Goulding was still actively planning a new campaign and in the May 1965 issue of *An t-Óglach* Goulding, with one eye on the forthcoming Convention, had promised that 'the next military campaign will be the final one. I work for that now.' In a letter circulated to Volunteers in September 1965 he referred to the plan for a 'military campaign against the British' and the need to raise money to finance it. That was despite the fact that the Army Council had not approved the plan and that Goulding himself was opposed to starting a new campaign. It is also interesting that, while presumably the majority of IRA members took Goulding at his word, the Irish government through its intelligence sources was able to assure London confidently that the IRA had no intentions of beginning a new armed campaign as was claimed by the RUC in late 1965 and early 1966.

In 1965 the Army Council gave its approval for armed robberies in Northern Ireland. All raids had to be sanctioned by the Chief of Staff and on 30 October £1,300 was taken from a Belfast bookmaker by the Belfast Brigade. £1,000 was sent to Dublin and the remainder retained by the local organisation. Given that the IRA had only a small income from draws, collections and donations and that GHQ had a balance of £990 at the end of 1965, it was not in a strong position to pursue its plans but the money that was raised became the source of future unrest over the use of these funds for political rather than military purposes.

While a Special Branch report on IRA training camps shows a high level of activity in 1965 and 1966, Garland, who was in charge of the programme, claims that this was largely in order to maintain internal cohesion and that there was no plan to embark on a military campaign.[24] Arms and explosives camps were permitted only under the strictest GHQ control and security. However despite the precautions, including the use of walkie-talkie radios that had been brought back to Ireland for the IRA, allegedly by the Clancy Brothers ballad group, Special Branch had detailed reports of the training camps and knew of 22 of the 'more important' camps held between February and November 1965.

A meeting of the IRA leadership took place in Dublin on 28 February 1966 to draw up a new training programme. The report states that it was held at a 'secret rendezvous' but that the Quartermaster General and other HQ officers were there which suggests that an informer was present but was not aware to what location he had been brought, as was the normal practice within the IRA. Instruction was given at the camps in short arms, rifles, Thompson and Bren machine guns, bazooka and explosives and there were also night exercises and firing practice. The biggest camp held in 1965 took place in Kerry and lasted from 10 to 23 July, when it was suspended owing to 'adverse weather conditions', and from 31 July to 14 August. Around sixty Volunteers including some from England and Northern Ireland attended: 'An unusually large amount of ammunition was made available' and the 'general feeling of those attending the camp was that an early resumption of Border activities was likely'. Again, this illustrates the disjuncture between the intentions of the Goulding leadership and those of the membership, and also that Garda Special Branch was well aware of the former, whatever it might have been hearing or observing at grassroots level.

According to Johnston the military plan was a 'sop' to Mac Stíofáin and Ó Brádaigh, who he claims were opposed to the general thrust of the political proposals.[25] He says that it was designed 'presumably to keep the militarists busy while the politicisers got on with the job'. He also believes that Mac Stíofáin wrote the military plan which later served as blueprint for the Provisional campaign.[26] Ruairí Ó Brádaigh believes now that there was never any

intention to implement the military plan and the intensive training programme was allowed to peter out.

Ruairí Ó Brádaigh also attributes the authorship of the military plan to
Mac Stíofáin but says that the traditionalists believed that it was an integral
part of a strategy that was broken into three phases: education in revolutionary principles and tactics, agitation around social and national issues, and a
resulting revolutionary situation in which there was a full-scale military offensive. Ó Brádaigh believes that Johnston wrote the political section[27] although
Johnston claims that Goulding and Costello wrote the text that was presented
to the Sinn Féin extraordinary Ard Fheis.[28] Costello wanted an immediate
change to electoral policy and was attempting to force the pace of internal
change against the wishes of Goulding and his closest allies. Later events
would also suggest that Costello saw no contradiction between the political
and the military aspects of the plan and may also have held a different view
of, or had a different insight into, the relationship between the IRA and the
Communists.

Johnston describes the plan as 'a transitional document of doubtful value'
and claims not to have been involved in writing it:

> I was far at that time from being 'in on' any of this. All I saw was what Goulding
> was trying to do in the public arena. This military stuff in the background must
> have been under pressure from Mac Stíofáin and co to which Goulding at the
> time had to pay at least lip service. By the time I got elected, which was at the
> 66 Convention, there was no trace of any of this sort of crap in anything I saw.
> That was my deal with Goulding.[29]

Johnston, however, was a member of IRA headquarters staff in 1965 and did
not have a high opinion of Dublin IRA members, most of whom he believes
were motivated to join by 'some kind of romantic militarism, or a sense of
adventure', which would complement his attitude to the 'crap' which the
majority of IRA members believed to be the organisation's *raision d'être*.

Johnston claims that 'The problem was how to keep the non-political military element contained while the political side was built up, to the extent that
the military side could safely be run down'.[30] According to the Official IRA in
1972, the decision not to organise another campaign in the Six Counties was
taken as early as 1963 and Peter Berry held a similar view.[31] If so, only a small
number of those close to Goulding, including the Special Branch source(s),
were aware of this although Johnston is no doubt correct in stating that this
faction was intent on neutralising the IRA as a military force and focusing on
the political aspects of the plan. Others like Mac Stíofáin were temporarily
appeased by being given responsibility for the military plan.

The centrality of Johnston to the new strategy was underlined by the range
of responsibilities that fell under his aegis. Among them were the

Joint Republican Education Centre, the Wolfe Tone Society, the Economic
Independence Committee, Housing Action Committee and Comhar Linn,
which was the republican co-operative organisation. These were clearly meant
to function in the manner of the 'front' organisations that were associated
with the Communist Party, of which the Connolly Association was a good
example. Someone could be a member of a group but not necessarily be a
member of the IRA or CPGB, or indeed be necessarily aware that one body
was a creature of another. The reference to the Wolfe Tone Society also belies
the claim that that organisation was not under IRA control.

The 1965 Sinn Féin Ard Fheis took place in Moran's Hotel, Talbot Street,
Dublin, on 30 and 31 October. According to a Garda report it was attended
by 135 delegates who represented 84 cumainn.[32] If so they represented only a
small part of the membership, which was estimated by the Gardaí at 3,897
organised in 283 cumainn at the end of 1964: this is evidence of resignations
or apathy due in part to dissent over the proposals put to the extraordinary
Ard Fheis. In his presidential address, Mac Giolla stated that while there had
been much condemnation of Communism in Ireland, little was said of the
harm done by capitalism. Communism was anti-religious and materialist and
did not commend itself to the Irish people. Capitalism was unchristian and
individualistic. Echoing earlier influences of Catholic social teaching, Mac
Giolla claimed that there was a third way between capitalism and Communism, the type of co-operativism that he claimed had been advocated by
Connolly.[33] Mac Giolla said that Lemass ought to have ordered the repatria-
tion of Irish capital, frozen British assets, established a national currency,
nationalised the banks and broken the Anglo-American grip on Irish
industry.

An Phoblacht ridiculed co-operativism and the claim that the policy was
influenced by Connolly. Socialism meant state ownership and if Sinn Féin
needed to know what Connolly had in mind it ought to look at China.[34] Sinn
Féin had come to realise that its economic policy up to that point was inher-
ited from Griffith but it couldn't abandon its suspicion of socialism. It
described the party's economic programme as a 'bizarre mixture of re-hashed
Proudhonism and the Social Credit theories of Major C. H. Douglas'.

According to Special Branch, Mac Giolla had not wished to remain as party
President but was persuaded by Goulding and Ruairí Ó Brádaigh to remain.[35]
The Ard Comhairle had a majority of traditionalists and, reflecting the centralisation and weakening of the movement, ten of the 15 members had
addresses in Dublin and none was from Northern Ireland. Special Branch also
pointed out that all except Clarke, who was almost 70, and the only woman
member, Mairín De Burca, were prominent members of the IRA. According
to Tom Mitchell only himself, Costello and Goulding were definitely in favour
of abandoning abstentionism at this point.[36]

There was a 'heated debate' on motion 46 from the Liam Mellows Cumann, Dublin, which asked the Ard Fheis to condemn Communism as the 'lowest form of slavery and makes it clear that such people are not welcome in Sinn Féin'. The party was to be forbidden to enter into any collaboration with Communist organisations and anyone who was known to have Communist links was to be expelled. The motion was withdrawn before the debate ended and no vote had been taken.[37] The motion on Communism was obviously directed at Johnston and the moves towards co-operation and merger. The Garda report claimed that Johnston's was behind the new strategy.[38] Johnston wrote an article entitled 'Whither Ireland' for the October issue of the *United Irishman* which claimed that there was now a theoretical system that could wed the concerns of ordinary people to the task of freeing Ireland, described as 'the identification of nationalism with the ownership of property'. Republicans had for a time lost sight of that even though the economic neo-colonialism that was described by the Ghanaian leader Kwame Nkrumah was first developed in Ireland after Partition. While republicans would continue to play a role in bringing about national independence a key element would be a broader alliance. One sympathetic observer, Proinsias Mac Aonghusa, who attended Wolfe Tone Society meetings, cautioned republicans that they would in the near future have to choose between real politics or remaining a 'backroom debating society discussing the finer points of the Second Dáil, Document Number Two and the integrity of abstentionism from Parliament'.[39]

Following the Ard Fheis the Education Department organised a two-day conference over the weekend of 18 and 19 December in Dublin 'to enable key people in each area of Ireland to participate in a study of the new Republican Social and Economic Programme'.[40] Mac Giolla chaired the first session and Seán Ó Brádaigh spoke on 'Social and Cultural Objectives'. Other issues included housing, rural life, the Irish language, education and the *United Irishman* as a tool for political education. The growing interest in civil rights was indicated by a seminar on 'Local Democracy as a Threat to Unionist Rule'. Johnston chaired the second session and spoke about the need for republicans to infiltrate trade unions. The Special Branch report claims that of the 50 people who were in attendance 42 were IRA Volunteers, two were in Cumann na mBan while Johnston, presumably, was a 'prominent member of the Irish Workers Party'. Seán Ó Brádaigh presented the education plan to the Ard Comhairle on 13 November 1965 as a joint initiative between Sinn Féin and the IRA, with Johnston as the key figure on the Army side. Johnston claims that it was part of Goulding's plan to integrate both parts of the movement. The Secretary's report given to the 1966 Ard Fheis by Mairín De Burca and Walter Lynch stated that the joint education centre had collapsed because of lack of support. Johnston claims that his intention was to use IRA training camps for political education purposes and that he knew nothing of any military aspect other than that he recalls lecturing Volunteers on nutrition. He does admit that the political education programme was not particularly successful.[41] Seán Dunne attended educational meetings where Volunteers were addressed by people such as Kadar Asmal and Anthony Coughlan. Dunne had no problem with this, or the perception that Asmal and Coughlan were communists, as it fitted with his own view of the Irish struggle as being part of an international revolutionary movement.[42]

The involvement of republicans in disputes such as the telephonists' strike revived accusations that the movement was instigating communist subversion. The Minister for Justice, Brian Lenihan, quoted from a Garda report which confirmed that such elements had been active; and that there was 'ample evidence that for some time anti-state organisations have adopted a definite policy of intervening under various guises in selected agitations and disputes'.[43] That had been the government's rationale for invoking the provisions of the Offences against the State Act in the ITA dispute. The IRA claimed that while it did support the strikers it had not been directly involved and denied stories in the *Evening Herald* and *Evening Press* alleging that Irish Communists and IRA leaders were meeting members of the Communist Party of France and that the latter was financing the IRA. The *Herald* also claimed that Irish Communists were attempting to infiltrate trade unions and 'to take leading positions in national movements'.[44]

In a January 1966 interview with the new *United Irishman* editor Tony Meade, who had taken over from Foley, Mac Giolla said that Sinn Féin's main problem was the need to redress its neglect of social and economic issues. In response to Meade's suggestion that it was only in 1965 that this began to be addressed, Mac Giolla said that it had taken time to change people's attitudes and that it was important not only to have a social and economic policy but also to take part actively in social struggles. Mac Giolla denied the claim that left-wingers had taken control of the movement and that Sinn Féin was opposed to private enterprise although they did prefer co-operative ownership as an alternative to both capitalism and communism. Mac Giolla said that the new political direction had nothing in common with the Republican Congress of the 1930s as the latter had been associated with the Communists. With regard to abstentionism, Mac Giolla said they had no intention of entering Leinster House 'until such a time as we are given a mandate by the Irish people to establish a Republican legislature for the whole nation'.[45]

Mac Giolla's remarks illustrated the extent to which the modernisers had been forced to pull back from their optimistic plan to change electoral policy and lay the basis for a 'radical alliance'. Goulding had clearly underestimated the strength of the traditionalists. The regular media references to communist infiltration also indicate that the state, armed with high-level intelligence on

IRA policy, was happy to use this to weaken the movement further. It is also evident that, while Garda intelligence indicated an increase in IRA and Sinn Féin membership after 1962, by 1965 the movement was in decline, not least because of internal unease over the new political strategy.

There is nothing to indicate that the state was concerned about an impending threat from the republican left and indeed it is noticeable that the periods when state concerns were most prominent, in spring 1965, early 1966 and 1969, all coincided with the run up to the General Elections in the Republic in 1965 and 1969, a Presidential election in the Republic in 1966 and the northern elections of 1966. Republicans took part in none of those elections but were regarded as a handy stick with which to beat the opposition, particularly where it could be claimed that they had associations with the IRA.

Notes

1 Mac Stíofáin (1974), p. 93.
2 Interview with Ruairí Ó Brádaigh, 22 May 2002.
3 Interview with Seán Ó Brádaigh, 21 May 2005.
4 *United Irishman*, February 1965.
5 *TCD Miscellany*, no. 1253, 19 February, 1965.
6 *Ibid.*, April 1965.
7 Interview with Seán Ó Brádaigh, 21 May 2005.
8 *United Irishman*, June 1965.
9 Taoiseach, 98/6/495, Garda Report on IRA 3C/15/66, NAI.
10 *Irish Democrat*, April 1965.
11 Document shown to author, p. 1.
12 *Ibid.*, p. 4.
13 Email from Roy Johnston, 1 June 2001.
14 *Ibid.*, September 1965.
15 Interview with Roy Johnston, 19 April 2001.
16 Patterson (1997), p. 96.
17 Justice, 2000/36/3, memo of 18 March, 1969, NAI.
18 *An Phoblacht*, Vol. 1, no. 1, September 1965.
19 Document from Óglaigh na h-Éireann GHQ, filed with Garda Report 3C/15/66, NAI.
20 *Ibid.*
21 Sinn Féin Ard Comhairle Minutes, 29 January 1966, in Swan (2006), p. 168.
22 Garda Report 3C/15/66, p. 9.
23 Garda Report 3C/15/66, p. 1.
24 Interview with Seán Garland, 28 February 2005.
25 Interview with Roy Johnston, 4 April 2001.
26 Email from Roy Johnston, 1 June 2001.
27 Interview with Ruairí Ó Brádaigh, 11 May 2002.
28 Interview with Roy Johnston, 19 April 2001.

29 Email from Roy Johnston, 26 May 2001.
30 Email from Roy Johnston, 1 June 2001.
31 Justice 2000/36/3, memo of 18 March 1969, NAI.
32 Garda Report, 3C/15/66, p. 52.
33 *Ulsterman*, November 1965.
34 *An Phoblacht*, Vol. 1, no. 3.
35 Garda Report 3C/15/66, p. 52.
36 Interview with Tom Mitchell, 11 January 2002.
37 Garda Report 3C/15/66, p. 53.
38 *Ibid.*
39 *Munster Express*, 27 August 1965.
40 Garda Report 3C/15/66, p. 21.
41 Interview with Roy Johnston, 19 April 2001.
42 Interview with Seán Dunne, 20 November 2001.
43 *Dáil Debates*, Vol. 218, col. 1218.
44 *Evening Herald*, 25 November 1965.
45 *United Irishman*, January 1966.

4

The Wolfe Tone Society
and the Communists

Goulding and those close to him after 1962 quickly came to the conclusion that by itself Sinn Féin was not an adequate vehicle for their political ambitions. Instead, they decided to establish an organisation that they hoped would draw in a wider group of individuals who were sympathetic to republicanism but antipathetic to Sinn Féin and the IRA. A March 1969 memo from Peter Berry suggests that they were persuaded of the merits of this by 'suggestions from left-wing sources' outside the movement.[1]

The main vehicle for the new departure was the Wolfe Tone Society, which was established to organise events around the bicentenary of the birth of the founder of the United Irishmen. The Wolfe Tone Directorates were established in late 1962 or January/February 1963 when Goulding, Cronin, Richard Roche and possibly Uinseann Mac Eoin met and issued the initial invitations to other potential members. Roche worked in the *Irish Independent*, where he had secured a position for Cronin following his release, and says that he was asked to become secretary on the basis of his writing skills and aptitude for publicity. Roche felt that the armed campaign proved that the IRA had outlived its usefulness and he regarded the Society as providing an alternative avenue for republicans. He believes that Goulding had decided that armed struggle was no longer an option by 1963 but that he did not exercise control over the Society.[2]

Although Roy Johnston, who joined the group in January 1964, acknowledges the role played by the IRA in its formation, he is adamant that the Society quickly outgrew its origins and 'ceased to be seen as "Army Council property"'.[3] Noel Kavanagh regarded it as a means to promote republican ideas and agrees with Johnston that it was not under the direct control of the IRA.[4] The references to the Society found in later IRA documents, however, would suggest that the IRA did regard it as under its control, in the same way as Sinn Féin. Seán Bermingham says that there was huge demoralisation following the end of the campaign and that he saw the Society as a political alternative to armed struggle and a means to circumvent the legislation and censorship that made it difficult for Sinn Féin to provide that outlet.[5]

The Sinn Féin Ard Comhairle approved the establishment of the committees on 23 February 1963 and among its original Dublin members were Martin Shannon who was editor of the *United Irishman*, Harry White, Uinseann Mac Eoin, Lorcan Leonard, Deasún Breathnach, who as Rex McGall wrote for the *Irish Independent*, and the solicitor Ciarán Mac an Fháili. Noel Kavanagh was asked to join by Seán Cronin, and Cathal Mac Liam, who remained a leading member of the Society into the 1970s, was invited to join by Goulding who was his cousin. Mac Liam had been a member of the Connolly Association and the Communist Party of Great Britain and joined the Irish Workers Party when he returned to Ireland in 1963.

Belfast members included the Sinn Féin Vice President Seán Caughey, Fred Heatley, Michael McKeown, Jack Bennett, who was a member of the Communist Party of Northern Ireland, and Liam Burke. The Belfast committee produced 12,000 copies of *Wolfe Tone Today* and sold 3,500 in the north and a further 3,500 in Dublin. When the Belfast group organised a commemorative parade on 16 June 1963, the RUC informed it that the tricolour could not be carried. The group agreed to this in order to avoid giving the police the excuse to provoke a disturbance.[6] IRA veterans of the 1930s, Seán O'Callaghan and Jack Lynch, established a committee in Cork but O'Callaghan had to drop out and Eddie Williams, later the Cork IRA OC, Jim O'Regan and Dáithí O Conaill became members.

Jack Bennett suggested in February 1963 that they organise a meeting in Belfast on unemployment[7] but most of the committee's work was taken up with organising a series of lectures in the Mansion House. In a letter to Alphonsus Ryan, who had expressed an interest in establishing a committee in Waterford, Roche emphasised that any platform for a commemorative event ought to be representative of 'all religions and all shades of republican opinion (repeat republican)'.[8] Máire Comerford, a veteran of the War of Independence, informed Roche of previous efforts which she had made to establish a similar group as a more 'constructive and worthy outlet for Republican energies than the existing war over the Border', but the IRA had been uninterested.[9]

A convention, attended by Goulding, in the Spa Hotel, Dublin, on 25 and 26 May 1963 agreed to pursue the idea of maintaining the committees although a further meeting in November decided that they would not organise as a political party. That suited the IRA's objective of building a group that would not be a direct rival to Sinn Féin and its role would be to propagandise among a broader target group and to help to formulate a new programme for the republican movement.[10] It would deliberately not attempt to build a large membership. The committees organised a series of lectures in the Mansion House in September 1963 under the direction of Roger McHugh of University College Dublin which were well attended and widely publicised in the press.

Roy Johnston began to attend Society meetings in January 1964 and presented a paper on the need for republicans to focus on the needs of different social groups. That would entail political engagement but he advised that they should not advocate an immediate end to abstentionism as that would 'split the movement'. Their relationship with the republican movement was defined as broadening 'the Republican outlook without whittling down its ideals'[11] and helping to provide 'a factual basis for republican programme'. They also agreed to co-operate with Sinn Féin in the rewriting of its social and economic programme, with Johnston, Breathnach, Leonard and Mac Eoin nominated to undertake that task. The Directorate met with Sinn Féin in April and agreed to support republican candidates in the Stormont elections.[12] In June the Directorate decided to sponsor the founding of an Economic Resistance Movement[13] and the Ard Comhairle decided to distribute Johnston's paper on economic resistance for discussion at cumann level. That was an indication of the key role that the Society had in promoting the new direction within the movement and the paper was published in the *United Irishman* in October 1964.

In April Johnston proposed that they establish a committee to draft a constitution for a republican 'ginger group' but Seán Cronin felt that the concept was too vague and provided no clear indication of what the Society could do: 'It can do no work that Sinn Féin cannot do better; it will draw no forces that Sinn Féin has not already attracted.'[14] Cronin presumably was one of those who abstained when the Draft Constitution was approved and it was agreed to reconstitute as the Wolfe Tone Society. The formation of the group had been signalled in the June issue of the *Plough*, edited by the Labour Party member Maisie O'Connell. Johnston had suggested this to Roche as 'a "kite" flown to test public reaction in Labour circles'. The *Plough* believed that the Society had done a certain amount to 'broaden the scope of Republican thinking'.

The future Labour TD Justin Keating was co-opted in September[15] and co-option of another future Labour TD, Michael O'Leary, had been discussed in June. Johnston's wife Mairin, also a former CPGB activist, was a member of the Labour Party in O'Leary's constituency, and Seán Dunne, who was elected as a Labour TD in 1965, was sympathetic. Roche recalls that Keating was never very active and that Michael O'Leary never actually attended a meeting although he did speak at public meetings organised by the Society and Roche and Coughlan assisted O'Leary in his successful election campaign of 1965. When Roche visited the United States in the mid-1970s he met Cronin, who joked that the Society must have great influence given that two of its members, Keating and O'Leary, were members of the Fine Gael / Labour Cabinet.[16] It would appear, however, that Greave's initial desire to exercise a similar influence within Labour as within the republican movement through former

Connolly Association members did not have the same success. A recent history of the Labour Party notes the strong 'informal contacts' between republicans and Labour activists at the time, but Puirséal perhaps misunderstands the nature of the relationship between people such as Johnston, Coughlan, O'Leary and Keating and its roots in the Connolly Association.[17]

The draft Wolfe Tone Society Constitution defined the Irish people as 'one nation sharing a common history on a common territory' and that Partition was the cause of 'all the exceptional political and economic problems from which Ireland has suffered for the past 40 years'.[18] The objectives of the Society were the establishment of a 'united, independent, democratic Irish Republic' and to educate the public on the nature of the subjection of the country to 'British imperialism'. They hoped that Ireland would be united and independent by the 1970s, exercising economic as well as political sovereignty. The key to that would be to unite different sectional groups and they would not stand candidates for elections but would support candidates who showed themselves to be in favour of the objectives of the Society. Any person who proved to be active in support of those objectives could apply for membership, which was open to persons active in the language, trade union, co-operative and republican movements.

A small piece in the *United Irishman* of November 1964 announced the formation of the Society which it said was 'composed of young Republican-minded Irishmen of various persuasions'. Patterson has described the group as being imbued with traditional republican ideology and claims that those involved in the Society saw Fianna Fáil's abandonment of its rhetorical anti-partitionism as providing political opportunities for republicans to exploit.[19] Patterson sees this as proof that the Society was not socialist, which it was not, and that this undermines the left republican thesis regarding the potential for socialist politics to develop out of republicanism. However, that is to neglect the fact that the Marxists involved in the Society were deliberately downplaying that aspect of their own politics, and their ambitions for the Society and the republican movement as a whole.

Efforts to involve Peadar O'Donnell, the iconic republican socialist figure of the 1930s, Séamus Ó Mongáin, one of the authors of the Sinn Féin Comhar na gComharsan policy of the late 1940s, and Dublin trade unionists in an ambitious strategy for the co-operative movement were unsuccessful. Johnston was also asked to lecture to the trade union Irish language group Scéim na gCeardcumainn, exploring whether there was an alternative to 'national capitalism' but the invitation was withdrawn, apparently with O'Donnell's encouragement.[20] Further encounters with O'Donnell persuaded the Society that he lacked 'an overall national view'. A meeting of 20 October heard a report from Justin Keating on a meeting he had with visitors from the Soviet Union and the possibility of establishing diplomatic and trade relations.

The first proposal for the Society to become directly involved in campaigning for civil rights in Northern Ireland came from Brian Murphy of Clann na Poblachta who wrote to Uinseann Mac Eoin in July 1964 to suggest that they organise a 'Freedom Bus' to Derry to highlight discrimination there, similar to the 'Freedom Bus' of 'US integrationists'.[21] Members of the Society attended a meeting on civil rights in the ATGWU hall, Belfast, on 8 May 1965 along with other representatives from the republican movement, CPNI, NILP and various trade unions. The Society then was involved, but by no means instrumental, in the early efforts to organise a civil rights campaign.

Sinn Féin decided not to contest the general election held in the Republic on 7 April 1965 but the Society organised a public meeting in the Clarence Hotel, Dublin, on 4 April at which a resolution was passed lamenting the failure of any party to make an issue of the buying up of Irish property or the objective of a united independent Republic 'despite the present amenability of the British Labour Government to pressure'. Johnston referred to Michael O'Leary as a politician who understood the integration of social and economic issues throughout the island.[22] O'Leary, with the assistance of Society members, was elected in Dublin North Central and Labour won six seats in Dublin. Fianna Fáil won an overall majority with 72 seats and 47.8 per cent of the vote. Labour increased its share of the vote to 15.4 per cent from 11.6 per cent and won 21 seats, an increase of six. It was that apparent growth in support for the left that became one of the key motivations for the modernisers and their desire both to form a radical alliance and to contest that support with Labour.

The first issue of *Tuairisc*, the journal of the Wolfe Tone Society, appeared in July 1965: 250 copies were sent to people within the Society's target audience of republicans, the Labour Party, trade unions and cultural groups, following Coughlan's proposal to Roche that circulation be deliberately restricted. Coughlan saw the purpose of the journal as helping to build bridges between republicans and activists in the Labour and trade union movements. Writing to Professor Michael Dolly of Queen's University, Johnston stressed that the Society was 'anxious to reach as wide sections as possible and are aware of the negative nature of doctrinaire republicanism. If any of the latter is creeping in to *Tuairisc* we would like our friends to tell us.'[23] *Tuairisc* expanded on the objectives set out in the Constitution and provided an analysis of the effects of the Free Trade Agreement almost identical to that found in the pages of the *United Irishman*. At its AGM for 1965 on 21 September it was decided to invite Tony Meade, recently appointed editor of the *United Irishman*, to become a member, and Roche felt that influential people were looking to the Society for 'leadership and advice'.[24]

Following a meeting in Belfast in October 1965, Johnston, Coughlan and Mac Eoin suggested that Belfast ought to concentrate on civil rights issues.

They had made contact with republicans who were active on this and a Committee for Democratic Elections had already been established. Fred Heatley was to be asked to be secretary of the Belfast Society that would retain the Wolfe Tone name. The Society's recommendation that the Committee for Democratic Elections should form links with the Campaign for Social Justice in Dungannon, and 'form a broad common platform on this issue with all similarly-minded organisations' might be regarded as the beginning of what was to become the civil rights movement but the Dublin Society expressed some frustration at the slowness of Belfast's response to its suggestions.[25] Johnston, speaking at Queen's University in January on the subject of 'The Function of Minorities', claimed that Unionism depended for support upon people who did not materially benefit from the Union and needed to use scare tactics focused on an alleged threat from the IRA. Johnston claimed that the lessons of this had not been lost on the IRA and foresaw the decline of sectarianism in politics and the emergence of a radical labour movement, and a union of republicans and socialists from the Protestant community,[26] which presumably included the CPNI.

A national consultative conference on free trade held on 14 November in Powers Hotel, Kildare Street, was the fruit of a decision made by the 1965 IRA Convention initiated by Johnston. It was attended by representatives from Sinn Féin, the Labour Party, Phoblacht Chríostúil, branches of the ITGWU, Workers Union of Ireland, Drogheda Trade and Labour Council, the Amalgamated Society of Woodworkers, the Free Ireland Organisation, Comhar Linn, the National Fisherman's Co-operative Society and others. The conference unanimously passed a resolution alerting people to the danger that free trade would lead to increased dependency on Britain and defended the right of the state to protect industry against unfair competition. They also called for a referendum on any agreement negotiated with the British. Following the conference the Wolfe Tone Society established the Economic Independence Committee which included members of the different bodies who had attended the conference. They noted that the Federation of Irish Industry had already spoken out against the proposed agreement with Britain and called on workers to pressure their unions to do likewise. They published a pamphlet in 1965 entitled *A Catechism in Free Trade* which argued that the Free Trade Agreement would destroy any prospect of economic or political sovereignty and that by 1981 the Republic would be as much a part of the British economy as Northern Ireland.[27] Lemass signed the FTA on 14 December.

Special Branch was clearly aware of the Society's connection to the IRA and Richard Roche recalls that Society meetings were kept under surveillance with cars parked outside the houses where they took place. On one occasion they discovered a detective standing outside a window trying to hear what was being discussed. When they went outside to remonstrate he departed leaving his notebook behind him. The notebook contained personal details and descriptions of Society members including an unflattering one of Seán Ó Brádaigh who was described as 'walking like a duck'. Richard Roche began to withdraw from the Society in early 1966, his secretarial role being assumed by John Tozer, another former member of Ailtirí na hAiséirghe. Roche felt that the Society was coming under the control of people who had ulterior motives and who had current connections to communist organisations and was once requested by Johnston to speak at a Communist Party meeting in Manchester but refused. He also recalls having confronted Johnston at a Society meeting and accusing him of being a malign influence.[28] Seán Bermingham shares Roche's view of Johnston and also agrees that Johnston exercised an enormous influence on Goulding.[29]

While most republicans were suspicious of any connection to people who were or had been members of Communist organisations, Irish Communists diplomatically chose to overlook any lingering anti-Communist rhetoric in their courtship of republicans. Michael O'Riordan's address to the February 1962 Conference of the Irish Workers League, which in a flight of optimism saw it substitute the title Party for League, looked forward to 'co-operation with all progressive forces'. The IWP was striving to help the Labour Party to become the dominant political force among the working class with a programme based on opposition to the EEC, positive neutrality, state industry, increased social welfare and a drive to end unemployment and bad housing.[30] In building an alliance of progressive forces, the IWP would not allow 'differences over tactics or the ultimate merits or demerits of Socialism affect such co-operation'. The weakness of the IWP itself, however, was illustrated by the fact that the *Irish Workers Voice* had a circulation of only four hundred.

Sinn Féin was considered to be one of the 'progressive forces' and the IWP saw the Ard Comhairle statement on the EEC of March 1962 as a token of 'maturity'. It could, 'in alliance with other labour and progressive forces, revolutionise Irish politics and lay the basis for a movement which would finally sweep imperialism from our shores'. Other 'progressive' forces were Labour, National Progressive Democrats 'and many in Fianna Fáil'. There was a reference to 'negative features' of Sinn Féin attacks on freemasonry and Communism. *Nation or Province* was given a warm welcome and 'should be in the hands of all progressive Irish men and women'.[31] Instead of concentrating on a purely historical criticism of the government, Sinn Féin was now beginning to tackle current problems. The IWP referred to the occasional co-operation that had taken place between James Connolly and Arthur Griffith's Sinn Féin as a model for future projects involving both republicans and the labour movement.

Even before the armed campaign ended in 1962, some on the left had begun to detect encouraging signs within the republican movement. Tom Mitchell, who was released from Belfast Prison before the end of the campaign, recalls that Anthony Coughlan came to see him soon after Mitchell had returned to Dublin. Coughlan tried to interest Mitchell in a campaign against the Republic's application to join the Common Market. Mitchell believed that Coughlan was acting on behalf of the Irish Workers League and he told Coughlan that he saw merit in such a campaign but was suspicious of the Communists.[32]

The IWL and the CPNI had opposed the armed campaign in the North and paid it scant attention. That was despite the initial reaction in the USSR to the first Saor Uladh attacks in 1956 that were described as 'a new stage in the struggle of the long suffering Irish people against hated English oppression'.[33] A definite shift could be discerned in the attitude towards the republican movement in late 1961 when, although the IRA campaign was still continuing, the IWL became more republican-sounding. The chief motivation behind the change in policy was the application by the Lemass government to join the EEC, as was admitted following the split by the newly reformed Communist Party of Ireland.[34] The CPI also claimed that the IWL had been the only group to oppose EEC membership in 1961, implying that the Communists had been responsible for persuading republicans to do likewise, whereas in fact opposition was central to the Sinn Féin election manifesto of 1961. Communist opposition to the EEC must be placed in the broader context of the Soviet Union's concerns around an enlarged European economic and political alliance with the German Federal Republic at its centre. In 1961 the Communist Party of Great Britain published a pamphlet outlining its reasons for opposing British entry. It must be stressed, however, that, while evidence has been uncovered which proves that the CPGB was in receipt of Soviet money,[35] no such connection has been made between Soviet intelligence and Irish Communists during the 1960s.

An article in the December 1961 issue of the *Irish Democrat* sketched what it foresaw as the future agenda facing Irish republicans. It recommended that Sinn Féin should embark upon a 'New Departure' that would focus on opposition to the Common Market and agitation around the issues of unemployment and partition. Republicans might enter an alliance with the labour movement that had the potential to topple the Unionist government at Stormont and to win over Protestant workers. Once that had been accomplished the national question could be addressed in earnest. What the *Irish Democrat* was promoting was in essence the strategy favoured by Goulding and his allies. Indeed the phrase 'new departure' was later used by Johnston as a member of Sinn Féin while writing for the *Irish Democrat* in 1965. An alliance with the Communists was anathema to the majority of republicans, and led to ongoing tensions as people like Johnston became influential within the IRA, and as Goulding appeared to be pushing not only a common political strategy but an actual alliance with the Communists. The change in the attitude of the

IWP had not gone unnoticed by seasoned red watchers. The Reverend Michael O'Neill wrote an article for *Hibernia* in April 1962 entitled 'Irish Communists and the Common Market' in which he accused the Communists of attempting to form a united front with republicans and but welcomed the apparent cold shoulder that had been given the Communists by both Sinn Féin and the Labour Party: 'Only the politically naïve could fall for the united front blandishments of the Irish Workers League.'

Two of the people to the forefront of the new strategy were C. D. Greaves, as a leading member of the Communist Party of Great Britain and the Connolly Association, and Roy Johnston, a former member of both. They, and in particular Johnston, were to become the *bêtes noires* for traditionalists and they certainly did not share their attitude to the Irish state. In an article published in the CPGB *Daily Worker* in June 1960, Greaves described the Republic of Ireland as the 'most progressive state in Europe'. Within the Moscow-oriented Communist movement that expressed the notion that any western European state that was not involved in NATO or in colonialism was 'progressive'. In an article he wrote for a local London Communist Party newsletter, Johnston used almost the same phrase as Greaves in describing the Republic of Ireland as 'the most progressive country in Western Europe'. The forces that would underpin the progressive alliance that could bring about an independent united Ireland were labour, farmers, intellectuals and that section of the bourgeoisie 'not interested in the British Connection'.

Johnston had been involved in the postwar reformation of the southern section of the Communist Party of Ireland as the Irish Workers League and had subsequently been active in the CPGB and the Connolly Association. Johnston took a job with Aer Lingus in 1963, resigned as Treasurer of the Connolly Association and returned to Dublin where he was associated with the IWP, but says that he severed his formal connections with the group in 1964. He instead chose to join the republican movement and work with Cathal Goulding in converting the IRA from a secret army into an open political movement involved in social struggles. Johnston's remained close to members of the IWP and remained in contact with Greaves who was a regular visitor to Ireland in the 1960s where he maintained close relations with members of the Irish Communist parties and came to know leading members of the IRA including Cathal Goulding, on whom he appears to have exercised considerable influence. Johnston's relationship with the IRA apparently began when he wrote to the former IRA Chief of Staff Seán Cronin while the latter was interned in the Curragh and then came to know Goulding. Johnston attended the Sinn Féin Ard Fheis in November 1963 and meetings of the Sinn Féin Ard Comhairle in 1964. In July 1964 a paper that he had written on economic resistance, for the Wolfe Tone Society, was passed for discussion by Sinn Féin cumainn and presented to the 1964 Ard Fheis.[36]

According to Johnston, the main effects of imperialism were regional depopulation, concentration of industry, increased dependency on trade and the foreign takeover of Irish businesses. This needed to be challenged but 'the danger is that the Republican Movement, by continuing to concentrate on one single aspect of British rule, namely the Occupation', would allow those forces to attain a level of control such that the possibility of creating an independent Irish state would be lost for ever. Republicans needed to help create a co-operative economy which could then develop independently of the state, 'thus foreshadowing the role of an organ of the future Republican Government'.[37] Apart from his economic proposals Johnston suggested that republicans might organise a petition to encourage the sponsors of British Labour MP Fenner Brockway's Anti-Discrimination Bill to have the legislation extended to Northern Ireland although both Johnston and Anthony Coughlan give Greaves the main credit for initiating this campaign.[38] Other republicans, however, claim that there was a general awareness of the importance of challenging the Northern state on civil rights and that this pre-dated any initiative from outside the movement.

Although the 1963 Ard Fheis had passed a motion to create a new political programme for the party, that process was put on hold because by the end of 1964 Goulding had placed the formation of policy in the hands of Johnston. Seán Ó Brádaigh says that the aborted programme was later revived by the Provisionals and became part of their Éire Nua policy and Dáithí O Conaill had apparently updated the document in the late 1960s as an alternative to Johnston's proposals for a National Liberation Front. Seán Ó Brádaigh claims that requests from the drafting committee to have the document published in 1964 were continually deferred because it no longer satisfied those within the leadership who wanted to have a formal relationship with the Communists, justified theoretically by Johnston.[39]

Johnston was a participant in a joint summer school held by the IWP and the CPNI in June 1964. This continued association with the Marxist left confirmed the suspicions of Johnston held by republicans, who were not without their own sources of information in the Communist movement. Johnston attended other IWP events through the 1960s, some of which Greaves was also at, and leading republicans like Goulding regularly met with Dublin Communists on a social basis. Others who were themselves on the left of the movement were of the opinion that there was more to Johnston's joining the republican movement than met the eye. One person, who subsequently took the Official side in the split, believes that there was formal support from the Communist Parties of Ireland and Britain for Johnston's entry into the IRA and that this was understood and accepted by at least one senior figure within the IRA. The same person believes that Cathal Goulding had come under the influence of the Soviet agent Klaus Fuchs while held in Wormwood Scrubs and that Goulding facilitated the entry of Johnston into the republican leadership as part of a strategy to influence the future direction of the IRA.[40] Ruairí Ó Brádaigh has also referred to Goulding's relationship with Fuchs.[41] Noel Kavanagh was convinced that Johnston and Anthony Coughlan were still members of the British and/or Irish Communist Parties, and that they were actively promoting Communist policy in their contacts with republicans.[42] Seán Ó Brádaigh is certain that Johnston maintained formal links with the Communist movement.[43]

Goulding was prepared to facilitate Johnston's membership of the leadership for a mixture of ideological and practical reasons. He was sympathetic to Marxism, and he believed that people such as Johnston had the intellectual skills to accomplish the transformation of the IRA that were lacking among the movement's own membership. Seán Garland dismisses any notion that there was a conspiracy involved in Johnston's membership and says that he was well received by most republicans.[44] Tom Mitchell admits to having had some suspicions regarding Johnston but more to do with what he perceived to be Johnston's lackadaisical attitude to security. Mitchell claims that Johnston would sometimes park his car in front of houses where IRA meetings were being held and that when challenged would say that he didn't believe they should be hiding from the Special Branch.[45] Seán Swan believes that there is a credible basis for the claim that Johnston was a Communist agent but that the evidence is not available to make a final judgement.[46]

Charles Desmond Greaves was a key influence on the modernisers despite the fact that he never lived in Ireland, nor was he at any time a member of the movement. His influence, however, was exercised over a long period through his membership of the Connolly Association and his close personal contacts with Roy Johnston and Anthony Coughlan and through them with leading republicans like Cathal Goulding. Greaves's ideas, particularly on the civil rights strategy, played a key role up to the early 1970s. Greaves is best known as a Marxist historian and he was the author of political biographies of James Connolly, Seán O'Casey and Liam Mellows. Most of his published work was concerned with Irish affairs and he was the long-time editor of the *Irish Democrat*, the newspaper of the Connolly Association. Greaves was a member of the Communist Party of Great Britain from 1934 until his death in 1986. He appears to have developed an early interest in Irish politics and joined the Connolly Association in 1941.

The Connolly Association was originally made up of former members of the Republican Congress and other exiled Irish Marxists. It was first known as the Connolly Clubs following its founding in September 1938 and published a newspaper called *Irish Freedom*, changing its title to the *Irish Democrat* in 1941. From the beginning the *Democrat* was published at the printing works of the Communist *Daily Worker*. An early difficulty that faced the

Association in its attempt to woo Irish workers was its attitude towards the Second World War. Greaves claimed that the Association defended Irish neutrality but he was referring specifically to the situation prior to entry into the war of the USSR in 1941. After that the Communist Party and its satellites did a *volte face* and the 'imperialist war' against Germany became the 'fight for democracy'. Indeed that led directly to the dissolution of the CPI which was unable to reconcile the contradictory shifts in Stalinist policy.

While Anthony Coughlan claims that Greaves was opposed to Stalinism,[47] Greaves was forthright in his defence of the Soviet Union on occasions like the invasions of Hungary and Czechoslovakia and ensured that the Connolly Association adhered to an orthodox Communist line. In 1958 Scotland Yard informed Irish officials that all the leaders of the Connolly Association were known to them as 'card carrying members of the Communist Party'.[48] A War Office report of March 1957 also described the Association as 'communist inspired' and said that it was 'completely ignored by those holding republican views'.[49] That situation was of course to radically change after 1962. In 1945 Greaves's anxiety to preserve the Association under Communist control from 'ultra leftists' appears to have led him to propose that it be dissolved and replaced by a support group based around the *Irish Democrat*. His proposal was defeated and the following year Greaves's attitude had changed to the extent that he was beginning to think of sending Connolly Association members back to Ireland to influence politics there.[50]

Greaves first met Roy Johnston when Johnston was a member of the Promethean Society in Trinity College Dublin. Some of this group attended a CPGB summer school in 1947. Johnston had already made contact with the remnants of the old CPI that had been disbanded during the Second World War. They had a bookshop called New Books and together with some former IRA prisoners like Ned Stapleton, who had formed a Connolly Club among Marxist IRA Volunteers, they founded the Irish Workers League in early 1948. Johnston toured Ireland with Stapleton in an attempt to recruit other former prisoners. Greaves attended the first meeting of the IWL as a representative of the International Affairs Committee of the CPGB that was to resume the supervisory role it had exercised on the old CPI through Bob Stewart and others.

Johnston wrote articles for *Irish Youth* which was the organ of the Socialist Youth Movement among whose members were Brian Behan, brother of the later to be famous Brendan. *Irish Youth* was strongly pro-Soviet and in September 1947 Johnston wrote an article that attempted to explain the 'scientific' basis of socialism. The Socialist Youth Movement and its paper were succeeded by the Democratic Youth Movement, which functioned as the youth wing of the IWL, and by a new periodical entitled *Young Ireland* that was edited by Johnston. The group was affiliated to the World Federation of

Democratic Youth, the Soviet-run Communist youth movement; in 1949 Johnston wrote a piece on the World Youth Festival held in Budapest.[51]

The TCD Promethean Society published *The Promethean* and proclaimed itself to be 'frankly socialist'.[52] An article by Johnston on 'New Farming' advocated the introduction of collectivisation.[53] An article by 'DOF' referred to the IRA's flirtation with fascism but admitted that some republicans still adhered to progressive ideas.[54] There was a report of a lecture that Greaves gave to the Society on 8 March 1947 in which he emphasised the theme that was to remain a hallmark of his politics for the next 30 years: 'Ireland must join the democratic forces. Only by doing so and making partition once more an international issue can she solve the problems which confront her.'[55] The 'democratic forces' naturally consisted of the USSR, its satellites and political apologists in the West. Of course the notion that the Irish state could become 'democratic' or indeed that it might align itself with the Soviet Union was anathema to most republicans.

Greaves clearly saw his role in London, through the Connolly Association, as one of influencing Irish workers towards socialism but was sceptical regarding the prospects for an openly Marxist organisation based in Ireland and this brought him into conflict with the leadership of the IWL. Greaves sought to influence the Irish working-class diaspora in Britain by taking a republican position on Irish domestic affairs and attempting to make Irish unification one of the priorities of the British labour movement. Greaves regarded the main issue as being the lack of civil rights in Northern Ireland and he was much less critical of the southern state.

This had already led to friction between the Connolly Association and Irish republicans based in London over the Communists attitude to the war, and towards IRA prisoners being held in the Republic. That was remarked upon by Seán Mac Stíofáin who described his suspicions of the Communist Party and the Connolly Association. Roy Johnston agrees that the attitude of the CPGB did much to alienate republicans.[56] Johnston himself, however, remained a member of the IWL although he did argue against what he believed was the League's mistaken attitude towards the national question. Johnston attended the 1954 republican commemoration at Bodenstown where Special Branch saw him in the company of other IWL members including Ned Stapleton and Packie Early.[57] In the November 1957 issue of the *Plough* Johnston argued that, while the Republic had secured a certain degree of freedom, it remained economically subservient to Britain. Economic independence was possible but not as long as partition remained, as republicans correctly said, but this was negated by the IRA's tactics.

In a subsequent article, Johnston argued that Irish unity would amount to a 'sound business proposition' that would benefit native enterprise and agriculture. Workers would benefit most of all while small farmers would be able to find jobs in native technology-based industry. The class basis of what Johnston described as 'Irish conservatism' would be destroyed by nationalising all British-linked large-scale industry, the banks and insurance companies. The Labour Party would not be capable of achieving this, and while Sinn Féin was better disposed to such a project 'its tactics are catastrophic for the causes that it wishes to further'. What was required was a 32-county socialist republican party allied to the British Labour Party.

The IWL for a time maintained a much more hostile attitude towards the republican movement than Greaves and Johnston. In November 1958 the *Irish Workers Voice* declared that 'Big business is the right wing of Fianna Fáil and its left wing, the small businessmen, shade off into supporters of Sinn Féin, Clann na Poblachta etc.'. The difficulties facing the IWL were not helped by the even greater unpopularity of Communism following the Soviet suppression of the Hungarian uprising in 1956. This apparently led one of the best known figures on the Irish left, Peadar O'Donnell, to propose to the League that both it and the CPNI should dissolve themselves and become part of a new broader left party.

According to Johnston, Greaves was unhappy with the manner in which the IWL and the Labour left approached the national question. Greaves defended the IRA on the basis that 'If there was no British occupation of North Eastern Ireland there would be no IRA. The issue is as simple as that.'[58] The *Irish Democrat* did publish the CPNI statement rejecting armed struggle but claimed that the IRA was only filling a vacuum caused by the absence of a national policy in Dublin. The CPNI condemned violations of civil rights in Northern Ireland and called on the labour movement to press for negotiations between Dublin and London 'to explore a way forward for the solution of the problem in dispute between the peoples of these countries'.

At its annual conference in 1957 the Connolly Association referred to the electoral revival of Sinn Féin and the unemployed movement as signs that the people of the 26 counties were searching for alternatives. The *Irish Democrat* noted that there were admirable points in the Sinn Féin election manifesto although it was deficient in its analysis of the property relations that underlay British rule: 'If they were to convert themselves into an all-embracing democratic republican party they might yet do Ireland untold good.' However, the continued adherence to abstentionism and neglect of theory stretched Greaves's patience with the republicans.

One of Greaves's key allies within the Irish Communist movement was Jack Bennett who was a member of the CPNI in Belfast. Bennett's articles for the *Sunday Press* under the pseudonym Claude Gordon were regarded as a formative influence on southern attitudes to the North. In August 1957 Bennett wrote an article for the *Irish Democrat* in which he declared that Irish socialists would 'find it impossible, in practicable politics, ever of securing a path to socialism without bringing partition tumbling down first'. If socialists abandoned the national question then they were also abandoning the struggle for socialism.

Paddy Carmody, writing as A. Raferty, responded on behalf of the IWL leadership. Irish socialists ought to concentrate on economic issues, as raising the national question at that stage would only worsen divisions between Nationalist and Unionist workers. He also rejected the notion that the IRA campaign was a continuation of the 1916–23 struggle: 'Both states have a political system which allows the majority of the Irish people to choose their Government.' Shorn of its commitment to armed struggle the republican position on partition differed in no way from that of the other parties in the south and the armed campaign was a 'God send to Unionist propagandists'.

While Greaves was more sympathetic to republicans than Carmody, the Connolly Association was opposed to the armed campaign. It urged the IRA to call it off and organise a mass movement of democrats that could appeal to Protestant workers over the heads of the Unionist party, and Sinn Féin needed to recognise Leinster House. The Association continued to place events in Ireland in a broader international context and lauded the fact that 'the Aiken proposals have differentiated Fianna Fáil from Fine Gael for the first time in years'. That was a reference to Aiken's suggestion at the UN that Khrushchev's offer to begin troop withdrawals from Europe should be given a chance.

Bennett and Carmody exchanged further polemics in the *Democrat* in January 1958 where Carmody referred to Aiken as proof that the proposition that Fianna Fáil members were merely the hangers-on of British imperialism was 'nonsense'. He contended that the notion of the national question having primacy in Irish politics was a 'fallacy'. Bennett wrote a detailed critique of the CPNI's *Irish Way to Socialism* but it was refused publication in the Communist press. The position argued by Greaves, Johnston and Bennett was bolstered by the change in political circumstances wrought by the Republic's application to join the EEC. The CPNI's 1962 programme, *Ireland's Path to Socialism*, was radically different in its approach to the republican movement and pointed to the 'domination of British imperialism' as the central factor in Irish politics.[59] It presented itself as part of a 'progressive' movement that would include republicans and criticised the NILP for its hostile attitude to republicanism. The republican movement in contrast was praised for its consistent opposition to the EEC and NATO. There was also an echo of Johnston's attempt to make socialism more attractive to republicans by referring to co-operativism. It was clear then that there were differences within the Communist movement over the attitude to be adopted towards the Irish republican movement but that the priority given to opposing Irish entry to the EEC shifted the balance in favour of the Greaves/Bennett position that was shared by Johnston. Ironically the modernisers were to adopt a position on the national question similar to that of Paddy Carmody in the 1970s and 1980s.

While the *Irish Democrat* campaigned for the abolition of the Special Powers Act, it was more reticent when it came to criticising the Dublin government over its security policy although it did welcome the release of the Curragh internees in 1959. While it criticised the reintroduction of the Special Criminal Court in January 1962, the Connolly Association did not take part in public protests and in April 1964 Greaves defended a decision not to picket Lemass on his visit to London: 'The Irish in Britain should never carry out hostile demonstrations against members of the Dublin Government when they visit this country.' Another article claimed that the Irish government was pulled between two tendencies: one that 'aimed at exploiting a politically independent part of Ireland as if it were still a colony; and the tendency of national democracy aimed at completing the national revolution and establishing an All Ireland Republic free not only politically but economically too'. The task of progressive forces was to support the latter.

Greaves's views on Ireland were summarised in a short book entitled *The Irish Question and the British People*. It was published in 1963 but had been circulated prior to that among leading members of the Connolly Association and some republicans. Greaves rehearses the traditional republican view of partition as a violation of Irish sovereignty.[60] Although Britain retained its power over the Republic through financial and economic power, the southern state unlike Northern Ireland constituted a 'viable independent state'. The bulk of the book deals with the mechanics of discrimination and repression against the nationalist minority in Northern Ireland and sets out an agenda of striving for legislation to bring it to an end, which in effect became the policy of the civil rights movement.

Greaves welcomed the revival of republican political activity that followed the ending of the armed campaign and claimed that it was recognition that there could be a vigorous and valid form of constitutional action. Republicanism had a potential point of contact with socialism through the movement's historic internationalism and this could form the basis for 'the complex process of securing a junction between the National movement and the working class movement'. Armed struggle could not provide a solution to Partition. What was required was to build an alliance of progressive forces in Northern Ireland to demand that the British Labour Party should legislate to provide the same democratic rights there as in the rest of the United Kingdom. The Republic could play its part by strengthening the state sector against economic imperialism and making it more attractive to northern Protestant workers. The Connolly Association was seen as the bridge between the progressive movements in Britain and Ireland. The relevance of that to the later civil rights movement is clear although it would be ridiculous to claim that the notion of campaigning for equality of citizenship between Northern Ireland and the United Kingdom came about only as a consequence of a strategy created by Communists. Rather, it was a case that the growing demands by northern nationalists for equality coincided with that strategy and were seen by the Communists and their republican allies as a suitable vehicle for their own political ambitions.

The chief obstacle to the Connolly Association gaining the kind of influence hoped for by Greaves remained the belief that the organisation was Communist. The *Irish Democrat* published a series of questions and answers about the Association in June 1960 and in response to a query as to whether it was Communist there was a disingenuous denial and a claim that a group that had attempted to 'introduce a Trotskyist flavour' into the Association had been expelled. In December 1961 the Standing Committee of the Association denied that it was Communist, in response to an allegation made in a letter sent to trade union officials which had referred to the 1959 Congress of the CPGB where the Connolly Association had been praised for having 'closely followed the Party line in domestic and international affairs'. A former leader of the CPGB, Douglas Hyde, writing in *Hibernia*, described the Association as an 'Irish fellow-traveller organisation' and accused it of exploiting Connolly in order to dupe Irish emigrant workers into joining the Connolly Association.[61] A leftist critic and former member of the Association claimed that Johnston had told him that emphasising Connolly's role as a nationalist martyr was a subterfuge designed to introduce Marxism into the republican movement.[62]

Shared opposition to the EEC was the one unifying issue capable of bringing together the Marxist left and republicans. As Milotte suggests, the Communist reorientation towards the IRA and Sinn Féin had 'nothing to do with any change in republican politics'.[63] It had much more to do with the potential threat that Irish membership posed to the interests of the Soviet Union. Seán Ó Brádaigh also suggests that Communist interest in the republican movement may have been motivated by a feeling that a demoralised and weakened movement might provide potential recruits or be more easily influenced.[64]

Coughlan claims never to have been a member of the Communist Party in either Britain or Ireland and denies that the Connolly Association was ever under direct Communist influence.[65] He remained close to members of the IWP and lectured at meetings of the Young Ireland Club which Special Branch described as consisting of 'mainly members of the "Youth Section" of the Irish Workers Party'.[66] Coughlan says that Greaves never foresaw the republican movement as replacing the Labour Party as the main party of the working class. This was based on his belief that the class composition of republicanism was inimical to its embracing socialism, and Coughlan shares that view of republicanism as a petit-bourgeois ideology.[67] Greaves's main objective was to republicanise Labour, which would explain why a number of Connolly Association members also joined the Irish Labour Party at the same time that Coughlan and Johnston were making contact with the IRA. Michael O'Leary, elected as a Labour TD for Dublin North Central in 1965 and later party leader, had been in the Association in London. The *Irish Democrat* in June 1965 described him as 'the most consciously republican in outlook of the Labour TDs'.[68] Coughlan and O'Leary shared a flat in Dublin at around this time.

Although the *Irish Democrat* lauded the role of former Connolly Association members in Dublin, it was also conscious of the rumours: 'Some people may fall for the bogey stories that the Association still directs their work. It doesn't'.[69] Coughlan also denied that Greaves had any responsibility for the subsequent political roles of any former members. Coughlan says that he did act as an adviser to himself and others but that this was purely 'informal'.[70] Coughlan had been the full-time organiser of the Connolly Association in London before returning to Dublin to take up the position of lecturer in Social Administration at Trinity College in 1961. Although Coughlan and Johnston shared a similar political background, Coughlan appears to have remained closer to Greaves. Johnston's actual policy proposals did not represent a huge shift in republican politics. His economic policies on the face of it were quite compatible with those of Comhar na gComharsan that in essence remained the official social and economic policy of the movement following his own taking over of policy formation. However, it was political strategy, involving as it did an alliance with the left and moves to end abstnetionism, rather than policy which was the main bone of contention.

At the same time that Johnston and Coughlan were making contact with the republicans, there were a number of stories in the media regarding Communist influence. Communists were accused of having been involved in organising the Dublin bus strike of 1962. In a *Sunday Independent* feature, Richard Beaumont warned his readers that there were almost '1,000 dedicated card-holding party members; led by some 20 Moscow-trained experts' active in the Republic and a similar number in the North who were responsible for strikes and protests and were infiltrating other organisations.[71] This was at a time when the IWL had fewer than a hundred members. One correspondent, however, suggested that Fianna Fáil at its Ard Fheis had initiated the red scare in order to discredit opposition to EEC membership.[72] During a debate in the Dáil in April 1963, Frank Aiken agreed with a Fine Gael TD's suggestion that the 'Connolly Clubs' (*sic*) were financed with Russian money.[73]

Johnston's prominent role within the Wolfe Tone Society and the IRA and Sinn Féin was possible only under the patronage of Goulding. The 1960s was not the first time that the IRA had looked outside its own ranks for political advice. It was a symptom of its failure to create within its own ranks what

Gramsci referred to as 'organic intellectuals'. For Gramsci one of the crucial steps in the struggle by any group for power was its ability to convince large sections of the traditional intelligentsia of the coherence of that group's ideology, and that this colonisation of the intelligentsia was facilitated by the creation within its own ranks of organic intellectuals capable of putting that case to those outside.[74] While the republican movement of the revolutionary period had clearly succeeded in both of those objectives, the IRA had patently failed to do so after 1925. In welcoming people like Johnston, and in facilitating the formation of the Wolfe Tone Society, Goulding was attempting to import from outside the movement the kind of intellectual talent that he was conscious was missing. In doing so he was also creating the basis for tensions that were to cause internal difficulties over the next decade. Seán Ó Brádaigh believes that Goulding was an 'intellectual lightweight' and that this made him more susceptible to the influence of people such as Johnston and Greaves.[75] Of course there were far more prosaic reasons than 'absence of theory' which accounted for the lack of support for the movement.

Johnston shared Goulding's view that the IRA rather than Sinn Féin was the means to politicise the republican movement because of the Army's structure and discipline. That was the reason he agreed to join but he now feels that its history and culture made it an unsuitable vehicle for the task. Johnston describes what was taking place at the time as a conscious attempt to demilitarise the republican tradition and that process was derailed by the outbreak of the northern crisis in 1969. Patterson supports Johnston's claim that, while this may appear to have been contradicted by ongoing military training and plans for a renewal of armed struggle, this was kept up only as a means of maintaining morale and discipline within the IRA.[76] This may have been the view of Johnston and perhaps even of Goulding but was not shared with the majority of IRA members including many supportive of the moves towards ending abstentionism and adopting socialism.

It is not clear when Greaves first met Goulding but it was before December 1964 when Goulding asked to meet Greaves who introduced Cathal Mac Liam, a first cousin of Goulding, to Goulding for the first time.[77] They discussed the fraught relations between the republican Clann na hÉireann based in Britain and the Connolly Association, with Goulding clearly in favour of a close relationship in opposition to most Clann members. Greaves's journal entry for 7 December 1964 is worth quoting in part for the light it sheds on the relationship between the Communists and the IRA modernisers:

> Taking all in all, things are progressing here 'as well as can be expected'. The younger people with the Connolly Association experience are becoming personally acceptable to the Republicans, and after Monday's meeting RHWJ[78] and Seán Cronin went off to AC's[79] flat which the young Labour hero Michael O'Leary is sharing, and so all heads clarify each other by mutual interaction.[80]

There is an interesting later entry from August 1965 regarding the prospects for 'unity' between the Connolly Association and the republican movement, with the former in effect displacing Clann na hÉireann.[81] It is clear then that Goulding was already discussing common political activity with the Communist movement. Greaves remained close to the Goulding faction for the remainder of the decade and was consulted at various points in regard to issues that arose. He may also have been the author of a key position paper in April 1967. Greaves was not acting in a personal capacity, nor was he simply the hibernophile that he is sometimes portrayed as. He was a member of the upper echelons of the CPGB and regarded as an expert on Irish history and republicanism. What influence he exerted, therefore, could only have been designed to benefit the CPGB. Jim Lane claims that Jim Savage, who was a member of the IWP in Cork, was influential in Sinn Féin as early as 1965 when he was urging left-wingers who had left the movement to rejoin. He told them that the IWP now had a foothold in the movement and that the Wolfe Tone Society would provide the vehicle through which Communists would form a link to republicans and the Labour Party.[82]

The IWP held its Fifth National Conference in Dublin on the same June 1965 weekend as the special Sinn Féin Ard Fheis. The Draft Political Resolution shared many areas of concern and policy with the republican movement and was almost identical to that being proposed by the Wolfe Tone Society and the left within the republican movement. It referred to increased economic growth that was making possible the realisation of the undertakings given in the Second Programme for Economic Expansion but that this was at the cost of increasing dependence on foreign and particularly British capital.[83] Fianna Fáil, which had formerly played a positive role, was now acquiescent to monopoly capital but had the support of workers, small farmers and small businessmen because of a lack of political alternative. The IWP believed that the labour movement could provide leadership to potential opposition from those groups and that Communists were not rivals to the Labour Party but a 'complementary fraternal partner in the Irish Labour Movement', and a 'comrade organisation in the struggle for Irish freedom'. It noted the strengthening of socialism and of the European left and welcomed the 'changed attitude to Socialism' on the part of the Catholic Church: 'Far from being in conflict with Christianity it is only through Socialism that the basic social idea of Christianity, the brotherhood of man, can be fully realised.'

The Connolly Association viewed the new direction being taken by the republican movement with satisfaction. Speaking at its 1965 Wolfe Tone commemoration in London, Coughlan claimed that republicans were 'consciously backing all those movements of economic resistance to the effects of imperialism in Ireland'.[84] Later in the year Coughlan wrote an article which stated that individual members of the Labour leadership had been in discussions with republicans to organise a campaign against the Anglo-Irish Free Trade Agreement.[85] In his editorial for the November 1965 *Irish Democrat*, Greaves predicted that Labour involvement in such a campaign would be the precursor to sending Fianna Fáil and Fine Gael the way of the old Redmondite Irish Parliamentary Party.

What the Communists clearly shared with republicans of both the traditionalist and modernising strains was an overly optimistic belief in any desire on the part of Irish people to resist economic modernisation in favour of the alternative of economic and political isolation allied with material self-sacrifice. The labour movement despite early misgivings was drawn into effective support for the new Fianna Fáil policy which brought benefits to trade union members in jobs and wages, and most of them continued to vote for Fianna Fáil. The modernist faction of the republican movement, as Official Sinn Féin and Sinn Féin the Workers Party, also came to embrace foreign-investment-led industrialisation, albeit from their perspective as the precursor to state socialism on the Soviet model.

Echoing Johnston's approach to abstentionism within the Wolfe Tone Society, the *Irish Democrat* in August 1965 claimed that, while there were definite advantages attached to republican participation at Stormont including the possibility of creating a 'progressive majority', caution needed to be exercised. The author, possibly Greaves, referred to the manner in which abstentionism had split Sinn Féin in 1926 when De Valera would have been better advised to wait until he had won over a majority of republicans to his view. Johnston and Greaves were content to leave the issue on the long finger as a secondary matter to building an alliance between republicans and the left.

Part of that alliance focused on Irish republican groups in Britain, but they were hostile to the Connolly Association. Sinn Féin in Britain was replaced by a new organisation Clann na hÉireann, launched in April 1964, and which according to Garda Special Branch hoped, while continuing to propagate IRA policy and raise funds, to attract more moderate Irish people through its 'non-militant' image.[86] In June 1964 the *Irish Democrat* welcomed the new group but criticised its call for Irish people in Britain not to have anything to do with groups that called for support for British parties. The *Guardian* claimed that the sentiments expressed at a Clann rally 'suggested that the speakers were blood brothers of that Legionary whose motto was "Down with intelligence and long live death"'.[87]

Greaves offered to co-operate with Clann na hÉireann but it reciprocated by excluding the Connolly Association from one of its rallies in October. The Clann's suspicion of Greaves was well founded in fact as Greaves contacted Tadgh Feehan of the Irish Embassy in April 1965 to assure him that he was totally opposed to the republican group and that the Connolly Association would never do anything that would embarrass the Irish Embassy or the Irish government. Greaves also gave the impression that he believed that Clann na hÉireann had been responsible for a petrol bomb attack on the Embassy on 22 April.[88]

Feehan noted the hostility between the different Irish groups in London and that the Clann shared the contemporary concerns of the republican movement including the sale of Irish land to foreigners, emigration, unemployment, Partition and the arrests of Easter lily sellers. However, while the Clann na hÉireann 1966 Ard Fhéis on 27 February demonstrated that it was on board with the political agenda of the Goulding/Johnston faction, it remained highly suspicious of Goulding's sponsorship of closer links to the Connolly Association. According to Keating it was continuing to grow especially outside of London. The Connolly Association, which Keating described as 'a front organisation for the Communist Party', was in corresponding decline.[89] Relations between the two groups remained cool and in June 1966 O Cionnaith wrote a letter to the *Irish Democrat* criticising those who 'subordinated themselves to British political and cultural interests'. The Connolly Association rejected the claim and called on the Clann to meet with it to discuss plans for unity. The obvious implication of Goulding's support for close ties with the Connolly Association was that republicans in Britain should align themselves with British parties, which, while superficially involving electoral support for Labour, actually entailed a link to the CPGB through the Connolly Association. Many younger Irish activists, including some who were members of the Clann, were in fact more attracted to the various Trotskyist groups, among whom Irish exiles such as Gery Lawless, Eamonn McCann and Brendan Clifford were involved.

The Clann continued to resist encouragement from Dublin to align with the Connolly Association and at its 1967 Ard Fheis, held on 19 February, two resolutions were passed rejecting any form of alliance with the Connolly Association. But that was negated by another motion, supported by Goulding, which removed the constitutional ban on members of the Association becoming members. There was also some controversy over an attempt to register 19 delegates from London and in all only 20 delegates were given voting rights. That represented a membership of two hundred and a notable decline even since the previous year when more than a hundred delegates had attended, mirroring the similar fall-off in Sinn Féin membership between 1966 and 1967.

The numbers are worth referring to as they provide an accurate picture of the real strength of the movement which the modernisers were hoping to push in a certain direction. It is clear not only that this was alienating traditionalist members, causing substantial numbers to leave or cease to be active, but that this loss was not being compensated for through the recruitment of large numbers of new members attracted by the new direction. All of the constituent parts of the radical alliance envisaged in the new strategy – the IRA, Sinn Féin, the Wolfe Tone Society and its adjuncts, the two Irish Communist parties and the Connolly Association – had small memberships, totalling probably no more than several thousand, and most of them were republicans many of whom were ceasing to be active, as is proved by the attendances at Sinn Féin Ard Fheiseanna in 1967 and 1968. That serves to put the modernisers' project into perspective and questions their belief that this was transforming the republican movement into a formidable opponent.

Notes

1 Justice, 2000/36/3, memo of 18 March 1969, paragraph 3, NAI.
2 Interview with Richard Roche, 26 April 2005.
3 Roy Johnston in email to author, 5 July 2001.
4 Interview with Noel Kavanagh, 7 March 2005.
5 Interview with Seán Bermingham, 20 April 2005.
6 *Irish Independent*, 17 June 1963.
7 Minutes of Wolfe Tone Bi-centenary Committee, p. 2. In possession of Cathal Mac Liam.
8 Letter from Richard Roche to Alphonsus Ryan, 13 May 1963, in possession of Cathal Mac Liam.
9 Letter from Maire Comerford to Richard Roche, 23 October 1963.
10 Minutes of Wolfe Tone Bi-centenary Committee, note of meeting of 24 November 1963.
11 Minutes of the Wolfe Tone Society, 1963–67, 14 January 1964.
12 *Irish Independent*, 11 March 1964.
13 *Ibid.*, 29 June 1964.
14 Letter from Cronin to Johnston, 2 June 1964, contained in Minutes Book.
15 Wolfe Tone Society Minutes, 1 September 1964.
16 Interview with Richard Roche, 26 April 2005.
17 Puirséil (2007), pp. 225–6.
18 Draft Constitution of the Wolfe Tone Society, pp. 2–3. Original in possession of Cathal Mac Liam.
19 Patterson (1997), pp. 100–1.
20 Minutes of Wolfe Tone Society meeting on Economic Resistance, 20 October 1964.
21 Letter from Brian Murphy to Uinseann Mac Eoin, 1 July 1964, in possession of Cathal Mac Liam.
22 *Irish Times*, 6 April 1965.
23 Letter of 10 August 1965 from Roy Johnston to Prof. Michael Dolly, in Wolfe Tone Society Minutes, 1963–67.
24 Minutes of Wolfe Tone Society 1963–67, AGM 21 September 1965.
25 Minutes of Wolfe Tone Society 1963–67, 2 November 1965.
26 Report of speech by Roy Johnston, 17 January 1966, in Wolfe Tone Society Minutes 1963–67.

27 *A Catechism on Free Trade* (Dublin 1965), p. 8.
28 Interview with Richard Roche, 26 April 2005.
29 Interview with Seán Bermingham, 20 April 2005.
30 Irish Workers League, Fourth National Conference 1962, *Draft Political Resolution*, p. 5. Copy in possession of Cathal Mac Liam.
31 *Irish Socialist*, no. 23, April 1963.
32 Interview with Tom Mitchell, 11 January 2002.
33 *Cork Evening Echo*, 15 December 1956, quoting from Soviet trade union paper *Trud*. Courtesy of Jim Lane.
34 Tom Redmond, 'The Forces in the Irish National Liberation Struggle', *Marxism Today*, June 1973, p. 168.
35 Beckett (1998).
36 'Roy Johnston's Apologia', *Hibernia*, 31 March 1972.
37 *United Irishman*, October 1964.
38 Interviews with Roy Johnston, 19 April 2001, and Anthony Coughlan, 12 December 2001.
39 Interview with Seán Ó Brádaigh, 21 May 2005.
40 Private information.
41 Interview with Ruairí Ó Brádaigh, 22 May 2002.
42 Interview with Noel Kavanagh, 7 March 2005.
43 Interview with Seán Ó Brádaigh, 21 May 2005.
44 Interview with Seán Garland, 28 February 2005.
45 Interview with Tom Mitchell, 11 January 2002.
46 Swan (2006), p. 103.
47 Interview with Anthony Coughlan, 12 December 2001.
48 DFA A12/1/A, dated 6 March 1958, NAI.
49 WO 32/17577, National Archives, Kew.
50 Private information from former CA member in London in the 1950s who later joined the Irish Workers Party and remained close to Greaves.
51 *Young Ireland*, November 1949.
52 *The Promethean*, Vol. 1, no. 1, September 1946.
53 *Ibid.*, Vol. 1, no. 2, October 1946.
54 *Ibid.*, Vol. 2, no. 2.
55 *Ibid.*, Vol. 2, no. 4.
56 Interview with Roy Johnston, 19 April 2001.
57 Department of Justice, 8/900, NAI.
58 *Irish Democrat*, January 1957.
59 CPNI, *Ireland's Path to Socialism* (Belfast 1962), Introduction.
60 C. D. Greaves, *The Irish Question and the British People*, typescript in possession of Cathal Mac Liam, p. 1.
61 *Hibernia*, August 1958.
62 Clifford (1984), p. 7–8.
63 Milotte (1984), p. 265.
64 Interview with Seán Ó Brádaigh, 21 May 2005.
65 Interview with Anthony Coughlan, 12 December 2001.

66 Department of Justice, 8/922 – report by Detective Garda Maurice Keogh, NAI.
67 Interview with Anthony Coughlan, 12 December 2001.
68 *Irish Democrat*, June 1965.
69 *Irish Democrat*, August 1964.
70 Interview with Anthony Coughlan, 12 December 2001.
71 *Sunday Independent*, 25 November 1962.
72 *Ibid.*, 23 December 1962.
73 *Dáil Debates*, Vol. 201, col. 1078.
74 Antonio Gramsci, 'The Intellectuals', in *Selections from the Prison Notebooks* (London 1991), p. 10.
75 Interview with Seán Ó Brádaigh, 21 May 2005.
76 Patterson (1997), p. 108.
77 Johnston, *Century of Endeavour* (Dublin 2007), p. 181.
78 Roy Johnston.
79 Anthony Coughlan.
80 Greaves Journal, www.iol.ie/~rjtechne/century130703/1960s/greave60.htm, viewed 13 April 2005.
81 *Ibid.*, Journal entry for 12 August 1965.
82 Jim Lane, *Miscellaneous Notes* on the republican movement in Cark (republished manuscript in his possession), p. 11.
83 Irish Workers Party, *Draft Political Resolution*, 27 May 1965, in possession of Cathal Mac Liam.
84 *Irish Democrat*, July 1965.
85 *Ibid.*, October 1965.
86 Garda Report 3C/15/66, p. 16.
87 *Guardian*, 20 April 1964, in DFA B113/122, NAI.
88 DFA B113/122, Report by Feehan, 25 April 1965, NAI.
89 DFA 98/3/17, report by Keating to Seán Ronan of External Affairs, 4 May 1966, NAI.

5

The year 1966 and the revival
of the IRA 'threat'

The Dáil passed the Anglo-Irish Free Trade Agreement on 7 January 1966 by 66 votes to 19. The Labour Party opposed the measure and Fine Gael abstained. Labour put many of the same arguments as republicans and one Labour TD, Denis Larkin, discerned signs of a realignment in the politics of the Dáil that would open up the kind of opportunities for the left that were being envisaged by some republicans and the Communists.[1] The Wolfe Tone Society, which had organised a lobby of the Dáil on 4 January under the auspices of the Economic Independence Committee, congratulated the Labour Party which it said had 'returned to the position of its founder, James Connolly'[2] but *An Phoblacht* regarded the lobby as part of the process of conditioning republicans to accept participation in constitutional politics.[3] Mac Giolla said that the Dáil opposition could not respond to Lemass's taunt that they had no alternative because the only alternative to closer integration with Britain was 'to break the connection completely'.[4] The *Irish Democrat* was fulsome in its praise of republican opposition to the FTA, although it gave pride of place to the Irish Workers Party, and depicted Sinn Féin and the IRA as 'fighting on many fronts'.[5]

A meeting of the IRA Executive on 30 January 1966 reviewed what progress had been made since the Army Convention. Special Branch obtained two copies of the minutes, one in Tom Mitchell's handwriting and one typewritten. Six members, all of whom are described by pseudonyms, attended the meeting. Goulding was McNeill, Costello was Clancy, Garland was Nolan, Mitchell was Flynn, and the others there were Rasputin, who may have been Mick Ryan, and one other whose name is indecipherable, probably Stynes, which was the pseudonym of Tony Meade.[6] It was reported that there had been 'a certain amount of unrest and reaction in various areas after the extraordinary Convention as a result of the many controversial issues dealt with there'.[7] But while the typed minutes claim that this had been dealt with 'satisfactorily', Mitchell's notes refer to 'desertion in certain areas' and say that Cork was 'not fully cooperating'. Mitchell recalled that many IRA members began to become inactive around this time although few formally resigned.[8]

The Department of the Adjutant General, Costello, was said to be 'function-ing efficiently', but Quigley had replaced Prior as Quartermaster General. Drew had been replaced as Director of Finance by Mackey, who was Denis Foley, and the Director of Intelligence had been relieved of his position at his own request but had not yet been replaced. Nolan (Garland) was working full-time as Director of Operations and Training Officer, Quirke, who was Seán Ó Brá-daigh, continued as Director of Publicity and Jones (Johnston) remained as Director of Education.[9] Agitation was adjudged to have been fairly successful in raising the profile of the movement although 'many of our people did not know exactly what they were at' and 'only Army people were active in this work'.[10] Progress was being made in establishing co-operatives under the aus-pices of Comhar Linn but Johnston claims that Comhar Linn was a failure.[11]

The Quartermaster General's department, responsible for arms procure-ment, was 'not so good', training camps were being conducted regularly, finance was 'fairly active' and there was a 'steady flow of capital' from the United States but Intelligence was 'not so good'.[12] Costello reported that many Command areas were weak, as was contact with GHQ. The Executive dis-cussed taking action against dissidents who were suspected of using IRA weapons but no decision was made. The committee that had been appointed following the Convention had just completed its work and its report would be considered by the Council at its next meeting.

The *United Irishman* was proving to be a drain on the movement although things had improved since the appointment of Tony Meade as editor. A north-ern edition, the *Ulsterman*, had run between March and December 1965 but had been discontinued owing to a lack of sellers and the conviction of some under the Special Powers Act. There was a curious reference to a briefing given by Irish Army officers to the CIA who were worried about republican influ-ence on the trade union movement. Apparently it was believed by the Ameri-cans that '500 dissidents in Ireland easily dealt with'. Overall, the picture that emerges is of an organisation that was growing weaker rather than stronger. Most of those who had been members during the armed campaign had become inactive and, as it became apparent that there would be no renewed armed offensive, many members drifted away. Nor were many enthused by the alternative role sketched for them in the 1965 Convention proposals. So, while the IRA was still able to maintain a public face through commemora-tions and occasional protests, there was little real activity. For most Volunteers the action they sought was military rather than participation in protests and that led to a significant number, including many who had been involved in the 1956–62 campaign, to embark on armed adventures against the orders of the Army Council.

Despite the evidence of internal weakness, in January 1966 the Ard Com-hairle adopted a plan, based on the 1965 proposals, to build Sinn Féin to a position of strength whereby within five years it would be capable of winning a majority of seats in Leinster House. Given how badly Sinn Féin had done in its most recent electoral outings in 1960 and 1961 such an ambition was delusory. Costello ordered that selected Volunteers should be made to join Sinn Féin to form cumainn where none existed, but, far from building an organisation capable of winning an election, Costello was probably thinking as much about ensuring a bloc of support for his own proposals on the future of the party.

The first bulletin of Johnston's Education Department was issued in January 1966.[13] It referred to the first education conference which had taken place in Dublin in December and outlined plans for a series of further events. According to the Gardaí, a member of the Irish Workers Party, most likely they meant Roy Johnston, addressed a two-day educational conference at the end of January on agricultural co-operation although the bulletin had planned that it should be on trade unionism. Further conferences were planned in February on local government, in preparation for the next local elections, and on trade unionism in the North. The conference was designed to organise support from Belfast trade unionists 'on a non-sectarian basis' for the fiftieth anniversary Easter commemoration, which if successful would 'make the Unionists shiver'. The Unionists did express concern about the event becoming the catalyst for an IRA uprising, but participation by 'Belfast trade unionists', in reality CPNI members, was minimal following objections from the Antrim GAA which owned Casement Park where the main com-memoration was held.

The *Republican Manual of Education*, which was designed to reinforce the lessons of the seminars, covered the period from the United Irishmen to the 1960s and linked political events to class in classical Marxist fashion. It was claimed that 'constitutional actions can be revolutionary' depending on 'the demands put forward and the composition of the leadership', and that this had been possible in the 1880s before the actions of the Invincibles in murder-ing the Chief Secretary had forced Parnell to compromise. Because the inter-ests of the working class had not been put at the head of the national revolution after 1916, the basis for the betrayal of the Republic was laid, the lesson being that the revolutionary movement needed to be properly educated and to identify itself with the social and economic struggles of the workers and small farmers. The movement needed to go beyond even that and, unlike the IRA in the 1930s, not only to be socially involved but also to constitute a 'viable alternative political movement' to Fianna Fáil, which would require the repub-licans to form a 'disciplined, incorruptible political movement that would be prepared to work as a minority within the Dáil, until it gained enough support to make it a majority'. That amounted to an unequivocal rejection of absten-tionism and went beyond the electoral strategy agreed by the Ard Comhairle in January. The 1956–62 Campaign had failed, mainly owing to a lack of popular support, and in place of its former attitude the movement required 'a ruthless realism' based on its better understanding of neo-colonialism and because it now had a programme that embodied the interests of those social groups opposed to imperialism. The key to that was integration between the political/military and the social/economic wings of the movement.

There was no reference to the traditional republican claim that the Republic retained *de jure* legitimacy after 1922. That was the fundamental difference between the traditionalists and the modernisers. Garland is dismissive of the belief that the IRA Army Council was the 'government',[14] whereas the Ó Brádaighs still hold that view.[15] At the same time, the IRA leadership still invoked its alleged status as the governmental authority of the Republic when that suited its own purposes, in for example ensuring that, while the 1965 Convention had rejected dropping abstentionism, the Army Council could interpret decisions of the Convention in a manner that facilitated a continuing erosion of the old policies.

On 6 February 1966 Cathal Goulding was arrested at Portlaoise in possession of a Luger pistol and 3,000 rounds of .303-rifle ammunition, at a time when critics of the leadership were claiming that weapons were being collected from units to be placed under the control of men whom Goulding trusted politically. Cathal Mac Liam had been with Goulding in Tipperary where Goulding met Dan Gleeson, an IRA veteran of the 1920s. Unbeknownst to Mac Liam, Goulding had collected the gun and hid it in a bag of vegetables where it was found when the car was stopped.[16] In April a jury failed to agree on the charges and he was acquitted but recharged. Goulding told the jury: 'If you find me guilty of this charge, you are finding every Irishman of every generation from Tone to the men of 1916 guilty because they used the same methods I am seeking to use now for the same reasons.'[17] Goulding's detention was also significant because he was replaced as Chief of Staff during his absence by Seamus Costello, who used the opportunity to push forward with proposals for internal change more radical than perhaps Goulding himself believed were acceptable at that time.

Goulding was sentenced to three months in June when he refused to pay a £50 fine, but the money was raised by Mac Liam with contributions from Johnston, Greaves, Keating and others. The heightened Garda pressure on the republican movement prompted Sinn Féin to mount a picket on Dublin Castle on 15 May. They demanded that the Special Detective Unit should be disbanded and accused it of using phone-taps, searches and intimidation against republicans. The Connolly Association called on the Minister for Justice to release Goulding, and the Irish Workers Group declared that 'the names of the officers who arrested Mr. Goulding and of the prosecuting officer have been noted by the Irish revolutionary movement'.[18]

That support from the left was grist to the mill of those who were alleging a communist takeover of the IRA. The *Sunday Independent* claimed that persistent efforts by the Irish Communist organisation to gain influence in the IRA had come to fruition in 1965. They saw this as a replication of the situation in 1934 when elements of the IRA leadership had been 'seduced' by the Republican Congress. The article alleged that 'a leading member of the Communist organisation' was now a key member of the IRA.[19] The Minister for Justice, Brian Lenihan, said that he did not 'dissent in any way from the facts given in this article'. The IRA admitted that it had supported the telephonists' strike but said that its only contribution was individual financial donations and advice that the workers should settle their dispute within existing trade union structures. Republican opposition to foreign takeovers 'should not be interpreted as implying connections with any ideology or doctrine other than that of the 1916 Proclamation'. Mac Giolla called on Lenihan to investigate the infiltration of Fianna Fáil by pro-British and anti-national elements.

The number of violent incidents that took place in the first part of 1966 forced the modernisers in the IRA leadership to confront the contradiction between their opposition to these and the military aspects of the 1965 proposals. The IRA never formally approved the plan and as far as is known did not actually kill anyone, or attempt to kill anyone, between the 1965 Army Convention and the outbreak of the northern conflict in 1969. What took place was a series of operations that one might have imagined belonged more properly to the second phase of 'stunt operations' but all appeared to have ceased by early 1966. Some of these, like the plan to attack the *Lofoten*, had been authorised but most were carried out by IRA Volunteers without official sanction, while still others were the work of people who had left the movement. As Hanley and Millar show, many IRA members were frustrated by the reluctance of the leadership to sanction actions and instead embarked on unauthorised operations, with many of those involved being expelled or resigning to become active in one or other of the dissident groups.

One of those involved in the incidents which brought public focus on the IRA was Richard Behal from Kilkenny. Behal was arrested and charged with involvement in the attack on the *Brave Borderer* at Waterford on 10 September 1965 and in November Behal and Walter Dunphy were sentenced to nine months for assaulting a Garda, while Edward Kelly received six months. What caused most concern for the IRA leadership were Behal's subsequent activities including a series of bombings in Kilkenny. Behal was attracting unwanted attention and was acting without sanction. Behal escaped from Limerick Prison on 20 February and went on the run and his group blew up the automatic telephone exchange at Kilmacow, County Kilkenny, on 13 April. A poster which read 'IRA Struggle for Freedom' was discovered at the scene.

Between 12 and 22 April eight incidents took place involving the blocking of roads and damage to telephone and telegraph wires. At the end of April Behal announced that the actions had ceased now that attention had been drawn to the treatment of republican prisoners. He also stated that he was not responsible for any incidents that had taken place outside of Kilkenny. On 17 April an attempt was made to blow up the automatic telephone exchange in Merrion Street, Dublin. Posters demanding the release of republican prisoners were discovered at the scene. On 20 April a petrol bomb was thrown through the window of the gymnasium of Cathal Brugha barracks in Dublin. The IRA abducted Behal and the former Dublin Brigade OC Phil O'Donoghue, who had been involved in the Dublin incidents. An IRA court martial sentenced them to death for unofficial actions and seizing weapons. The sentence was lifted on condition that they take no further actions. Behal was later banished from the country by the Army Council to prevent him forming a splinter group. Tony Meade was chairman of the court martial and says that he accepted that Behal had been provided with the weapons on request: 'This saved him, I believe, from a possible sticky end. It was not thought that Behal's actions were a deliberate provocation, but then you would want to have known Richard.'[20] Behal eventually made it to New York where he described himself as a 'political refugee'.

The run-up to the fiftieth anniversary of the 1916 Rising encouraged others to embark upon military escapades. On 24 February the British Legion hall near the Dublin docks was set on fire. The *Evening Herald* suggested that a Communist organisation was responsible.[21] The IRA denied responsibility for the attack and stated that 'all such incidents are contrary to declared Republican policy'.[22] On 1 March the home of the British Military Attaché Brigadier R. N. Thicknesse, at Eglinton Road, Donnybrook, Dublin, was petrol-bombed. The bomb was thrown through the kitchen window and caused extensive damage although the family were out at the time. No group claimed responsibility but the attackers left a note calling on the Attaché to leave Ireland by Easter Sunday or he would be shot. The most spectacular incident took place on the morning of 8 March when Nelson's Pillar in O'Connell Street was blown up. At least eight people were arrested but all were released without charge. The IRA denied it had anything to do with it even though it was popularly attributed to the organisation. The Gardaí were aware that it was not a sanctioned action and blamed it on 'the IRA splinter group'. Some of its members and members of the IRA were arrested but although incriminating documents were found in their possession no evidence was found to implicate any of them in the bombing. The Gardaí were 'reasonably satisfied as to the identity of some of them' but did not find sufficient evidence to bring charges.[23] Phil Suthcliffe, a former member of the IRA in Dublin, admitted in 2000 that he had been involved in the bombing, as had former Saor Uladh activist Joe

Christle. Special Branch believed that there were two groups of former IRA dissidents, one based in Dublin and the other in Cork. There were 41 in the Dublin group based around a 'hard core' of former Volunteers, described as 'vicious and undisciplined' and 'likely to engage in violent acts of disorder'.[24] They had arms and explosives and were trained in their use. Besides being suspected of various violent acts, the group had also become involved in social and economic agitation.

A more considered IRA statement pointed out that since 1954 it had been the policy of the movement to avoid any activity that would bring Volunteers into conflict with the southern state. The only authorised military operations since then had been directed against the British navy: 'We have refused to settle for the destruction of the symbols of domination; we are interested in the destruction of the domination itself.' The statement claimed that the incidents would provide a pretext for the state to reactivate repressive legislation.[25] The IRA leadership was praised for having demonstrated 'quite high standards of leadership' by Michael McInerney of the *Irish Times*, a member of the Wolfe Tone Society.[26] According to Ruairí Ó Brádaigh the IRA was genuinely worried that the state's unfounded fears of a republican offensive to coincide with the 1916 anniversary would lead to a crackdown on the movement.[27]

A large number of people were arrested under the Offences against the State Act in April 1966, leading to republican fears that another round of internment was about to begin. It is likely that the Irish government wanted to be seen to be acting on the claims from Belfast that the IRA was planning a new campaign, while at the same time assuring both the Unionists and London that the IRA had no such intention. It may also have suited Fianna Fáil to play up the alleged danger presented by subversives in the run up to the Presidential election campaign. Roy Johnston claimed that the state was concerned at the IRA's new departure 'and is actively engaged in trying to force the movement into the Forties mould, aided by "physical-force" splinter groups; no doubt under the leadership of agents-provocateurs'.[28] In May *An Phoblacht* claimed that the IRA statement amounted to 'felon-setting', by narrowing the focus of the police investigation and that the operations exposed the contradiction between the IRA's constitutional path and its claim to be a revolutionary organisation. The attacks were raised in the Dáil by the Fine Gael leader, Liam Cosgrave, who wanted to know what measures the government proposed to take against those responsible.[29] Minister Lenihan stated that the Gardaí were taking all possible measures but that it was not believed that extra powers were required. Another Fine Gael TD, Richie Ryan, accused him of hiding something and claimed that the 'country is full of rumours'.

While some of those who believed the IRA had blown up Nelson's Pillar regarded it as an occasion for levity, or even as a 'service to the nation' as the ballad popularised that year by the Dubliners put it, others took a dim view. A week after the event an article in the UCD magazine *Campus* saw it as perhaps a portent of things to come:

> Although many of the trappings of the IRA and its preposterous newspaper seem laughable and even quaint, we shall ignore at our peril the threat that this body poses to law and order in Northern Ireland and in the Republic…It looks as if many more bombs, north and south, will shatter the silence of the night before the year is out.

An editorial in *Hibernia* in November 1965 expressed similar fears that the Anniversary would provide the occasion for an 'IRA renaissance'. Concerns within the IRA that the state might take pre-emptive action against the organisation led to the moving of dumps from early January. Another motive was to remove arms from the reach of volunteers who the IRA suspected were involved in planning unauthorised actions.

Goulding's allies meanwhile attempted to use the Easter Rising anniversary and the heightened interest in republicanism to press forward with their attempts to alter radically the structure and direction of the movement. Roy Johnston's article for the Trinity 1916 anniversary publication praised the Wolfe Tone Society for 'refraining from didacticism…stressing practical objectives' and 'helping the learning process which the Republican Movement is undergoing at present'.[30] He accepted that the term 'socialist' had been debased in its European usage but that because of Connolly there was 'no need for us to go abroad for our revolutionary theory'. Johnston outlined the main features of Sinn Féin's Social and Economic Programme still under discussion and its emphasis on co-operatives and the nationalisation of major industries and finance. The new strategy was described as 'a return to classical republicanism' and a departure from the tradition of 'shoot first and explain afterwards'. Johnston claimed that republicans understood that going the same way as Fianna Fáil and Clann na Poblachta was to go into politics without clear social objectives, fear of which was the basis for the traditional republican attitude to Leinster House.

Johnston further upset traditionalists when he wrote to the *United Irishman* in June condemning the recitation of the Rosary at republican commemorations. Mac Stíofáin ordered that the paper should not be distributed in his Command area and was suspended for six months, reduced on appeal to two but he was re-elected to the Army Council at the IRA Convention in October. In his autobiography Mac Stíofáin makes the point that his suspension had nothing to do with Goulding, who at the time was being held in prison.[31] Garland supported the suspension and describes Mac Stíofáin as having been 'more Catholic than the Pope'.[32] Johnston did receive support at the Ard Fheis in November but a motion from the Palmerstown cumann in

Dublin calling for a 'prayer common to all denominations' to be recited at commemorations was not taken.[33]

The commemoration of the Easter Rising of 1916 provided the movement with an opportunity to stake its claim to be the true inheritor of the mantle of the revolutionaries. As in previous years, the Gardaí were directed to prevent the sale of Easter lilies and this led to more clashes. The incidents were of a relatively minor nature but a number of people were charged with assault on Gardaí. The most serious incident took place at Midleton, County Cork, on 11 April when an off-duty Garda was attacked by two members of the IRA in apparent reprisal for the seizure of Easter lilies. Two men were later charged. Officially, Easter Week began when De Valera reviewed a defence forces parade at the GPO on Easter Sunday, 10 April. Six hundred veterans of the Rising took part. That night RTE broadcast *Cuimhneachán*, an hour-long film celebrating the events of the Rising. The Garden of Remembrance was formally opened on Easter Monday, and on 12 April Tomás Mac Anna directed a pageant in Croke Park involving thousands of schoolchildren. There were also events organised in other parts of the state. Daly and O'Callaghan note Lemass's reference to Connolly as the most important of the 1916 leaders and say that there was intense competition between the state and republicans over the organisation and control of commemorative events. Daly does not accept, however, that the commemorations initiated an IRA revival,[34] and there is no evidence that the occasion led to a significant boost to recruitment. On the contrary 1967 saw a notable fall-off in the numbers attending the Ard Fheis, although that was partly the consequence of increasing internal dissatisfaction at the direction being taken by the movement.

The largest republican demonstration, attended by five thousand people, took place in Dublin on Easter Sunday. In his address at Glasnevin, Mac Giolla described Lemass's meeting with Terence O'Neill as a 'total surrender' and recognition of British rule in Ireland. Attempts were made by the Gardaí, under Chief Superintendent Michael Fitzpatrick, to seize the flag of the Dublin IRA. This was unsuccessful and the subsequent violence led the Labour Party to claim that the Gardaí had acted 'without any provocation from members of the procession'.[35] The National Civil Liberties League also condemned the Gardaí and noted 'that it is the declared policy of the Republican Movement at the present time to forego [*sic*] policies of violence in favour of more constitutional means of achieving their ends'.[36] Speaking at the Belfast Easter Commemoration, the acting Chief of Staff Seamus Costello harked back to the brief display of solidarity between Protestant and Catholic workers during the 1932 Outdoor Relief dispute, one of the favourite references of the republican left.

Another Army Council member, Seán Garland, was arrested by Gardaí at Mountrath, County Laois, on 7 May 1966. When searched, Garland was found to be in possession of the document which had been drawn up by the committee established following the 1965 IRA Convention. On 9 May Garland was sentenced to two months for possession of illegal documents and membership of an illegal organisation. The capture of the documents, and their partial publication in the media, was an embarrassment to the IRA, especially as they were being moved to avoid their capture in expected raids, and caused disquiet among ordinary Volunteers who had heard rumours of the content of the material. An IRA statement of 15 May claimed that what the newspapers had christened the 'Garland Plan' was only 'a suggested outline for a policy'. The organisation also found it significant that the government had only released those parts of the material that related to the 26 counties whereas most of the proposals concerned the British presence in Northern Ireland. The IRA accused Lenihan of attempting to stir up an atmosphere that would be conducive to the introduction of internment. Significantly, however, not only did the June *United Irishman* publish excerpts regarding the need to reorganise and reorient the republican movement but Meade's editorial also welcomed the ideas in the document as the basis for avoiding the mistakes and failures of the past. In that way the capture of the documents was used by both the modernisers and the state to highlight those aspects of the draft report that were most likely to cause unease among traditionalist republicans.

The press had been given only the section that discussed the political reorientation of the IRA. The Military Plan was not released but was handed over to the RUC and later turned up as part of its evidence to the Scarman Tribunal in 1971 in order to prove that the IRA had deliberately instigated the disturbances of 1969. The Irish government knew that the IRA Army Council had not approved the military plan. On foot of the Scarman disclosures, the Official IRA issued a statement on 23 May 1971 that again stressed that the 1965 plan was 'never in fact more than a draft for discussion purposes'.[37] The Scarman Tribunal was told that the document was passed to the RUC by an 'A.1 source' in mid-1968. The IRA claimed that the document must have been passed over in 1966 and that the source was Dublin. It is clear from the exchanges between Belfast and London in late 1965 and early 1966, however, that RUC Special Branch had reliable information on IRA intentions before Garland was arrested. While the RUC claimed that the plan had begun to be implemented in 'Autumn 1965', presumably it also knew that the military plan had not been approved. It chose to ignore this or to view the plan as a signal of intent and believed that, similarly to the situation that preceded the 1956–62 campaign, Army Council procrastination would either end or be ignored.

Lenihan told the Dáil that it would not be in the public interest to release all of the documents. The *Irish Times* of 14 May published extensive extracts from the political section, and the 'Garland Plan' received wide coverage in all of the national newspapers. The authorities obviously hoped that this would both embarrass the IRA and create public unease. Ironically the effect of publishing the 'Garland Plan' was not exactly what might have been intended. The presidential election campaign was in progress at the time and, speaking in support of the Fine Gael candidate Tom O'Higgins, Oliver J. Flanagan, TD for Laois/Offaly, accused Fianna Fáil of attempting to use the IRA document as an election gimmick. He even appeared to imply that the whole thing might have been a fabrication designed to distract attention from strikes, unemployment and taxation. The election was held on 1 June and De Valera won with a majority of less than 11,000. Interestingly, one of the documents captured with Garland was a draft of a leaflet calling on people to vote against De Valera. That was raised at the Ard Fheis by the Brugha Sábht cumann from Limerick, and the North Kerry Comhairle Ceantair whose motion accused the Army Council of 'supporting one of the candidates'.[38]

Others chose to see the plan as evidence of the political progress being made by the republican movement. A meeting of the Universities branch of the Labour Party congratulated the IRA for its insight into the social and economic situation.[39] The June *Irish Democrat* regarded it as evidence that the movement was grappling with real problems: 'If the attempt is successful it will undoubtedly be a development of major importance in modern Irish politics.' Writing in *Hibernia* in July, Francis Grose, perhaps more perceptively in the light of the election campaign, claimed that the release of the 'Garland Plan' was another example of the use of the IRA 'bogeyman' by Fianna Fáil and questioned the manner in which Special Branch was allowed to operate and criticised the 'belligerently uncooperative attitude' taken by the Minister for Justice Brian Lenihan. Republicans themselves may have gained an exaggerated view of their own importance from the fact that both Dublin and Belfast unveiled the 'bogeyman' when it suited them politically.

The Northern government was concerned over the threat posed by the IRA in the run-up to the fiftieth anniversary of the 1916 Rising. On 9 December 1965 O'Neill wrote to the British Secretary for State at the Home Office, Frank Soskice, to report that 'we have been advised by the RUC that preparations are on foot for an early resumption of IRA activities in Northern Ireland'.[40] The Northern Cabinet had discussed the security situation on 23 November but no details are available.[41] The RUC closely monitored the preparations for Easter, and a memo of 1 December, 1965 expressed fear that the IRA or a splinter group might mark the occasion with 'some spectacular and publicity winning coup'. Most of the Home Affairs file consists of complaints from Unionist associations, the Orange Order and even B Specials over republicans being allowed to organise commemorations, and RUC concerns over potential clashes between unionist and republican marchers.

O'Neill told London that Goulding and Garland had visited IRA units in the North and that arms had been brought in from the Republic. He believed that those who had been trained were 'impatient for action' and that in 'many aspects the present situation is on a par with that which prevailed immediately before the last IRA campaign was mounted in 1956'.[42] Seán Garland states that there were no such plans and that the IRA in the North was too weak to carry out any sort of offensive.[43] On the other hand Garda reports confirm that there was an expectation on the part of IRA members that a campaign was imminent. The fact that the Irish government was confident that this would not happen was based on intelligence from within the leadership which indicated that Goulding and his allies were opposed to a campaign. Nor did Dublin believe that any of the splinter groups possessed such a capability.

There had been a number of minor incidents in 1965 including the breaking-up of an Army film show in Belfast in October, and five men in semi-military uniform had been arrested close to the home of the Army GOC in November. The RUC were also aware of 34 training camps held in the Republic in the course of 1965,[44] the same ones known to Garda Special Branch. Soskice passed the report on to Harold Wilson and suggested that the Prime Minister should raise it with Lemass 'on some suitable occasion when the talks on the trade treaty have been concluded'.[45] When Wilson broached the issue Lemass said that he was aware of the intelligence but that 'on the whole he thought that reports of the IRA tended to be exaggerated' but that he was not 'taking them lightly'.[46]

On the basis of the RUC warning the British Joint Intelligence Committee discussed the IRA for the first time since the late 1950s on 9 December 1965. The MI5 Director General Sir Martin Furnival Jones reported that security on Northern Ministers and RUC Special Branch personnel had been increased, an indication that the alert was based on knowledge of the emphasis in the first stage of the putative IRA military plan on individual assassinations. The Irish government was showing little inclination to take action against the IRA although it could do so if it chose. Security service assistance to the Northern Ireland authorities, established during the 1956–62 campaign, was still in operation and 'coverage of IRA activity in Ulster was good'.[47]

Air Marshal Maguire wondered whether it might be useful to present what they knew of the IRA's plans to Dublin in the hope that the Irish would take action but Furnival Jones said that it would be difficult to prepare such a report as 'IRA plans so often outran performance'. They had no intelligence on when operations were likely to begin, and in any event it was probable that the Irish government had access to the same intelligence as London. Furnival Jones's comment is interesting in that it would seem to indicate that the British security service was perhaps closer to Dublin's view that, while the IRA might have had theoretical plans for an armed campaign, the Army Council had not approved any such plan nor was it likely to. The British view, however, appears to have shifted somewhat in the immediate run up to Easter 1966 as RUC warnings intensified. Ironically the fact that nothing came of it, and that London may have believed that Belfast had exaggerated the IRA threat, made the British less inclined to have a direct security service input and thus just as dependent on the RUC in 1969 as they had been three years previously.

Unionist fears were heightened by a petrol bomb attack on an RUC land rover in Andersonstown on 10 February 1966, for which the IRA denied responsibility and there was no evidence that they had been involved. The Home Affairs Minister Robert McConnell intervened to ensure that orders for new arms and equipment, including riot control equipment, for the B Specials were fulfilled in March.[48] On 15 February the *Belfast Telegraph* claimed that the Gardaí were preparing for an IRA campaign to begin at Easter, but in an interview with the *Telegraph* on 19 February Mac Giolla denied that the IRA had plans for a campaign and was badly equipped for such a venture.

A RUC report of 4 February referred to the military plan's emphasis on EOKA-type attacks and Furnival Jones thought that its warnings were based on good intelligence on the IRA's intentions. He hoped that it would resume the periodic reviews of the type provided during the 1956–62 campaign and emphasised that they contained information from a 'very sensitive source',[49] perhaps referring to the informant codenamed HORSECOPER. The JIC noted on 24 February 1966 that the expected campaign had not begun but that the threat still existed. The British Ambassador McLennan suggested that the Irish government might be receptive to a request to curtail IRA activities.[50] That was considered at a meeting of the security service, the Special Branch and the Commonwealth Office which decided to defer an approach pending the outcome of a meeting between the Gardaí and RUC[51] which was later said to have produced 'little of value'.[52] The JIC considered that it was not necessary to appoint an Army Intelligence liaison between Northern Ireland Command and the RUC, and that MI5 would remain as the most effective channel to transmit IRA intelligence to the Committee. It also needed more regular reports from Scotland Yard Special Branch.[53] Furnival Jones said that MI5's main input was to protect defence installations in Britain and that the police had primary responsibility.[54]

K. A. L. Parker of the Home Office was to approach Special Branch with a view to securing its co-operation in establishing a 'central plot' of IRA activities. The Committee referred to the IRA practice of deciding on attacks only at the last minute, which made providing adequate forewarning difficult. That suggests that the intelligence source(s) within the IRA were at a high level and were not themselves privy to immediate operational decisions. It was decided that an informal approach to Peter Berry of the Department of Justice by his opposite number in Home Affairs, William Stout, would be more effective than contacting the Taoiseach. At a Northern Cabinet meeting on 3 March McConnell briefed his colleagues on security measures,[55] and on 7 March the *Daily Mirror* published a lead story claiming that the Army was being requested to train the RUC in anticipation of a renewed IRA campaign. Belfast then was clearly upping the ante. Wilson was assured by the Home Secretary, Roy Jenkins, that his office was in contact with its counterparts in Dublin 'who were being very co-operative'.[56] On 4 April Jenkins also reported to Wilson on the provision of security service assistance for the RUC's Operations Room during the 'expected danger period' at Easter.[57] According to Jenkins, intelligence 'both from Scotland Yard and the Northern Ireland Government shows that the threat is a real one'. This was based on the growth of the IRA, which had an estimated membership of three thousand: 'Military training has been carried out at camps held secretly in various parts of Ireland, and an adequate supply of arms and ammunition is held.'[58]

Although Dublin had the same intelligence and although the Gardaí emphasised the growth in IRA membership, although not to the same level as the RUC, it did not share the same assessment of the current threat posed and it conveyed this to the British both prior to Easter 1966, and later in December 1966 when Lynch, furnished with the latest Garda intelligence, met Wilson. Although there has been recent criticism of the alleged failure of the JIC to take the RUC warnings in 1965 and 1966 seriously,[59] not only does this assume that what happened in 1969 was the consequence of a serious plan on the part of the IRA, but it neglects the fact that the deteriorating political and security conditions in the North were ignored for the period after 1966. It also overlooks the extent to which RUC intelligence was simply wrong or reports based on it greatly exaggerated.

In response to its own assessment, the RUC had stepped up protection of personnel and installations and there were plans to reinforce the police with the Army if that was necessary. It was also satisfied by the 'growing evidence of the Republican Government's desire to take a firm stand against IRA lawlessness and to co-operate with the Northern Ireland authorities'.[60] That would indicate that the noticeable intensification of Garda pressure on the IRA in early 1966 was in response to representations from London and Belfast rather than any belief in Dublin that a campaign was imminent. As we also saw, government and media speculation about the IRA threat also coincided with the Presidential election and Fianna Fáil fears that De Valera would be defeated, as indeed he almost was. Wilson trusted that the arrangements being made in both jurisdictions would prove to be adequate.

Apart from minor incidents Easter 1966 passed off peacefully so far as the IRA was concerned. Indeed there were complaints from republicans that no protests were organised against a visit to the North by the Queen. Despite the calm, the Northern Ireland authorities were still planning to take action against republicans. London expressed concern that, as the IRA had been quiescent, any aggressive security policy would, in tandem with the planned move of troops to the North, 'lay us open to blame for provocation of any disturbance or violence that might follow these arrests'.[61] Unionist fears had centred on plans for an Easter commemoration at the Casement Park GAA grounds in West Belfast and the danger that this would provoke a counter-demonstration by Paisleyites. In consequence, the authorities had introduced a ban on cross-border rail traffic and monitored road movements. They did not, however, believe that they would require military assistance. Despite what might be seen as inadequacies in intelligence the Ministry for Defence had decided that this should be left to RUC Special Branch and that MI5 would not have a role.[62]

On 21 April the JIC was told that the absence of incidents was due to the 'high order of police work' but that the danger had not passed. No relaxation was possible until IRA intentions were better known. There was also the danger posed by groups outside of IRA control like the one in Waterford, presumably Behal's followers. The Communists had influence on the IRA, exercised through a 'Professor at Trinity College Dublin who had a communist record and was well versed in communist techniques' and was currently Director of Education.[63] The new Home Affairs Minister, William Craig, who had replaced McConnell following the jostling of NI Governor Lord Erskine by Paisleyites at the Presbyterian General Assembly, defended the actions of the Northern government as 'necessary precautions'[64] and said that republicans still posed a threat. The Stormont Republican Labour MP Harry Diamond ridiculed this as a 'mare's nest' and contrasted the hysteria over the IRA to the actual murders that had been carried out by the UVF, who had killed John Scullion in Clonard on 27 May, and Peter Ward on 26 June. Gusty Spence and two others were arrested and charged with Ward's murder and the Unionists had agreed to proscribe the UVF. Craig claimed that the RUC had dealt with this and that the 'Garland Plan' proved that the threat posed by the IRA was real.

In July Furnival Jones told the JIC that the RUC retained its previous view with regard to the level of threat.[65] The IRA, however, disappeared from the JIC's agenda and ceased to be of any apparent interest to the British security services until 1969. That fact would indicate that RUC warnings were no longer treated very seriously but also that the security service was content to rely on Belfast and Dublin to monitor the IRA with London possibly more disposed to take the Irish government's view regarding any possible threat posed.

The intelligence neglect of Northern Ireland mirrored the overall neglect by the Wilson government which failed to act in time to prevent the civil rights crisis developing into civil disorder. It is also the case, however, that, although the security service reacted in somewhat of a panic in 1969 and was inclined to partly blame the situation on RUC incompetence, the fact is that there was little to report in the way of an IRA plot to overthrow the state. RUC Special Branch had not actually missed much although it did appear to compensate for that by claiming, *post facto*, that the IRA had organised the civil rights campaign with a view to creating an insurrection. That claim is not given much credence by the RUC's own clumsy response as evidenced by those it interned in 1971.

There was also a suspicion that the Northern government had exaggerated the threat in 1966 to coincide with the Westminster election campaign in which polling took place on 31 March. Republicans stood in five of the twelve constituencies. Gerry Fitt, standing as a Republican Labour candidate, was given a free run in West Belfast and won the seat with a majority of over two thousand. The republican candidates took 82,089 votes with Tom Mitchell coming closest to being elected in Mid Ulster with 47.75 per cent. The overall vote in the five constituencies contested was slightly down from 1964. Roy Johnston says that republicans in Mid Ulster felt that they would have taken the seat but for the abstentionist policy.

Catherine O'Donnell believes that the 1966 commemorations in the North did not act as a direct catalyst for the post-1969 conflict but rather that they did heighten the pressure on Unionist reformists from the Paisleyites and that this increased London's interest in Northern Ireland.[66] I would argue, however, that while Wilson, reflecting the pressure from within Labour from those MPs who were close to Gerry Fitt, did try to move O'Neill on reform, London was content to allow the Unionist reformists time to get their house in order and real British interest was little evidenced until the civil rights movement began to provoke the same sort of loyalist reaction in 1968. Certainly there is no evidence that the British security service was in any way concerned about the prospect of serious unrest in the North until then.

The Northern Cabinet minutes of later 1966 also cast an interesting light on the earlier fears of an IRA uprising. O'Neill met with Wilson and the Home Secretary, Roy Jenkins, on 5 August when the discussion 'centred largely on Paisleyism' and there was no reference to the IRA.[67] Wilson claimed that he was under pressure from within his own party to enforce reform in Northern Ireland and O'Neill expressed the view that up to now Belfast had been successful in having 'bought time' in resisting change. Even Tory support was not to be taken for granted and his colleagues agreed that 'a threat seemed to be hanging over Northern Ireland'. O'Neill had told Wilson that reform was 'politically impossible' owing to unrest among Unionists and claimed that Wilson had 'tacitly' accepted this. All of this perhaps indicates that real Unionist concern focused on resisting reform and the challenge of right-wing

Unionists rather than any fear of a nationalist insurrection. Security fears are absent from the Belfast records until 1968 when Stormont was forced to respond to growing demands from nationalists for political and social reform. London too seems to have been content to maintain its convention of non-intervention in 'domestic' Northern Irish affairs until the threatened breakdown of order forced it to commit itself.

As with the Anti-Partition Campaign of the 1950s, the official commemorations of 1916 contributed to a heightening of interest in militant republicanism. Some of this led to young people deciding to join Sinn Féin and the IRA. Certainly, up to this point, the movement had made little impact on public consciousness. Maria McGuire, who later joined the Provisionals, and was elected as a Conservative Party Councillor in the 1990s, described her awareness of the IRA while a student at Trinity College Dublin 'only as figures from the past who wore trench coats and carried Thompson sub-machine guns...the single event that impinged on our consciousness was an explosion in March 1966 which wrecked Nelson's Pillar'.[68]

Seán Dunne joined Sinn Féin some time after the 1916 commemorations. The blowing up of Nelson's Pillar had affected him but his opinion of the movement was informed more by reading the *United Irishman*. He found it exciting because of its references to Connolly, Cuba and Vietnam. His initial contact with the movement was through a girl he knew whom he saw dressed in a uniform at the GPO. She advised him to call to the Sinn Féin office at 30 Gardiner Place, which he did, in the belief that he was going to join the IRA.[69] When he called around he was met by Proinsias De Rossa who questioned him on his reasons for wanting to join the movement. Dunne joined the Seán Russell cumann and formed the impression that Sinn Féin had very few members. He remembers listening to a debate on abstentionism and thinking that it had something to do with alcohol! The majority view in the cumann was extremely hostile to entering Leinster House. De Rossa was an advocate of change but Dunne says that he was listened to with respect as he had been interned. Dunne joined in the belief that he was now part of the global ferment of radical politics but discovered that Sinn Féin was extremely dull. Only later did his perception change as he became involved in the Dublin Housing Action Committee of which he became Chairperson.

The Separatist, a pamphlet published by the IRA in 1966, noted Sinn Féin's commitment to abstaining from parliament but that the party was increasingly involved in social issues, and claimed that that 'has led to the tag of Communism being levelled at Republicans'.[70] An article entitled 'Ireland in the Seventies' looked forward to the successful creation of a united independent republic. The prescription for an independent economic policy was identical to the four points that had emerged from the Wolfe Tone Society conference on the Free Trade Agreement. But despite the new realities there was a harking back to the appeal to some putative instinct for self-sacrifice and 'the hardship of the birth-pangs of a new independent nation than the hardship of a slow death and decay'.

An IRA Volunteer who was interviewed in *The Separatist* declared that before the IRA could face the British in a military campaign they would have to 'unite the people in a mass freedom movement'. Such a campaign would, however, assuredly come and the authors were confident that the IRA possessed the capability to ensure that the next time they would be successful: 'They are experts in guerrilla warfare and are confident that military action in the future, coupled with economic resistance now, will win them the support of the Irish people.' That was merely bravado when measured against the poor state of the IRA and the apparent decision not to organise another military campaign. In the October *Hibernia*, Wesley Boyd described *The Separatist* as 'perhaps the most significant statement of republican policy of recent years' and a signal that the younger and more radical elements were rising to positions of power within the movement who 'could easily become an intellectual force in Irish politics – if they emerged from the shadow of the gun into the clear light of democracy'.

The pamphlet was declared to be an illegal document under the Offences Against the State Act and Rory Scanlon, whose address at Inverness Road, Fairview, appeared on *The Separatist*, was charged with offences arising from the Easter commemoration and with possession of the pamphlet. Scanlon said that he was a member of Sinn Féin and that he had written most of the articles in *The Separatist* and had attempted to give an impartial analysis of the IRA. The Labour TD for Dublin South West, John O'Connell, raised the seizure of *The Separatist* in the Dáil;[71] it was justified by the Minister for Justice, Brian Lenihan, on the grounds that it contained 'much matter which was a direct incitement of subversive activity'. When O'Connell pressed the Minister on the violence at the Easter commemoration Lenihan retorted: 'If the Deputy wants to join some of these subversive organisations, let him do so openly.' When Labour challenged the operation of the Offences against the State Acts through a Private Members Bill, claiming that it was a means by which 'the bedrock of freedom may be shattered', Lenihan defended the Acts on the basis that there was a possibility of a return to violence. The Bill was defeated by 57 votes to 23.

The August 1966 issue of *Tuairisc* carried a long article entitled 'Our Ideas' which was written by Coughlan and which Eoghan Harris read at a meeting on 13 August in Kevin Agnew's home in Maghera which planned the meeting in Belfast on 28 November in the Memorial Hall that led to the formation of the Northern Ireland Civil Rights Association. The purpose of the Society was to provide the movement for a republic with 'intellectual equipment' and convince the Irish people that it deserved to be given the 'leadership of the nation'.[72] *Tuairisc* described itself as 'small and select in its circulation' and aimed at 'opinion leaders'. It was critical of the intellectual poverty of the republican movement, stressed the need for it 'to take ideas and theory seriously' and said that it needed to overcome the 'stupid counterposing of the "practical" men and the "intellectuals"'. Coughlan attacked dissidents such as the *An Phoblacht* group who were using 'pseudo-revolutionary rhetoric and phraseology' to attack the republican movement. Coughlan claimed that the Wolfe Tone Society was 'making an indispensable and powerful contribution to the movement for a free and independent republic'.

Northern Ireland was undergoing rapid change which placed the onus on republicans to develop the 'utmost flexibility and political astuteness and to strive to free their minds from outdated forms of thought'. There was a possibility that British-imposed reform might lead to the coming together of Catholic and Protestant workers by destroying the mechanism of discrimination. The key to that was organisation at the broadest grassroots level and through the trade unions around the issues of the franchise, housing etc. Such a strategy would help republicans to break out of their isolation and impotence. Coughlan predicted a victory for the O'Neill faction in the Unionist Party and said that this would destroy the illusions of Protestant workers in orangeism and open up the 'long-term possibility' of reaching out to them. *Tuairisc* also carried a piece by Jack Bennett who described Paisleyism not as an ultra-right-wing fringe but as 'the uninhibited expression of the fundamentals of Unionism'. The logic of this was that Coughlan's prognosis was overly optimistic but Bennett drew the same conclusion and claimed that most Protestants were repulsed by Paisley and that this would lead them to reject Unionism.[73] When Mac Giolla was asked about the proposals in 'Our Ideas' he said that it did not necessarily reflect Sinn Féin policy. They supported political action but if force was used against a political campaign then force might be justified.[74]

The meeting in Maghera is regarded as the formal beginning of the civil rights movement. Mac Eoin and Coughlan made the arrangements for the meeting and contacted republicans in Belfast regarding the participation of Betty Sinclair of the CPNI who was a delegate to the Belfast Trades Council.[75] Goulding was there along with the Belfast OC Liam McMillen. Others included Michael Dolley of Queen's, Jack Bennett and Fred Heatley. There was general agreement with the overall thrust of the proposals but unease with the nature of the language used. Heatley and McMillen demurred from the optimistic analysis of the northern trade unions[76] while Dolley claimed to have found the paper 'embarrassing'.[77] There was a clear disjuncture then between Coughlan's optimistic vision of the prospects for working-class unity, and the more practical view of people actually living in the North.

The meeting did agree to establish a civil rights committee and to invite various organisations to participate, and to shun any overt connection with the republican movement and to abandon the Wolfe Tone Society name in connection with any future activity. That placed the role of the republican movement in more realistic terms and it had little influence on the way in which NICRA functioned. That suited the IRA as it wished to remain in the background but also led to a situation in which while the IRA did not control NICRA its connection to it allowed Unionists to claim that it was a republican front. NICRA itself came to be dominated by non-republican reformists in competition with the radical left, neither of which had much time for the republican movement.

The meeting in Belfast on 28 November decided not to organise a civil rights convention 'under circumstances in which it would be rapidly torn asunder by political rivalry'. Uinseann Mac Eoin attended the meeting and reported to the Wolfe Tone Society AGM that Fred Heatley, Jack Bennett and Michael Dolley of the Belfast Society were on the committee. It is clear, however, that Heatley and Dolley were distancing themselves from the Society and thus reducing the influence of the republican movement on NICRA. Johnston had written to Terry O'Brien of Magee College, Derry, requesting that John Hume speak at a meeting but O'Brien said that while Hume would be willing to address a 'mixed gathering' he would not speak at an event organised by the republican movement.[78]

In September 1966 the Wolfe Tone Society only had 33 members but six – Johnston, Seán Ó Brádaigh, Goulding, Tony Meade, Seán Bermingham and Éamonn Mac Thomáis – were members of the Sinn Féin Ard Comhairle and the first four were also on the IRA Executive or GHQ Staff. Proinsias Mac Aonghusa, who was a member of the Labour Party National Executive, began to attend meetings in November. The involvement alongside these of Cathal Mac Liam, and Michael O'Riordan of the IWP and Jack Bennett of the CPNI meant that in effect the Society was in embryo the 'shadow cabinet' of the reorganised radical movement envisaged by the modernisers. Seán Ó Brádaigh and Éamonn Mac Thomáis left the Society when this became more apparent in 1967.

The group referred to in Coughlan's attack on 'pseudo-revolutionary rhetoric' was the Committee for Revolutionary Action, the *Phoblacht* group which was based in Cork and attacked the IRA leadership not from a traditionalist perspective but from the left. Some Goulding supporters suspected that Seán Mac Stíofáin was involved but he was hostile to the group. Jim Lane was a member. There were some similarities between *An Phoblacht*'s critique and the concerns of traditionalists like Ó Brádaigh and Mac Stíofáin, and some of their supporters later joined the Provisionals, but *An Phoblacht* did not share the traditionalists' attachment to the *de jure* Republic, nor their antipathy to Marxism.

Ruairí Ó Brádaigh knew that some of them were still IRA Volunteers at the time. He says that *An Phoblacht* was circulated to people who were perceived to be 'players' within the movement, and that it did clarify for many republicans the motivations and objectives of the Goulding faction.[79] The journal's circulation was small and, like *Tuairisc*, it was aimed at an internal republican rather than an external readership. In November 1966 Special Branch put the strength of the group at 13.[80] *The People* described the group as one that was possibly contemplating a return to violence and quoted extensively from what it described as its manifesto referring to the need for republicans to 'put their ranks in order so as to be in a position to hit the Free State with something weightier than mere words'.[81] In July 1966 *An Phoblacht* boasted that it was one of the groups described by the republican leadership as 'extremists' and 'splitters'. *An Phoblacht* described the Wolfe Tone Society as 'a front for the clique which presently aspire to take over the IRA lock, stock and barrel', and also claimed to have information on the plan to disarm the IRA. Jim Lane says that Jack McCabe, who was strongly left-wing and later Quartermaster General of the Provisional IRA (he was killed in an accidental explosion at his Dublin home in 1971), supplied information regarding the centralisation of weapons under people loyal to Goulding.[82]

In January 1967 *An Phoblacht* claimed that the Wolfe Tone Society was outside the constitution of the republican movement and was aiming to bring about an alliance between the movement and the Labour Party and that this was the policy of the Communist parties, of which the instigators were 'former' members. They admitted that the republican movement had been hampered by a reactionary social and economic programme but 'we'll be damned if we will subscribe to the notion that all of this can be rectified by importing a few "party hacks" from the BCP'. They described the Society as a 'caucus of party hacks who are split between the Sinn Féin and Labour Parties', but said that not every Society member was aware that the Society was under their control.

An Phoblacht characterised as 'amazing' the recent interest displayed by the Communists in the republican movement: 'A few years back they viewed Republicans as a bunch of degenerate bourgeois nationalists. Of course we are well aware of the reasons for this change of heart but we'll let it pass for the time being.' *An Phoblacht* claimed that the position of the Irish Communist parties reflected the worldwide shift of Moscow-directed parties towards 'the peaceful road to socialism'. They also questioned the autonomy of the Irish parties as both had permanent representatives on the Central Committee of the CPGB, and IWP publications were printed in London. That meant Irish Communists were 'subservient to directives initially formulated by a British political party' which was pushing parliamentarianism on the republican movement. They accused the 'social democrats' in the movement of wanting to get rid of the IRA and said that as revolutionaries they could not condone a situation where the IRA was to be made 'the serving boy to constitutional political aspirations'.

An Phoblacht was not, however, entirely consistent in its critique and occasionally discovered encouraging portents in pronouncements by the IRA leadership. It praised Costello's speech at Bodenstown in 1966 as evidence that 'the militant spirit of the IRA is once again asserting itself'. Costello had spoken of the need for republicans to organise social agitations and to 'maintain a disciplined armed force which will always be available to strike at the opportune moment'. They noted that Costello's speech had been criticised in the *Irish Democrat* for privileging the power of the gun. In November *An Phoblacht* praised a speech made by Goulding in which he had made similarly militant noises and referred to the struggle as one between classes, but contrasted it to an article in the November *United Irishman* in which Tony Meade predicted that in the future the IRA would resort only to 'defensive' violence.

The new Taoiseach, Jack Lynch, met Wilson on 19 December 1966. While the main topics of discussion were the EEC and trade, they did spend some time on the IRA. Lynch had made soundings regarding a further meeting with O'Neill but had recognised the difficulties posed to O'Neill by Ian Paisley and from within his own Cabinet. Lynch stressed the importance of reducing political and religious discrimination in the North. Lynch was provided with a substantial Garda 'Review of Unlawful and Allied Organisations', on the basis of which he was able to reassure the British that there was no threat of a renewed IRA campaign. In an accompanying memo Berry emphasised that, while Craig's fears of renewed violence were not shared in Dublin, violence was possible 'unless signs become evident that the large block of nationalists in the Six Counties will not be denied their fair share of public appointments and participation in public affairs'.[83] If Belfast was intent on using the IRA threat to pressure Dublin into taking action against the organisation then Dublin was clearly equally willing to refer to the same threat as evidence of the need for the British to encourage Belfast to introduce reforms.

The Gardaí estimated an IRA membership of 1,039, an increase from 657 at the end of 1962.[84] The IRA was strongest where it had managed to retain a core of Volunteers who had been active during the 1956–62 campaign. While there was some overlap between membership of Sinn Féin and the IRA, the overall strength of the army was just over one-quarter that of the political wing. Dublin was the only Garda division that reported more members of the IRA than Sinn Féin. Sinn Féin in Kerry had 610 members but only 31 IRA members as many had resigned following the 1965 Army Convention. Interestingly, while some have cast doubts on the accuracy of the Garda report, the figure given for IRA volunteers in Kerry, 31, is close to 'around 22' estimated by Tony Meade. Goulding was described as a 'forceful and dedicated member' who had 'great influence with other members of the organisation'. The basic IRA unit consisted of five to seven men under a section leader. All the units in each of the 18 Command Areas came under the Command OC who had a staff which replicated the GHQ structure and which was in contact with GHQ. GHQ appointed the OC and the Intelligence Officer and the OC picked his own staff including the new position of Political Education Officer. Tony Meade and Denis Foley had drawn up a plan to replace the old company and battalion structure with cells but it was not implemented.[85]

Tomás Mac Giolla chaired the IRA Convention on 15 and 16 October 1966. There were approximately 55 delegates in attendance. The Executive elected at the convention comprised Ruairí Ó Brádaigh, Tony Meade, Cathal Goulding, Seamus Costello, Seán Garland, Seán Mac Stíofáin, Frank Driver, Larry Grogan, Roy Johnston, Tomás Mac Giolla, Denis Foley and Tom Mitchell. The Army Council which was then selected by the executive was Mac Giolla, Mac Stíofáin, Goulding, Costello and Brian Quinn from Tyrone. Johnston was asked to join the Army Council but refused. Goulding remained Chief of Staff and Costello Adjutant General. Larry Bateson was made assistant Adjutant General and the Quartermaster was Malachy McGurran. Departmental heads were Foley, Director of Training; Mitchell, Director of Finance; Liam Nolan, Director of Intelligence; Seán Ó Brádaigh, Director of Publicity; Roy Johnston, Director of Political Education, and Larry Bateson, the Six County co-ordinator.

The convention mandated GHQ to concentrate more in training the Army for a military campaign and said that only men who supported a new campaign should be elected to the Executive. It is also interesting to note, however, that a majority of both the Executive and the Army Council were supporters of Goulding although it has been argued that the balance on the Council was much more evenly balanced and that the position of Mac Giolla in regard to abstentionism was not really clear until the split in 1969. The success of the traditionalists in passing the motion on military policy was indicative of their continued strength following the modernisers' failure to pass changes to electoral policy in 1965. It also indicated, however, that some modernisers like Costello were supportive of the military plan.

Although the report makes it clear that Johnston was a member of the IRA Executive and a GHQ officer, 'since early in 1965', he is described by Gardaí as a member of the Irish Workers Party: 'The appointment of Johnston was a complete departure from former IRA policy to have any association with Communist or left-wing groups.' In the appendix containing personal details of leading members, Johnston is described as 'an active member of the Irish Workers Party'. Unlike those opposed to him within the IRA there was no reason why the Gardaí in a confidential report should have had any motive for describing Johnston as a Communist if he was not in fact known by them to be a member of the party. Presumably, therefore, they had information to that effect although no files on IWP membership are available. A former IRA member who like Johnston later joined the reformed Communist Party of Ireland is convinced that Johnston was always a member of the party and in fact may have been working directly for Soviet Intelligence. He also claims to have been asked to join the IWP in 1968 while still an IRA member.[86] The claim that Johnston was a Soviet agent is extremely far-fetched and unlikely. Undoubtedly there were Soviet intelligence connections to the CPGB and possibly through it to the IRA but there are more obvious candidates as agents among the characters in this narrative than Johnston.

It is important to note from an intelligence perspective that the information on the IRA available to the Gardaí dates from after Garland's capture and must have come to them almost immediately given that the report in which it was contained was written just a month after the Convention. This would indicate that Special Branch had a source with access to the documents and was not dependent on windfalls like the capture of the documents found when Garland was arrested. According to a person who attended all of the IRA Conventions between 1962 and 1969, it is unlikely that there was more than one copy of the minutes; this would have been made available to very few people.

The Convention proposed that the Army Council should examine areas where disagreement had arisen between the Army and Sinn Féin but that the Army Council statement to the Sinn Féin Ard Fheis should contain 'a strong directive to the body on the necessity for bringing its policy into line with Army policy'. For traditionalists that was a double-edged sword. Ó Brádaigh and Mac Stíofáin held a similar view of the party's subservient position vis-à-vis the army but were opposed to using the IRA's authority to force Sinn Féin to abandon abstentionism. The Convention had however effectively postponed any decision on abstentionism to some future date and thus deferred a split.

A resolution proposed that if there were more sectarian killings in the North then the movement would organise protests to call upon the Dublin government to take action, rather than the IRA retaliating as proposed in 1965. A similar decision was taken to use public pressure where republican prisoners were being denied political status. The germ of what was to become one of the main features of IRA activity in the Republic was contained in a proposal 'that action be taken against foreigners taking possession of Irish property'. There was also a decision to establish 'a shadow cabinet drawn from the Movement and friendly elements...under the control of the Army Council'. Among the 'friendly elements' were the Communists, which increased suspicions that an eventual merger was the aim. The only reference to electoral policy was a proposal that the Army Council should examine the possibility of contesting future elections in Northern Ireland and taking seats won, and a decision to refer any decision to contest elections in either state to the Army

Council and Sinn Féin Ard Comhairle. Mitchell and Meade argued in favour of dropping abstentionism but that was not accepted.

While the emphasis in the North would be on trying to involve Protestant workers in actions that would undermine Unionism, any advances along that line would be accompanied by preparations for armed struggle. It was agreed to maintain the IRA so that 'when the time comes the Movement will be prepared to back up its political and economic advances with such force and popular support as will ensure rapid and complete victory'.[87] Likewise the educational course would explain the 'logical sequence of events towards successful revolution, viz. (i) Economic Resistance followed by (ii) Political Action which in turn is followed by (iii) Military Action'. If the economic resistance campaign was successful in building popular support, 'militant and punitive action' might then be taken 'at the discretion of the Army Council', and the Army Council might also order operations against 'opportunity targets'. All of which would eventually lead to military confrontation with the British in the North. Mac Stíofáin proposed the resolution and there was a 'long discussion' on the 'feasibility of an early resumption of Border activities' following which it was agreed 'to leave the matter entirely in the hands of the incoming Army Council'. However the author of the *Republican Education Manual*, Roy Johnston, claims that military action was no longer any part of the strategy of the movement, and Special Branch did not believe that there would be a resumption.

When the new Army Council met on 3 November all of the really contentious issues were again avoided. It was decided 'that as soon as feasible at least 80 seats be contested in the 26 Counties with a view to forming a Government'. Both policy commitments then, to a possible armed campaign and to winning political power, bore little relationship to reality. GHQ was mandated to obtain modern weaponry, and it was agreed that each branch of the movement should be given a role in any military plan and that selected members be given military training. Measures proposed to deal with internal discipline, while ostensibly directed at dissident groups, led to suspicions on the part of some members that Goulding would use any enhanced powers to isolate and remove those opposed to his plans. A proposal that all decisions of the leadership should be made binding on all members of the movement was also passed, as was a proposal that speakers who made statements contrary to Army policy should be removed from the panel of speakers for republican events. Costello proposed that 'unless Sinn Féin carries out Army policy, a new political organisation be set up'. That was replaced by a more vague formulation to the effect that 'the Army Council wishes it to be known that steps have been taken to ensure that Sinn Féin brings its policy in line with that of the Army'.

Special Branch had a detailed report on IRA training camps, referring to 35 separate training camps or other exercises. The camps, locations and weapons used were on the same pattern as those in 1965. There were some innovations such as the fact that seven women from the Six Counties attended one camp on the border in January 1966. The informant claimed that they already appeared to be trained in the use of firearms. At another session in Cavan, Volunteers were instructed in the use of a time bomb. While it was not possible to provide a reliable estimate of IRA weaponry 'it is known that the organisation still have a fairly considerable amount of arms, ammunition and explosives at its disposal'. Efforts to secure new weapons were not meeting with much success. It was also noted that GHQ made regular enquiries with the local OCs regarding the weapons they had and that the QMG stressed the importance of maintaining and securing supplies. The weaponry was not very modern although the IRA had at least one 57 mm recoilless rifle that was test fired at a camp in 1965. Up to the end of October 1966 the Gardaí had captured four machine guns, 14 revolvers, two pistols, over 3,500 rounds of ammunition and 360 detonators.

The IRA's Intelligence Department had been reorganised in 1963 and it had achieved a certain level of success in cultivating contacts within the Gardaí itself, in the Army, Prison Service, Civil Service and among professionals who had contacts in the state services. The Intelligence Department had issued orders at regular intervals requesting local units to supply detailed reports on the Gardaí with particular emphasis on Special Branch. It would appear, however, that they did not have much success and following the Convention the Intelligence Department was reorganised under Seán Mac Stíofáin who replaced Liam Nolan. Mac Stíofáin claimed that 90 per cent of the files that were passed on to him were of no value whatsoever.[88]

The IRA's financial position was poor and dependent on a weekly levy of two shillings from each Volunteer and a Command levy of £1 per month as well as collections from supporters. The Gardaí were convinced that the restrictions being placed on republican collections, most notably on sales of the Easter lily, had added greatly to the movement's financial woes and in 1965 the Army Council had given its approval for armed robberies in Northern Ireland in order to address the situation. Part of the IRA's financial difficulties arose from the fact that there had been a split in Clan na Gael in the United States. Although leading figures like George Harrison supported the ceasefire, others had been unhappy with the move and were reluctant to fund other aspects of the movement's strategy. The IRA sent two GHQ officers, Vincent Conlon and Manus Canning, to the US to take over the Clan but despite this the amount of money crossing the Atlantic was believed to be 'very small'. There had been a debate over whether to use funds raised by An Cumann

Cabhrach, for the support of IRA prisoners, directly for current army needs but it was decided that they should be retained for the intended purpose in case of a resumption of an armed campaign. The chairman of the group was Donal O'Connor who owned the Castle Hotel in Gardiners Row. The *United Irishman* was printed by Record Press in Bray and had a monthly print run of thirty thousand. The paper had a credit balance of £857 at the end of 1965. *An t-Óglach* was issued occasionally by GHQ for internal distribution to Volunteers.

The Gardaí believed that, although the republican movement was serious about preparing itself for a three-stage campaign culminating in an armed campaign in Northern Ireland, it did not pose an immediate threat and it had little support: 'In regard to Sinn Féin, it is not anticipated that this organisation will gain any marked increase in support in any forthcoming national or local elections.' Far from the state being concerned over the threat posed by a growing 'left-republican' movement as believed by people like Johnston, it remained vigilant but confident that the movement was in a position of relative weakness. It is also clear that Special Branch was extremely well informed on the internal workings of the IRA and thus in an excellent position to anticipate and perhaps even to influence future policies and actions. The manner in which the state was able to infiltrate the IRA over this period, and indeed its successful penetration of the IRB in an earlier period, and of the Provisional IRA during the most recent conflict, raises other questions regarding the nature of secret revolutionary organisations. That is outside the scope of this book but worthy of further investigation.

The 1966 Sinn Féin Ard Fheis took place on 26 and 27 November in Moran's Hotel, Talbot Street. Abstentionism was the main issue but motions 8, 9 and 10 from Waterford, Armagh and Tyrone calling for it to be dropped were either withdrawn or defeated.[89] Motion 11 proposing to expel any person who advocated entering parliament was not taken. Mac Giolla moved an amendment to motion 10 putting the position agreed at the IRA Army Convention whereby the party would take its seats if it won a majority. That was passed as was an amended motion from Coalisland in Tyrone calling for an examination of the feasibility of taking local authority seats in the North. Kerry South called on the Ard Comhairle to establish itself as a 'shadow cabinet' while a similar motion from the Seán McCaughey cumann in Belfast referred to both Sinn Féin and 'other branches of the Movement' as constituting such a body.

Kerry North, representing the traditionalists, had another swipe at the leadership in their proposal that no member of the Army Council should be a member of the Ard Comhairle but that was defeated. That indicated a desire on the part of some traditionalists to take control over the party away from the IRA leadership which they distrusted. They also called for an explanation of policy 'as there is confusion and dissatisfaction in the movement since the Extraordinary Ard Fheis'. The role of the *United Irishman* came in for particular criticism from traditionalists. Kerry North condemned it for 'advocating entry into Leinster House' and called for the paper to be brought under 'proper control'. A Roscommon cumann wanted it to 'reflect the Republican spirit more closely' while the Seán Mistéil cumann from Dublin demanded that the *United Irishman* should not promote 'Free Statism'. None of those motions was taken.

The modernisers managed to reverse the Special Ard Fheis rejection of republicans involved in 'agitationary activities' defending themselves in court. An Ard Comhairle motion proposing to establish a Coiste Seasta that would meet on a weekly basis was also carried and was designed to tighten the grip of the IRA Army Council on Sinn Féin and was composed of Goulding, Mac Stíofáin, Seán Ó Brádaigh, Costello, Johnston, De Burca and Mac Giolla. There were a number of other motions proposing that the party should become more involved in working-class politics including the taking over of businesses as worker-run co-operatives. A cumann from Costello's hometown of Bray called for the 'creation of agitation on every possible issue in order to create a feeling of violent opposition to the Establishment'. The Ruiseal cumann, of which Seán Dunne was a member, instructed the Ard Comhairle to examine the structure and ideology of 'Socialist International Organisations'. It was hardly a wonder that the more traditional elements were becoming alienated and beginning to drift away. Northern Ireland was surprisingly little discussed and was underrepresented at the Ard Fheis. Only ten of the 112 motions were in the name of cumainn based in the Six Counties and only five dealt explicitly with northern issues. Interestingly, there was a proposal from the Kevin Barry cumann in Dunamore, County Tyrone, for the Ulster Executive to be given the authority to establish a 'People's Rights Movement'.

Mac Giolla was re-elected President and made it clear that the party would not be abandoning the policy of abstentionism. He said that it had been thoroughly debated and that it was decided that to abandon it would be to abdicate its position as a revolutionary organisation.[90] It was a clear indication that for the time being the more impatient elements within the leadership, particularly Costello, had been forced to moderate their position in the face of opposition. Ruairí Ó Brádaigh, however, feels that this was a tactical move and that Goulding and his allies realised that Costello was alienating people. They were content to bide their time until they were able to effect the change without provoking a major split and only after the alliance with the Communists was in place.[91]

According to Special Branch, IRA GHQ had ordered all Command OCs to instruct Volunteers who were delegates to the Ard Fheis to support the nomination of Mac Giolla as President; Mairín De Burca and Costello as Secretaries; O Loinsigh and Ruane as Treasurers; Grogan and Clarke as Vice-Presidents; and Mac Stíofáin, Goulding, Quinn, Seán Ó Brádaigh, Mitchell, Williams, Mac Thomáis and McBurney as the other members of the Ard Comhairle.[92] The actual elections returned a somewhat different outcome. Mac Thomáis was elected as Secretary along with De Burca; Niall Fagan and Ruane were Treasurers; and Grogan and Clarke were elected as Vice-Presidents. Costello's failure to be elected reflected his unpopularity within the party although he was co-opted to the Ard Comhairle along with the other IRA nominees with the exception of Williams and McBurney. Roy Johnston and Frank McGlade, the Chairman of Belfast Sinn Féin, were also elected to replace Ruairí O Drisceoil and the disgraced Behal.

Seán Ó Brádaigh's report as Director of Publicity was critical of the *United Irishman*, for not having carried a number of press statements. Five of the nine statements that were not published had been issued by the Ard Comhairle. Significantly perhaps, they dealt with more militant topics such as the British royal visit, enlistment in the British army and arrests. He also referred to the paper's accusation of lethargy on the part of Sinn Féin. He explained the continued failure to produce a Social and Economic Programme on the grounds that the process had become bogged down in statistics and that they would require expert advice.[93] It was, however, finished after three years' work and was over twenty thousand words long. Seán Ó Brádaigh claims that the real reason for not publishing the document was the ongoing stalling by the leadership over the new programme because they wanted to have a more explicitly socialist policy.[94] The document did, in revised form, eventually see the light of day as *Éire Nua*, published by Provisional Sinn Féin in 1971. In the introduction it was claimed that 'those who were involved in an attempt to take over the Republican Movement had it suppressed'.[95]

Notes

1 *Dáil Debates*, Vol. 219, col. 1801.
2 *Tuairisc*, no. 5, January/February 1966.
3 *An Phoblacht*, no. 4, March 1966.
4 Garda Report 3C/15/66, p. 53, NAI.
5 *Irish Democrat*, January 1966.
6 Email from Tony Meade, 18 April 2005.
7 Typed minutes in Garda Report 3C/15/66.
8 Interview with Tom Mitchell, 11 January 2002.
9 Handwritten minutes in Garda Report 3C/15/66.
10 Typed minutes in Garda Report 3C/15/66.
11 Email from Roy Johnston, 1 July 2001.

12 Handwritten minutes in Garda Report 3C/15/66.
13 *Republican Educational Bulletin*, Vol. 1, no. 1, January 1966, p. 1.
14 Interview with Seán Garland, 28 February 2005.
15 Interviews with Seán and Ruairí Ó Brádaigh, 21 May 2005 and 22 May 2002.
16 Interview with Cathal Mac Liam, 15 March 2005.
17 *Irish Times*, 20 April 1966.
18 *Irish Workers News*, 20 February 1966.
19 *Sunday Independent*, 2 January 1966, 'Communist's Quiet Revolution in IRA Proves New Threat'.
20 Email from Tony Meade, 18 April 2005.
21 *Evening Herald*, 25 February 1966.
22 IRPB statement, 25 February 1966 in NLI Ms. 22,938.
23 Taoiseach, 99/1/22, NAI. Note from Peter Berry to Runaí Department of Taoiseach, 17 January 1968.
24 Garda Report, p. 56.
25 IRPB statement, 22 April 1966 in NLI Ms. 22,938.
26 *Irish Times*, 4 May, 1966.
27 Interview with Ruairí Ó Brádaigh, 22 May 2002.
28 Daly and O'Callaghan (2007), p. 5.
29 *Dáil Debates*, Vol. 222, col. 21.
30 Daly and O'Callaghan (2007), p. 1.
31 MacStíofáin (1974), p. 96.
32 Interview with Seán Garland, 28 February 2005.
33 Sinn Féin Ard Fheis 1966, *Clár*, Section I, Motion 1, Sarsfield Cumann, Palmerstown.
34 Daly and O'Callaghan (2007).
35 *Irish Democrat*, May 1966.
36 *Irish Workers News*, 1 May 1966.
37 *Violence and Civil Disturbances in Northern Ireland in 1969: Report of the Tribunal of Inquiry*, Cmd. 566, Vol. II (Belfast 1972), Appendix B, p. 52.
38 Sinn Féin Ard Fheis 1966, *Clár*, Section G, Motion 20, Comhairle Ceantair, Ciarraí Thuaidh.
39 *Irish Times*, 23 May 1966.
40 PREM 13/980, O'Neill to Soskice, 9 December 1965, PRO.
41 CAB/4/1319, PRONI.
42 PREM 13/980, O'Neill to Soskice, 9 December 1965, PRO.
43 Interview with Seán Garland, 28 February 2005.
44 PREM 13/980, O'Neill to Solskice, 9 December 1965, PRO.
45 PREM 13/980, Soskice to Wilson, 10 December 1965.
46 *Ibid.*, memo from Wilson to R. F. D. Shuffrey of the Home Office, 13 December 1965.
47 CAB 159/44 JIC 9/12/1965, PRO.
48 HA/32/2/20, PRONI.
49 CAB 159/45, JIC (66) 10 February 1966, PRO.
50 CAB 159/45, JIC 24 February 1966, PRO.

51 *Ibid.*, JIC 3 March 1966.
52 *Ibid.*, JIC 17 March 1966.
53 *Ibid.*, JIC 3 March 1966.
54 *Ibid.*, JIC 17 March 1966.
55 CAB/4/1326, PRONI.
56 PREM 13/980, memo of 4 March 1966, PRO.
57 CAB 159/45, JIC 6 April 1966, PRO.
58 PREM 13/980, memo from Jenkins to Wilson, 4 May 1966.
59 Percy Craddock, *Know Your Enemy: How the Joint Intelligence Committee Saw the World* (London 2002), p. 301.
60 PREM 13/980, Jenkins to Wilson, 4 May 1966, PRO.
61 PREM 13/980, note of meeting between Frederick Molloy, Army Minister, and Lord Stanham, Parliamentary Under-Secretary of State at the Home Office, 13 April 1966, PRO.
62 DEFE 4/197 MOD, Chief of Staff memo of meeting of 17 March 1966, PRO.
63 CAB 159/45, JIC, 21 April 1966.
64 *Hansard*, Commons Debates, Vol. 64, col. 2280.
65 CAB 159/45, JIC, 7 July 1966, PRO.
66 Catherine O'Donnell, 'Pragmatism Versus Unity: The Stormont Government and the 1966 Easter Commemorations', in Daly and O'Callaghan (2007).
67 CAB/4/1338, Cabinet discussion of O'Neill's report on meeting with Wilson and Jenkins, PRONI.
68 Maria McGuire, *To Take Arms: A Year in the Provisional IRA* (London 1973), p. 14.
69 Interview with Seán Dunne, 20 November 2001.
70 *The Separatist* (Dublin nd. [1966]), p. 3.
71 *Dáil Debates*, Vol. 222, col. 1429.
72 *Tuairisc*, Vol. 7, 31 August 1966.
73 *Ibid.*, p. 12.
74 *Irish Independent*, 23 August 1966.
75 Wolfe Tone Society Minutes, 5 July 1966.
76 Purdie (1990), p. 132.
77 Bishop and Mallie (1987), p. 50.
78 Wolfe Tone Society Minutes, 7 February 1967.
79 Interview with Ruairí Ó Brádaigh, 11 May 2002.
80 Garda Report 3C/15/66, p. 56, NAI.
81 *The People*, 6 March 1966.
82 Interview with Jim Lane, 14 May 2005.
83 Department of Justice, memo of 9 December 1966, attached to Garda Report, Section 6, NAI.
84 Garda Report 3C/15/66, p. 1. Even though the Garda figures do not include Northern Ireland, it is unlikely that there were the two thousand members there to justify the RUC estimate of three thousand members as relayed to the British JIC. Indeed other evidence would suggest that the IRA in the North was extremely weak at the time with probably as few as two hundred members.
85 Email from Tony Meade, 18 April 2005.

86 Private information.
87 Garda Report, p. 6.
88 Mac Stíofáin (1974), p. 98.
89 Sinn Féin Ard Fheis 1966, *Clár*, Section A, Motions 7, 8, 9, pp. 1–2.
90 *United Irishman*, December 1966.
91 Interview with Ruairí Ó Brádaigh, 22 May 2002.
92 Garda Report 3C/15/66, p. 55.
93 Tuarascáil Bhliantúil an Stiúrthóra Poiblíochta don Ardfheis, 1966, p. 1.
94 Interview with Seán Ó Brádaigh, 21 May 2005.
95 *Éire Nua*(Dublin 1971), Introduction, p. 3.

6

Towards the National Liberation Front

In 1970 Cathal Goulding claimed that 'by 1967 the movement had become dormant'.[1] Sales of the *United Irishman* had fallen to a few thousand by mid-1967, while publicly claiming a circulation of thirty thousand.[2] When Mick Ryan was asked to travel around the country to collect debts and to report on the movement he found it to be in an 'awful state'.[3] An IRA document on the *United Irishman* from February 1967 recognised the need to boost circulation by setting proper sales targets under the responsibility of county organisers and becoming a 'campaigning paper' on social issues.[4] The paper's editor Tony Meade was in favour of disbanding Sinn Féin and turning the IRA into a new party. He resigned in August 1967 to be replaced by Seamus Ó Tuathail. Those opposed to the new direction had no difficulty in identifying the reasons for the malaise, and traditionalists were resigning in large numbers or being forced out. Goulding, meanwhile, was publicly referring to the IRA's 'new tactics' based on an alliance with the labour movement and campaigning for civil rights and democracy in Northern Ireland.[5]

According to *An Phoblacht*, the leadership was wholly committed to pursuing electoralism and abandoning the movement's revolutionary past[6] and claimed, accurately enough, that a 'retinue of informants' meant that the state was more aware of what was going on internally than most republicans. They did admit that the republican movement had in the past been hampered by a backward socio-economic outlook: 'But we'll be damned if we will subscribe to the notion that all of this can be rectified by importing a few "party hacks" from the British Communist Party.' *An Phoblacht* also claimed that Volunteers were being persuaded to hand over weapons on the basis of 'grandiose, but mythical, plans for action'. They took the credit for making republicans aware of this and aware that Volunteers were now refusing to hand over weapons to the leadership.

The most serious allegations made by the group concerned the infiltration of the IRA by what it described as a 'foreign directed clique'. This group had wormed its way into the leadership with the aim of 'directing the efforts of the Republican Movement along lines advantageous to the interests of a foreign power'. The 'subversives' were members of the British and Irish Communist parties and were 'directed from Moscow'. Their entry into the movement had been facilitated by an 'IRA Hq officer' who they initially had believed had been 'exploited' but who they were now convinced was a willing participant who had been 'recruited into that network which covers Britain and Ireland and which is managed by the British Communist Party'.

Although he was not named they were referring to Goulding. While *An Phoblacht* had previously suggested jettisoning the existing republican organisations, in particular Sinn Féin, it now urged those in the IRA who had contacted them not to leave the movement as that would play into the hands of the leadership. While the group offered itself as a co-ordinating centre for oppositionists *An Phoblacht* was not yet advocating the formation of a new organisation, and believed that the IRA could still form the cornerstone of a reinvigorated revolutionary movement.

The Wolfe Tone Society met with Sinn Féin representatives for talks which focused on Meade's desire to expand the Society into an organisation that would supplant Sinn Féin. Nothing came of this as suspicions grew among traditionalists regarding moves towards an alliance with groups outside of the movement. Meade's proposal would have meant that Sinn Féin and IRA members would have been part of the same organisation as members of the IWP and CPNI and indeed some members of the Labour Party. When Meade resigned as editor of the *United Irishman*, Coughlan was asked to replace him but declined.

Despite Meade's frustration the modernisers proceeded with their plans for a merger with other groups. A special conference of the Wolfe Tone Soicety on the weekend of 24 and 25 June in Dublin was given a paper by Johnston on radical movements in Ireland. His analysis of the Communist movement in earlier years referred to its 'relative isolation', a 'negative tradition of Stalinism' and 'failure to come to grips with the existence of the national question', but it did have 'members with considerable influence in the trade union movement', and its members were prospective allies. Anthony Coughlan delivered a paper on the development and uniting of republican, labour and cultural organisations which stressed the need for the Society to concentrate on 'quality rather than quantity' in its recruitment.[7] The Belfast Society was to focus its energies on NICRA for which it was said to be 'largely responsible'. Mac Eoin's call for the Society to expand conflicted with Johnston and Coughlan, who saw it as a small ginger group bringing other organisations together. In contrast to Mac Eoin and Meade they favoured recruiting members of the leaderships of those organisations rather than opening up the Wolfe Tone Society as a new party.

Apart from its ongoing opposition to the EEC, the WTS was also involved in the Irish Voice on Vietnam, among whose sponsors were the IRA War of

Independence hero Dan Breen, a Fianna Fáil TD until 1965, and Peadar O'Donnell. The South/O'Hanlon cumann objected to the support given to the Vietnamese Communists. Jerry Boyle of San Francisco claimed that republican involvement in the Vietnam issue was damaging the movement in the United States and that republicans had to tend 'towards the Green, not the Red'. In October the *United Irishman* published seven letters on Vietnam, four of which supported the paper's stance, and three opposed. One of those objecting to the support for the Vietnamese echoed Goulding's call for republicans to become more involved in day-to-day issues and drop abstentionism, an illustration that the different tendencies within the republican movement sometimes cut across one another.

Goulding was sent a paper in April 1967 entitled 'An Interim Analysis of the Irish Republican Movement'. It is not signed but the author describes himself as someone 'unhampered by the restrictions of Republican principles'.[8] There is a reference to the author having formed his view by having met and interviewed people over the course of previous months. It is my belief that the author may have been Desmond Greaves, whose journals record him as having spent a considerable amount of time in Ireland between 1963 and 1967. Ostensibly his visits were to research his books on Liam Mellows and Seán O'Casey but he had regular contact with Johnston and Coughlan and with Goulding. Indeed it is clear that Goulding increasingly looked to Greaves for political advice. In his journal Greaves records that Goulding would have attended a March 1967 IWP seminar, which Johnston was at, had it not been on the same weekend as an Ard Comhairle meeting. There is also an entry from July that records a late night meeting in Mac Liam's, over drinks, with Goulding, Costello, Coughlan, Ryan and Garland after which Greaves wrote that its 'only value was to enable me to see what theoretical points need explanation'.[9] In his comment on this Johnston 'wonders of what earlier encounter was it the aftermath'.[10] Perhaps it related to a discussion of the paper.

The paper refers to the 'agonized reappraisal' of republican policy during which the key dividing line that had emerged was attitudes to parliamentary participation. Despite the lack of interest on the part of most people in republican objectives the movement had 'assets' including its historical heritage, the sympathy of those not necessarily supporters and the obvious failings of the two Irish states. However, that was outweighed by the 'impractical illusions' of the movement, its rigid ideology, an outdated organisational structure and a 'self imposed isolation' from similar revolutionary movements, although they are not named. Finally republicans had an historic suspicion of 'compromisers and fair weather friends' which it might be taken to refer to the reluctance of many to engage with those revolutionary allies.

The paper said that republicans ought to focus their attention on an 'alliance with Labour', northern civil rights, 'non abstentionism', expanding the Wolfe

Tone Society, the university republican clubs, housing and, intriguingly, 'international connections'. There was also a reference to the 'unofficial dialogue' between republicans and unnamed others which had bolstered its education policy and exposed the membership to 'new ideas'. With whom the republicans were in dialogue is not suggested although the evidence would point to the Connolly Association and the Communists, particularly if the author was Greaves or someone from a similar background. The author expressed the hope that there would be a further shift in the desired direction without too many resignations or a 'schism'. Although there had been no 'formal decision' on key issues, the author's impression was that 'the Republican Movement has already made its vital decision' and was 'committed to policies on a far more conventional level than its public declarations or organisational decisions indicate'. The key issue was the timing of a public announcement and couching it in a manner 'tolerable to the reluctant minority'. All of this was leading inevitably to 'participation in Parliamentary politics – a half way house to revolution with the gun out of sight but not beyond reach'. That project was strengthened by the fact that the traditionalist 'physical force' element had shown itself to be 'unproductive'. Finally the movement needed to focus on clear priorities and reconsider its expending of resources on 'highly inefficient organisations', which could be read in the context as a reference to the IRA.

The paper is fascinating, not just for the fact that it outlines clearly the policies being pursued by Goulding and his allies, and that 1967 witnessed a more vigorous pursuit of the same, but also because the author was evidently not a formal member of the movement. Not only that, but he was writing with the confidence that those reading his recommendations shared his view and were conscious of the need to basically string along the traditionalist element until such a time as the strategy came to fruition with the embracing of parliamentary politics, a decisive turn away from militarism and an alliance with unnamed allies on the 'revolutionary' left. In documentary terms the paper is the best available evidence of IRA policy being framed in co-operation with people outside of the movement.

At around the same time, Goulding was sent a lengthy report outlining the prospects for an IRA campaign in Britain. That was something that had not been referred to in the 'Garland Plan' nor is there any evidence that serious consideration was ever given to it by the Army Council, even in theoretical terms. The author of the manuscript was, however, clearly *au fait* with the Mac Stíofáin proposals and discussed at length how they might be applied in Britain.[11] It is interesting that an IRA operative in Britain was motivated to write such a document even though Goulding at least had no intention whatsoever of implementing the proposal. On the other hand IRA actions began relatively quickly in Britain following the outbreak of the crisis in 1969 which suggests some prior preparation.

As recommended in the 'Interim Analysis', one of the main focuses of republican activity in Dublin was the Republican Club in Trinity College which attracted a number of young people who later became influential members of the movement. A UCD Republican Club was formed in April 1967 and there was also a body at Queen's in Belfast. The TCD Club Vice-Chairman Des White, in an interview with *Campus* magazine in February, described Sinn Féin as an outmoded movement: 'The IRA have given up their policy of using physical force. In fact I find them far more progressive and intellectual than Sinn Féin.' In November 1967 the Trinity Republican Club became the first political society to be formally recognised by the University and was to the forefront of student radicalism and said by *Campus* magazine to be under surveillance by Special Branch. A *TCD* piece in May 1967 attacked Special Branch harassment of republicans and described them as 'the scum of society'. Naturally the Gardaí held a different view. In June 1968 *Irís an Gharda* warned of a new and sinister element that was taking control of certain organisations. It pointed to the growing 'red influence' – 'much of it carefully cultivated among our emigrants in Britain' which was gaining a foothold in existing organisations including community and co-operative groups.

Sinn Féin stood 110 candidates in the 1967 local elections, compared to 1,107 for Fianna Fáil, 893 for Fine Gael and 525 for Labour, and appealed for support to the WTS. Johnston advised Noel Kavanagh that this would need to be done discreetly to avoid being seen to be 'bulldozing Wolfe Tone Society members into Sinn Féin'. The party's manifesto committed it to abolishing rates and replacing them with an income-based local tax. It also proposed that there should be a ceiling on the price of land and that local authorities would become the sole dealer in land.[12] The *Irish Times* claimed that the party was doing well during the campaign with an 'excellent programme' and that 'the party's future depends on this election'. Seán Bermingham, however, believes that Sinn Féin was too weak to fight elections properly.[13]

The estimated crowd of fourteen to fifteen thousand that attended Bodenstown on 19 June must have encouraged notions that Sinn Féin would do well. In his speech, Goulding echoed the main themes of the 'Interim Analysis', calling for unity among all radical elements and for Sinn Féin to put an end to its isolation and exclusivity. In doing so, it would need to move away from the traditional policy regarding the *de jure* legitimacy of the Republic. His description of the movement as a small 'traditional and sentiment-bound body' whose 'dog-in-the-manger attitude' was preventing 'others' advancing the revolution[14] infuriated traditionalists who would have been even more annoyed had they read the 'Interim Analysis'. The CPNI and IWP attended Bodenstown, and *Unity*'s report on the commemoration referred in glowing terms to the 'veteran and still active' Goulding and the crowd as comprised of 'the most politically conscious people in Ireland'. *Unity* emphasised the part of Goulding's speech in which he attacked 'those whose sterile thought could only invoke dead heroes, and who spurned the hard grinding necessary work of political and economic activity'.[15] It was clear that the Communists believed that they were closer to what Goulding desired than traditionalist republicans were.

Despite the optimism surrounding the elections in Dublin, Sinn Féin won no seats and a total of just 5,328 votes, 3.9 per cent, compared to 52,676 for Fianna Fáil, 37,339 for Fine Gael, 41,761 for Labour and 23,041 for others.[16] In the rest of the state Sinn Féin took seven county council seats, down from 16 in 1960. A number of candidates also managed to take seats on Urban District Councils. One of the few successes for the modernisers was the election of Seamus Costello to Wicklow County Council and Bray UDC. However, in Kerry organisational problems meant that there was no candidate in the north of the county. Most of the membership had resigned during the year following the expulsion of three IRA Volunteers including former candidate Kevin Barry. Interestingly, when Costello proposed to expel the entire North Kerry organisation in September 1967 he was seconded by Seán Ó Brádaigh.[17] The party lost its seat in Killorglin where the vote fell by 50 per cent, but Redmond O'Sullivan did manage to retain his seat in Killarney with a reduced vote.

Tomás Mac Giolla admitted that the party had suffered a setback and that they had expected to do better. However he was pleased that despite limited resources they had mounted an 'intensive and well organised campaign'.[18] Meade's last editorial in the July *United Irishman* declared that Sinn Féin would need to become more active or step aside. The *Irish Democrat* did point out that Sinn Féin had been disadvantaged by not having the party name on the ballot paper, but that in general the results were confirmation that the abstentionist policy was holding the party back.[19] Seán Garland felt that the election results were disappointing but that they were not seen as a serious setback, as electoral success was a long-term objective.[20] Tony Meade was not surprised at the results: 'None of us who were close to the candidates were a bit disappointed. The candidates were a pretty hopeless lot, especially those in Dublin.'[21]

The disappointing election results contributed to a decision to call a meeting of IRA members in August where, according to Goulding, they 'suddenly realised that they had no Movement at all. They only thought they had a Movement.' One of the decisions taken by the meeting was to emphasise the centrality of radical social objectives and to declare as its aim a socialist republic.[22] Roy Johnston admits that the IRA was being deliberately run down and that when traditionalists became aware of this they began actively to organise in opposition to the leadership.[23] Mac Stíofáin was now Director of Intelligence and on touring units became aware of the scale of the demilitarisation that had already taken place. He established an economic intelligence unit on the effects of free trade, which was to be used as the basis for local agitations. He also proposed that, if an English company pulled out when its grant expired, the IRA would burn its home base. Johnston says that Goulding was opposed to Mac Stíofáin's plans to attack economic targets[24] but when they took place the IRA claimed responsibility. Despite Mac Stíofáin's role, such attacks were later claimed by some modernisers as evidence of their involvement in the 'people's struggle' and the sort of activity which the state saw as evidence of the threat posed by the republican left.

Goulding's call for co-operation between republicans and other radicals at Bodenstown was complemented by the joint initiatives with the Communists on Vietnam and the EEC after the Irish government made a new application in May. The Defence of the Nation League was a creature of the Wolfe Tone Society, and the Irish Workers Party was asked to join. The *Irish Democrat* of August 1967 hailed the formation of the League as 'the broadest united front of Irish radical opinion since the days of the war of independence'. Apart from the hyperbole which obscured the fact that the republicans and Communists represented almost no one, such a vision represented exactly what the republican modernisers sought to achieve and which they hoped to give substance to in the National Liberation Front. The Defence of the Nation League also struck an older note in claiming that the alternative to the EEC 'would not be a bed of roses'.

The 1967 Ard Fheis was held in Liberty Hall on the last weekend of November. Seamus Costello was court-martialled by the IRA for attempting to influence the selection of Ard Fheis delegates as part of Costello's plan to force a confrontation with the traditionalist element on abstentionism. His suspension was seen by some as an attempt by the leadership to placate that section of the movement but also reflected the wish expressed in the 'Interim Analysis' to avoid for as long as possible any split. Costello was on the Steering Committee and used the position to influence votes. Attendance was lower than in previous years with around a hundred delegates present, reflecting the loss of cumainn in places like Kerry. Cathal Mac Liam and Dalton Kelly attended as representatives of the Wolfe Tone Society and reported on the 'strong diversion of opinion on the question of attending Leinster House'.[25] Motions on electoral policy included one that sought to limit discussion of the issue to every three years. Another proposed that participation in parliament be decided on a tactical basis by the Ard Comhairle. The Ard Comhairle itself proposed a compromise motion that sought to balance the desire of the majority to take seats with the need to bring along recalcitrant members. Goulding and Johnston argued that the time was not right to drop abstentionism and were hoping that the 'left alliance' would be in place first and that this would lessen the impact of the inevitable loss of traditionalists.

The successful amendment proposed that Sinn Féin should at some time in the future adopt a policy of 'revolutionary parliamentary action...linked with outside agitational work and mass organised pressure', and 'discrediting the claims of the Leinster House parliament to be the legitimate repository of political sovereignty over the Irish nation as a whole'. That would be part of a strategy to transfer 'real legitimacy, sovereignty and power to a 32 county assembly with the mass support of the organised people and the armed revolutionary movement'. The leadership would assess the prospects for this and report back to the Ard Fheis.[26] In the election for the Ard Comhairle, Goulding topped the poll with 95 votes followed by Seán Ó Brádaigh 71; Johnston 70; Costello 67; Mac Thomáis 64; and Mitchell 51. Seven of the body – Goulding, Garland, Mitchell, Johnston, Monica Ryan, Mick Ryan and Costello – were known to be in favour of abandoning abstentionism. The Coiste Seasta consisted of Goulding, Garland, Lynch, De Burca, Mac Giolla, Johnston, Seán Ó Brádaigh and Ruane.

The other major change at the Ard Fheis was the commitment to establish a 'Democratic Socialist Republic based on the 1916 Proclamation' which was passed by 68 votes to 8. The actual motion was another compromise, amending one from Costello's cumann in Bray which called for a 'Socialist Workers Republic' affiliated with 'revolutionary socialistic parties throughout the world.' Delegates from Limerick and Belfast were prominent among those opposed to the motion, with some declaring that socialism was incompatible with Christianity. The Constitution did retain traces of the influence of Catholic social teaching and still pledged the party to 'establish in the Republic a reign of social justice based on Christian principles, by a just distribution and effective control of the Nation's wealth and resources'. The unease at the use of the term 'socialist' had prompted the Galway republican Caoimhín Mac Cathmhaoil to write to *Hibernia* in December 1966 pointing out that republican policy was 'distributionist and not socialist'.

A discussion document on socialism distributed to members admitted that the definition of a socialist republic 'in accordance with the 1916 Proclamation', was 'not the last word in precision'. It then proposed what might be regarded as a similarly imprecise definition of socialism as the 'application to the ownership of the means of production of the democratic principle of the Republican ideal'. Socialism rejected private ownership of the means of production but alternative forms of social ownership could include those owned by local authorities and various types of co-operatives. There was no reference to outright state ownership, and indeed the state, while providing capital, would play a lesser role. Social services, for example, would be mainly provided by trade unions and co-ops with the state reduced to national defence and law enforcement.

The document was written by Johnston, who had introduced it for discussion at a meeting of the WTS stressing its 'tentative and preliminary character'.[27] It also emphasised the 'Garland Plan' strategy of uniting different social and political groups. Most members regarded the socialist aspect as a long-term vision and that the practical need was for a medium-term programme 'more appropriate in terms of contemporary Irish politics'. There was also a preference for co-operative over state or municipal ownership and concerns over the danger of a one-party state. Some respondents preferred a 'no-party' option based on elections to local committees.

In the November issue of *An t-Óglach,* the IRA reiterated its objectives in more traditional form; to force the British out of Ireland and to abolish both existing governments, and to establish a democratic republic. The IRA was necessary as the enemy would never concede power except to 'armed men who are determined, committed and trained in every field of revolution'. The IRA was not committed to any ideology of East or West but to the ideas of people like Mellows, who they claimed had 'understood the need to have a strong social base for the defence of the Republic...Our strategy, if it is to succeed, must be the perfect blending of Politics and Violence'.

An interview with a member of the Cork IRA, published in the November issue of *Spectre,* the journal of the University College of Cork Labour Party branch, illustrated some of the contradictions that existed. While asserting that the IRA's objective was to establish a socialist republic, it said it was unlikely that Sinn Féin would enter Leinster House but that if it did 'the IRA would have no alternative but to break with them'. *An Phoblacht* welcomed the statement and claimed that such sentiments had caused the leadership to pause in its efforts to drop abstentionism as they were now more concerned over the possibility of a split.[28] The Cork OC, Eddie Williams, was a close friend of Jim Lane.

An Phoblacht, sensing that the internal divisions within the movement were close to coming to a head, counselled secret preparations by those opposed to the leadership. It reiterated that it was not attempting to win the allegiance of dissidents to a new organisation: 'Many of our organisation's members continue their membership in the Republican Movement; and many of those who have joined us over the past year or so have remained in the movement on our advice.' Jim Lane claims that *An Phoblacht* had substantial support even at middle leadership level and that many of those stayed in the IRA and took the Provisional side in the split.[29] That the group did have support is proved by a directive issued by the Sinn Féin Ard Comhairle ordering members not to associate with what it described as a 'reactionary group outside the Republican Movement' and pointing out that, while some favoured a more 'militant' policy, the movement was pursuing a different strategy. It warned against infiltration by splinter groups 'and their attendant Special Branch contacts'. *An Phoblacht* took umbrage at this, warned that it would hold leading figures of the 'fake left' responsible for the slander and claimed the right to take 'corrective measures' against them.

An Phoblacht did not endorse the position of the 'traditionalists' who it claimed were equally as reactionary as the 'progressives'. They agreed that 'abstentionism' was a ridiculous policy' and claimed that the traditionalists were advocating not merely abstentionism from parliament but 'abstention from society' because of their unwillingness to confront the real social and economic nature of neo-colonialism. The 'progressives', on the other hand, were proposing to accept the political structures of neo-colonialism. The alternative was for republicans to link social and economic liberation with a rejection of the state, and from there they would be faced with 'the unavoidable fact that violence, either in the sense of its direct use, or by posing the threat of its use, represents the only Method of struggle capable of solving their problems'.

The third part of the internal education manual, published in October 1967, reflected the extent to which Marxism had gained ground, and the ideas in the 'Interim Analysis.' It outlined a three-stage programme including the election of a 'progressive Republican Government' committed to achieving national unity and independence.[30] There was a reference to the 'signal failure of *purely* military methods', and it was the recognition of this which had led to the theoretical work begun in 1962/63, but it had been weakened by its concentration on the goal of a united Ireland rather than civil rights agitation in Northern Ireland, and electoral politics. The delay in producing a new social and economic programme was due to the realisation that it needed to be redrafted to take those factors into account. The need to involve a broad social alliance of those who were not involved in large-scale ownership was stressed, and the need to avoid alienating them through a demand for a 'Workers Republic' which was inimical to owner-managers and small farmers. Co-operativism was an appropriate alternative form of ownership for small property while socialist state ownership was to replace the private ownership of large property. Although an analysis of Marxism concluded that Stalinism was an autocratic suspension of democracy, the dialogue between Catholicism and Marxism internationally made the time ripe for Irish people to study objectively the experience of other countries and movements, and while the CPNI and IWP had been isolated because of their Stalinism they were rooted in the trade union movement, had accepted republicanism as part of their revolutionary heritage and were thus potential allies.

Hostile political forces were all who in the Republic supported EEC membership including Fianna Fáil, Fine Gael, the Employers Federation, the

National Farmers Association and some trade union leaders. In Northern Ireland that trend was represented by the Unionist Party, the Orange Order and the Federation of British Industry. Within the NFA, Employers Federation and the Unionist rank and file there were people in conflict with that position and it was therefore wrong to class Paisley's rank and file supporters as the enemy, as there was potential in uniting dissident elements in opposition to the EEC. The republican movement, IWP and CPNI which had a 'consciously thought out political position', were distinguished from 'opportunist' groups including the Irish Labour and NILP leadership, and the leftist anti-Unionist 'splinter groups' who would lead principled groups into isolation. Traditionalists were accused of advocating armed struggle and abstentionism as principles rather than tactics and depicted as 'gombeen-nationalist' elements who would have been at home in Fianna Fáil in the 1930s. While republicans had re-embraced radical theory the movement was still handicapped by hangovers from the 'barren period' of the 1930s and 1940s, epitomised by the abstentionist policy that had developed into a 'refusal to play any part whatever in the everyday struggles of ordinary people'.[31] The WTS was praised as the 'generator of theoretical ideas and analysis' which helped people to avoid pseudo-revolutionary sloganising.

Northern republicans needed to be able to work legally and to agitate on work-related issues where there was a possibility of uniting Catholic and Protestant. In the Republic the main issue was opposition to the EEC, and the campaign to revise the Anglo-Irish Free Trade Agreement which needed to be a trade-union-based campaign. The object was to bring about a position in which 'the principled radicals of the Movement are accepted in leading positions in the mass organisations of the people'; only then could the achievement of political power become a credible aim. Republicans had to organise trade unionists to make more radical demands such as calling for the nationalisation of firms threatened with closure. Seán Garland agrees that work within the unions was very localised and slow but that it did yield results at a later stage. He also felt that there was reluctance among many republicans to be directly associated with specifically working-class issues.[32]

While there was a reference to the IRA as a logistical source of transport, accommodation and information which would be the 'specialist function of the activist group' there was no reference to any armed role. The basic unit would remain the cumann but there was a recommendation that it should be factory-based. Their minimum required activity would be to sell the *United Irishman* and to hold political discussions and be responsible for deciding tactics on local issues. Electoral policy was recognised as a constraint, as the building of a radical leadership within the mass organisations was 'self-defeating unless a credible political alternative is similarly made public. This, in the present time can only come from the Labour and Republican

Movements.' The problem of course was that it was the Labour Party, as evidenced by the 1967 local elections, which was benefiting politically not Sinn Féin.

Johnston has said that he was consciously attempting to promote the idea of an alliance between politicising republicans and the IWP as he believed that this would bring together the most radical and ideologically coherent elements.[33] Others like Seán Ó Brádaigh were convinced that they were aiming at an actual merger.[34] An objective view would suggest that the 'National Liberation Front' had little relevance to the groups targeted in Johnston's schema who were hostile to anything suggestive of Communism. Patterson has also made the point that the republican left had little comprehension of why workers, whose wages and living standards were improving, found the new economic policies of the state attractive.[35] While the notion that a politically weak republican movement might benefit from an alliance with the Communists appears ill-advised, for the Communists it made sense to align with, and exercise influence on, an organisation with a much larger membership and support base, and greater access to resources.

While Mac Stíofáin claimed that by 1968 the movement was basically stagnant and he considered resignation, he and other traditionalists were involved in IRA actions against foreign-owned property and in support of strikes. On 28/29 May the IRA burned buses belonging to a company that was carrying non-union workers to the EI factory at Shannon where there was a dispute over a refusal to recognise the ITGWU. Apparently the attack had been requested by a leading ITGWU official who was friendly with Goulding.[36] A statement from Adjutant General, Seamus Costello, published in the June *United Irishman*, described the IRA as 'the revolutionary army of the Irish People' and issued a warning against strike breakers. James Dunne, President of the ICTU, who condemned the IRA attacks, was cited by Sinn Féin as evidence of how far the trade union leadership had deviated from Connolly and was now part of capitalist society.

Garland referred to the bus burnings in his speech at Bodenstown in June and promised that it would not be an isolated incident. Garland defends such actions as having been designed to identify the IRA with workers' struggles.[37] The EI action was praised in a motion from the Liam Mellows cumann, Dublin, at the 1968 Ard Fheis. That conflicts with Johnston's claim that the leadership did not approve of such actions. Garland also stressed the need for a change in the relationship between the IRA and Sinn Féin, and signalled the proposal for a formal alliance with the Communists: 'We must be prepared for any structural or organisational changes as we are prepared for changes in tactics and simply regard the movement and its policies as a means to an end.'[38]

There were similar attacks during 1968 including the burning of a foreign-owned lobster boat in Galway which was justified on the basis of protecting national resources. Increased IRA militancy may have reflected the same sort of *frisson* that swept the European left in 1968, and which Simon Prince believes was a key factor in the student left that was part of the civil rights movement. Goulding for a time appears to have countenanced a more militant strategy than hitherto and against the advice of Johnston. The 1968 events were also the inspiration for other armed groups such as the Rote Armee Fraktion, and the revivified ETA as well as the radical left in general. Without doubt that did influence the attitudes of individual IRA members and must have had a similar impact among some IRA leaders persuaded of enhanced opportunities for radical agitation. The Army Council approved armed actions in 1968 which contradicted the move away from them after 1965. The activities of the Official IRA even after their ceasefire in 1972, as explored by Hanley and Millar, would also indicate that Goulding and others maintained a pragmatic if not opportunistic view of the use of force.

There were high expectations of Costello's candidature in the March 1968 by-election in Wicklow. At first Costello refused to sign the pledge required of all Sinn Féin candidates that they would not take the seat if elected but relented under pressure from Mick Ryan and Malachy McGurran who were appointed by the Ard Comhairle to run the campaign. Costello said that he was standing not to win a seat but to demonstrate the level of support that existed for Sinn Féin as a 'revolutionary socialist organisation'.[39] According to the *Irish Democrat* in April Sinn Féin had indicated that it would not have stood a candidate had the Labour Party selected Noel Browne. Although Costello performed moderately well with 2,009 votes, that was a long way short of what was required to win a seat in a general election. It must also be adjudged an expensive failure given that £1,254 15s 6d had been spent on the campaign.[40] The leadership had rejected a request from Sinn Féin in Clare to contest the by-election held there despite the fact that P. J. Burke had won a County Council seat in 1967 with over 1,400 votes.

Roy Johnston is convinced that the movement was making ground and that the state was frightened of the advance of left republicanism. He claims that it was that fear which led to the intervention in the movement at the time of the split. He also believes that Mac Stíofáin may have been an informer whose task it was to frustrate the politicisation of the movement.[41] He further claims to have known the identity of another informer but did not wish to name him as Johnston believed that the person in question might have been working within the IRA in furtherance of the Goulding plan'.[42] Johnston believes:

> that there were two members of the Army Council exchanging information with two different government departments during the 60s. I am inclined to think that the Govt [*sic*] actually wanted the IRA to remain in existence as such, because it gave them the excuse to use repression against any emergent left. They made sure it happened from two angles. The 'arms trade' story sort of confirms

this because there is no doubt that the effect was to nip in the bud effectively what the politicisers were trying to do.[43]

According to Peter Berry's diaries there were two informers on the Army Council. One reported to McMahon and had been active since the 1950s and the other to Chief Superintendent John Fleming.[44]

Johnston, meanwhile, was under intense attack from those within the republican movement who regarded him as the main influence behind the drift towards constitutionalism. Speaking at the Dripsey ambush commemoration on 3 March 1968, Gearóid Mac Cárthaigh, who had resigned from the Cork IRA, attacked Johnston for ruling out the use of force. Mac Cárthaigh claimed that this was a betrayal of republicanism and urged that republicans 'rid the movement of Roy Johnston and his associates – wherever they come from'. Jim Lane of the Cork *An Phoblacht* group clashed with Jim Savage who was a member of the IWP and Secretary of the Cork Wolfe Tone Society. Savage was in correspondence with Michael Flood, a supporter of *An Phoblacht* who was living in England at the time, but who Savage believed was hostile to the Cork dissidents. Flood passed his letters to Lane. Savage described the *An Phoblacht* group as 'shams and chancers' and claimed that it was a 'police job'. He also told Flood that he had passed his details to Greaves and that Savage had suggested to Greaves that they get together on 'the Clann Ard Fheis so as to work out some plan of campaign, otherwise it will be lost again'.[45] This clearly indicates that Goulding supporters, the Communists and the Connolly Association were co-operating in attempting to have Connolly Association members admitted as members of Clann na hÉireann. In another letter Savage related having met Goulding and Johnston at the 1968 IWP Conference in Dublin.[46] Savage was the editor of *Republican News* which appeared in Cork in July 1968. In his first editorial Savage said that their task was to 'abandon the outmoded attitudes of the past and bury them reverently as they were a hindrance rather than a help to the development of the Movement which in fact were only a variety of irrelevant and empty formulas'.[47] The above is an interesting insight into the dynamics of the relationship between the Communists and the Goulding faction. It is also worth noting that dual membership of Clann na hÉireann and the Communist Party of Great Britain was not uncommon after the split.[48]

Despite Johnston's claim that the IRA had turned its back on militarism, efforts were made by the IRA to acquire weapons. Costello was in charge of this and he organised raids as well as procurement missions to eastern Europe. Costello's attempt to source arms from the socialist states, apparently facilitated by Michael O'Riordan of the IWP, did bear fruit although the first consignment was not sent until after the split.[49] Seán Dunne, who admired Johnston, doubts that he could have been unaware of the arms or of other military operations as Johnston was a GHQ officer.[50] The fact that the IRA in 1968 was engaged in serious arms procurement raises interesting questions regarding the attitude of some of the modernisers towards militarism and the difference between people like Costello and Johnston. It also suggests that the apparent move away from militarism after 1963 was a pragmatic rather than an ideological much less a moral imperative, and that Goulding and others were prepared to sanction violent actions when it suited them. Hanley and Millar illustrate this succinctly in their treatment of the Official IRA even at a time when it was adopting a pseudo-moralistic attitude towards the Provisional IRA and Costello's Irish National Liberation Army.

The IRA may also have contemplated the kidnapping and possible killing of the British Ambassador Sir Andrew Gilchrist in 1968. This was uncovered in June but Special Branch was not certain if the 'official' IRA or a splinter group was involved. Following an attempted break-in at the Embassy in August, Scotland Yard was told by its sources that it had been the IRA. Apparently the IRA later decided to tar and feather Gilchrist rather than shoot him, but this threat had receded. So too had the danger emanating from the less predictable Saor Eire Action Group following the arrest of four of its members during a foiled armed robbery.[51] Gilchrist was perhaps understandably concerned when the four were released on bail.[52] He had earlier threatened to resign but changed his mind.[53] Joe Doyle, Padraig O'Dwyer and Charlie O'Neill, all of whom were members of the Saor Eire Action Group, were charged with shooting with intent to kill during the course of the robbery. The case against Doyle and O'Neill collapsed in January 1970. O'Dwyer absconded to England while on bail but was extradited and convicted in June 1970. He was given a character reference by Inspector Corriston of Special Branch and had his sentence of two years backdated. He was released in November 1970 on the recommendation of the Minister for Justice, Des O'Malley.[54]

The Secretary for State in the Foreign and Commonwealth Office, Micheal Stewart, met Lynch and Molloy on 30 October to impress on them the seriousness of the situation. Lynch said that he had been unaware of the threat although Molloy had been informed and claimed that sufficient precautions were in place. Lynch expressed some concern over the threat posed by the IRA and said that his own home had been broken into; he claimed that the British were fortunate not to have to put up with such subversive actions.[55] Scotland Yard, however, was convinced that the Irish authorities would not move against the IRA for fear of provoking public sympathy. In November Molloy reported that security measures remained in place but that he had no idea who was behind the threat.[56]

The IRA's ban on Volunteers carrying out armed robberies in the Republic seemed to be less strenuously enforced after 1968 and there was a growing tendency on the part of dissident groups to resort to this means of collecting funds. The first major bank robbery took place at the Royal Bank in Drumcondra on 27 February 1967 in which around £3,000 was taken. The individuals involved were quite well known and indeed tended to flaunt their notoriety and their relative affluence. Dublin Volunteers were warned to stay away from them and there was a general suspicion regarding the relative impunity with which those involved seemed to be able to act and the manner in which legal proceedings against them often appeared to collapse. Several of those active in the IRA at the time are convinced that leading participants were working for the state and cite the O'Dwyer case as proof. They refer also to Joseph Carey who admitted having joined the IRA in 1967 in order to supply information to Special Branch and to encourage the organisation to carry out robberies.[57] This issue was to become particularly important in the immediate aftermath of the split in the movement and the murder, allegedly by the Saor Eire Action Group, of a Garda during the course of a bank robbery. There has also been speculation regarding the connections between Dublin Saor Eire and Fianna Fáil members who were involved in importing arms in 1969. Charles Haughey's brother Jock was filmed while in London buying arms in the company of the Saor Eire member Martin Casey, later injured while attempting to steal weapons from a Dublin Army barracks.

Saor Eire was founded in November 1968 by the Cork *An Phoblacht* group, almost a year after the final issue of that paper in December 1967. According to Jim Lane, the decision to form Saor Eire came about because they believed that the initial tactic of attempting to influence the republican movement, or sufficient persons within it, to adopt their proposals had exhausted itself, and that the time was right for launching a separate organisation. Lane also stresses the fact that Saor Eire was not meant to be a military organisation although the group was not ideologically opposed to armed struggle.

Saor Eire began publishing *Peoples Voice* in November 1968 and it appeared for six issues ending in April 1969. The group styled itself as a Marxist-Leninist organisation and had chosen the name Saor Eire in tribute to the IRA-controlled organisation established in 1931 when the IRA was ostensibly committed to revolutionary socialism. Saor Eire also rejected electoralism. Lane says that, while most of the *An Phoblacht* group publicly aligned themselves with Saor Eire, they continued to advise supporters within the IRA to retain their positions and that in this manner they were able to access a continuing flow of information from IRA Volunteers, some of whom were in prominent positions. Lane says that many in the republican movement who were supportive of *An Phoblacht* and Saor Eire joined the Provisionals. Colm Daltún was a supporter and later took part in a hunger strike in Portlaoise Prison in the 1970s. Daltún died, while still a member of the Provisional IRA, in 1983. Richard Behal, who joined the Provisionals, was also believed to have been close to Saor Eire for a time. The British seemed particularly interested in this group, and more particularly Behal's connection to it.[58]

As with *An Phoblacht* Saor Eire was viewed with hostility by the republican leadership and Lane claims that Ruairí Ó Brádaigh told him that Roy Johnston urged that action should be taken against them by the IRA and that Tomás Mac Giolla was the main opponent of this on the Army Council. Lane also claims that Garland had threatened that Lane himself would be 'dealt with' and that, in response, Lane and Brendan O'Neill abducted the Cork IRA OC, George O'Mahony, and told him that they were aware of the threat and that if anything happened they would retaliate against the IRA leadership.

Saor Eire made contact with the Irish Communist Group which shared its position on the ideological differences within the international Communist movement, both taking the 'anti-revisionist' position that was supportive of the Chinese. Saor Eire later joined the ICO, on the suggestion of Colm Daltún, but left when that group began to adopt a two-nationist position on the national question. Lane and others then established the Cork Workers Club which published a wide range of pamphlets, mainly historical reprints, during the 1970s and early 1980s. Lane joined the Irish Republican Socialist Party and was Party President until his resignation in 1985.

There is some confusion regarding Saor Eire because of the existence of the separate Dublin organisation the Saor Eire Action Group. Lane says that the Cork group had nothing to do with the establishment of the Dublin group although it had contact with it in 1966 prior to either adopting the Saor Eire name. In summer 1969 the Dublin group proposed that they should establish a formal relationship in which Cork Saor Eire would 'run the political side of the organisation and they would organise the armed struggle'.[59] Lane rejected this and says that the Cork organisation had nothing to do with the Dublin group's activities, which were mainly armed robberies. After one of those robberies, in September 1969, the Dublin group issued a statement in the name of the Saor Eire Action Group. Cork Saor Eire responded publicly stating that it was not associated with it. Lane was arrested following the Arran Quay bank robbery in April 1970 during which Garda Fallon was killed, allegedly by the Saor Eire Action Group. Special Branch claimed to have discovered Cork Saor Eire material in a house that was used by some of the suspects following the robbery. Lane says he knew nothing about it.

The Saor Eire Action Group was founded by, among others, Frank Keane, a former member of the Dublin IRA Brigade staff. Other prominent members included Peter Graham, who was killed in a dispute over money in 1971, Joe Dillon who was still an active republican and supported the 32 County Sovereignty Committee that split from Sinn Féin and the IRA in 1998, Mairín Keegan, who died of cancer in 1972, Liam Dalton, who committed suicide, and Liam Walsh, who was killed in a premature explosion in October 1970 while attempting to take arms from McKee Barracks. Unlike the Cork group, the Saor Eire Action Group was Trotskyist in sympathies and had links with the United Secretariat of the Fourth International which was led by the Belgian Ernest Mandel. Most controversially the group was also alleged to have been a conduit for arms and money supplied by Fianna Fáil Ministers in 1969, and Keane was allegedly a friend of Neil Blaney, one of the Ministers forced out of the government because of his role. In May 1973 Saor Eire members being held in Mountjoy Prison issued a statement announcing that they were resigning from the organisation because they claimed that 'political weaknesses' had allowed 'undesirable elements' to operate on its fringes.[60] Their role in the events of the time still remains murky and unexplored.

Their brief prominence also illustrates the way in which a political space was created for militant radicalism in the midst of the northern crisis. The republican movement also benefited from that rather than the upsurge in support which they enjoyed being the fruit of the political reorientation of radical republicanism initiated by the modernisers. It was the possible implications that this had for the stability of the Republic which exercised Irish governments during the northern conflict, and the Irish state has proved to be remarkably successful in neutralising and even incorporating ostensibly revolutionary threats, including those presented by both the Official and Provisional wings of the republican movement, as has been illustrated by the subsequent trajectories of both organisations.

Co-operation with the IWP led to internal disputes in 1968. At Bodenstown in June, Mick Ryan, who was OC of the Dublin Brigade, gave permission for the Communists to carry their banner in the commemoration and Cumann na mBan refused to take part. There were also a number of motions seeking to ban Communist participation tabled at the 1968 Ard Fheis. Goulding retaliated by attempting to have Cumann na mBan disbanded with reliable women Volunteers taken into the IRA. Suspicions of Communist influence were heightened by the invitation to a delegation from the IWP and its youth wing, the Connolly Youth Movement, to attend the Sinn Féin Ard Fheis. In turn, delegates from the TCD Republican Club attended the Connolly Youth Movement conference and at its Sixth Conference the IWP welcomed 'the growth of friendly and fraternal relations with other Labour and Republican forces'.[61]

Republican suspicions of the Communists were not helped by the fact that 1968 was a year of major upheaval within the Communist movement following the Soviet invasion of Czechoslovakia in July. It might not, therefore, have been adjudged the most propitious time for republicans to be seen forming an alliance with the Irish parties. The invasion caused disagreements within the IWP where an attempt by Michael O'Riordan to have the party support the Red Army was defeated. The *Irish Socialist* avoided the issue although the opposition within the party was reported in *Unity*. The CPNI expressed its support for the invasion and defended the trials of dissidents in the Soviet Union while the IWP had criticised them. Sinn Féin condemned the invasion and stated that socialism could flourish only under national independence. For Ruairí Ó Brádaigh it was confirmation of the malign nature of Stalinist totalitarianism.[62] Greaves supported the invasion and the September *Irish Democrat* carried an article which urged its readers to avoid 'enlisting under the banner of British imperialism in showing sympathy with the Czechs'. Following the Soviet invasion the Wolfe Tone Society invited a Czech Communist called Hudek and a Czech who was not a party member to address one of its meetings. Hudek emphasised the 'progress' that had been made since 1948 and said that 'The capitalist class, as a class, was destroyed. There was a need to induce initiative among the people, as full employment was now a fact.' The other Czech claimed that there was 'widespread support for socialism, which they considered the best system'.[63]

The 1968 Ard Fheis was held in Liberty Hall on 7 and 8 December with delegates from 64 cumainn. As a measure of the weakness of the party it can be recalled that Sinn Féin was estimated to have had five thousand members in 336 cumainn in 1961 and 3,839 members in 295 cumainn in 1966. On that basis, there were probably fewer than one thousand members in 1968, which places Johnston's view of the threat posed by a left-wing Sinn Féin in perspective. In his Presidential address, Mac Giolla signalled support for the civil rights movement but stated that there could be no internal reform of the Six Counties. However, an amendment to a motion urging the establishment of civil rights committees in every county and calling for a withdrawal of British armed forces was rejected on the recommendation of the Ard Comhairle. Clearly sceptical of the Johnston/Coughlan blueprint, Seán Ó Brádaigh spoke of the need for the movement to be prepared to take retaliatory action if the civil rights movement was subject to physical attack. Mac Giolla claimed that republicanism and socialism were one and that socialism had nothing to do with atheism or totalitarianism.[64] The *Irish Democrat* saw the Ard Fheis as evidence of the new 'radical mood' in Sinn Féin.[65]

Motion 9 from the Kildimo-Patrickswell cumann in Limerick and the Limerick Comhairle Ceantair called on Sinn Féin to have no association with the IWP, the Connolly Association or the Connolly Youth Movement.[66] Motion 10 from the Brugha-Sabhat cumann, also in Limerick, proposed that no member of the above should be allowed to join Sinn Féin and that no member of the party be allowed to associate with them. Motion 67 from the Seán Caughey cumann, Belfast, called for members of the Young Socialists and Communists to be banned from taking part in republican commemorations while Motion 68 stated that only national and provincial flags and banners of the republican movement should be permitted at Bodenstown.

The Seán Caughey cumann also proposed that 'Sinn Féin concern itself with the establishment of an Irish Republic and that the name Irish Workers Republic be dropped'. The anti-Communist motions were defeated and instead delegates voted in favour of co-operation with other radical organisations.

The IRA Army Convention had been held in Kildare prior to the Ard Fheis. A proposal to effectively abandon abstentionism was defeated by a 3 to 1 majority. Seán Ó Brádaigh also claims that when the leadership proposed the National Liberation strategy that it was in terms of an actual merger with the IWP, CPNI and Connolly Association and that it had only been the strength of the opposition that forced them to back down in favour of an alliance.[67] Membership of the Army Council was expanded to 20 and had a pro-Goulding majority. In an attempt to reproduce that majority on the Ard Comhairle, Motion 34 from the Pearse Cumann, of which both Goulding and Johnston were members, proposed that, as the current system of election to the Ard Comhairle was not representative, only five members be elected at the Ard Fheis with the remainder elected by the Comhairle Ceantairs. However the motion was not taken and instead an amendment, proposed by Garland, to expand the Ard Comhairle to 25 with 12 regional representatives as well as the President, was passed.

The election to the Ard Comhairle seemed to indicate that those in favour of changing electoral policy had the support of a majority of the delegates. Goulding topped the list, followed by Costello, Garland, De Burca and Mac Stíofáin. Johnston did not put his name forward although he had been re-elected to the Army Council. Johnston admits that he was 'uneasy' with the direction in which the republican movement was going at the time, which may perhaps have reflected his displeasure at IRA actions of which he disapproved. He says that the reason he did not seek election to the Ard Comhairle was that he wished to concentrate on the Wolfe Tone Society and research. Greaves appears to have formed the impression that both Johnston and Coughlan were again active in the IWP. Greaves recorded in his journal that Johnston 'draws our Marxist ideas without acknowledgement and retails them to republicans opportunistically tailored to their prejudices'.

Several motions proposed that abstentionism be retained. Dan Moore of Newry claimed that it was illogical to propose abandoning abstentionism just as the policy had been vindicated by the withdrawal of the Nationalist Party from Stormont. Motion 11 from the Brugha-Sabhat cumann sought to restrict debate on the issue to every third Ard Fheis. Kerry South Comhairle Ceantair along with the Limerick Comhairle Ceantair and the Kildimo cumann proposed that Sinn Féin should not contest the next general election unless there was a chance of winning a majority. Motion 17 from the Belfast Comhairle Cenatair proposed that elected Sinn Féin candidates should take their seats in

Leinster House. Motion 18 from the Tony D'Arcy cumann, Galway, proposed that Sinn Féin should 'involve itself in the existing political institutions in the 26 Counties'. Motion 19 from the Janesboro cumann in Limerick proposed that Sinn Féin TDs, if elected, should take their seats in Leinster House on a five-year trial basis. The Gleann Columcille cumann from Donegal wanted any elected TDs to satisfy the growing demand among the public that they should take their seats under the direction of the supreme authority of the republican movement. Reflecting frustration at previous attempts to resolve the issue, the Pearse cumann proposed that, if abstentionism was retained, Sinn Féin should not contest elections in the Republic. Motion 29, proposed by Johnston, deleted the requirement for party members to support abstentionism. Significantly, this was passed by 66 votes to 20. The proposal not to contest elections was the only positive decision on electoral policy taken by the Ard Fheis and meant that Sinn Féin did not nominate candidates for the general election in 1969, which made the party even more irrelevant at a time when the Labour Party was reaping the benefits of an apparent leftward swing among the electorate, one of the key arguments for abandoning abstentionism made in 1969.

While there possibly was the required two-thirds majority in favour of changing electoral policy, Motion 17, which proposed that Sinn Féin should 'allow its elected members to take their seats in Leinster House', was amended. Uncertain of winning the required two-thirds majority or wishing to avoid the inevitable split that would follow such a decision, Garland proposed that a committee comprised of Sinn Féin and the IRA be established to examine the issue and that it would submit its recommendation to an extraordinary Ard Fheis within three months. Costello, despite having argued in favour of the motion, seconded the amendment but made clear his own desire for the issue to be pushed to a conclusion. Garland spoke after Costello in an effort to dispel what the *United Irishman* described as the 'distinct anti-abstentionist complexion of the proposal'. The paper saw the amendment as a compromise that would allow the movement to steer a course 'between the Scylla of Abstentionism and the Charybdis of Anti-Abstentionism'.[68]

The Sinn Féin members of the Commission elected by the Ard Comhairle in December were Mac Giolla, Costello, Seán Ó Brádaigh, Derry Kelleher, Liam Cummins, Paddy Callaghan, Denis Cassin and Malachy McGurran. Only Ó Brádaigh was known to be opposed to any change in electoral policy and he resigned before its first meeting to be replaced by Seamus Rattigan, another Goulding supporter. The balance of power was reinforced by the appointment by the IRA of a further eight members although one of these was Seán Mac Stíofáin. Seán Ó Brádaigh believed that participation by traditionalists was pointless given that there was a clear majority on the commission that supported ending abstentionism.[69] So, although it had not yet been formalised, the fault lines of the split that was to take place a year later had already been defined. Within the IRA, dissident Volunteers had already begun to withdraw their allegiance from the Goulding-dominated Army Council and the beginnings of a separate organisation had been made.

Two members of the IWP attended the Sinn Féin Ard Fheis, and the Communists welcomed the party's acceptance if the 'twin aims' of independence and socialism.[70] They had, however, misgivings concerning the move towards the left and the need for republicans to be very clear about what they meant by socialism, perhaps because the Irish parties were uneasy about the change in republican ideology as it threatened their own niche. They favoured an alliance with the IRA and Sinn Féin as representative of radical republicanism rather than the movement becoming formally socialist. Greaves shared a similar view and did not wish to see Sinn Féin replacing the Labour Party or presumably the Communists.

A faction of the leadership led by Costello attempted to pre-empt the Garland Commission by proposing to convene a special Ard Fheis to select a candidate for the Mid Ulster election who would take the seat if elected. That proposal was defeated and reflected a desire to postpone what must have appeared as an increasingly inevitable split. Another proposal from Éamonn Mac Thomáis was that Tom Mitchell would stand as an abstentionist but that was unacceptable to a majority of the Ard Comhairle. Alternatively, Mitchell would resign from Sinn Féin and take his seat, or a sympathetic non-republican like Conor Cruise O'Brien would be asked to stand. What happened instead was that Bernadette Devlin ignored the theological ruminations and decided to run, thus forcing the IRA to support her campaign. Johnston believes that this was a mistake and that Sinn Féin would have won the seat if it had decided to nominate a candidate.[71] The election caused friction within the Wolfe Tone Society where those who were not members resented the manner in which the IRA attempted to dictate policy. This became public when Uinseann Mac Eoin wrote to the *United Irishman* in February to attack the '1918 mutterings of those Old Men of the Sea, the Sinn Féin Party' who he claimed were completely divorced from popular feeling.

On 26 January 1969 Johnston, Goulding, McMillen and McGurran met with representatives of the CPNI at a meeting chaired by Michael O'Riordan to discuss the draft of the Garland Commission report on the North. The Communists approved the draft but were apparently more cautious than Johnston with regard to support for civil rights among the Protestant working-class.[72] The report, entitled *Ireland Today and Some Questions on the Way Forward*, was published in March 1969. It advised that it was not to be taken as the final word on the issue and that every member of the movement was to give his (*sic*) opinion. The Commission was not yet making any recommendations.[73] However, as Seán Swan says: 'what was intended here,

communism, the subordination of the IRA and the dropping of Abstentionism must have made a split seem not only possible but inevitable'.[74] Garland
says that he personally welcomed the prospect of a break with the traditionalists.[75] Roy Johnston also believes that it would have been preferable had the
anti-abstentionists resigned following the 1968 Ard Fheis, and that, if the split
had occurred then, the Provisionals would not have been able to mobilise
from within the republican movement after the August 1969 events and
NICRA would have held the middle ground, thus averting the Orange
pogrom. The mid-Ulster election might have been won by a 'politicising left-
republican', rather than Devlin whom he regarded as an 'ultra-leftist', and the
strategy would have proceeded apace.

According to the report, the key objective of the republican movement in
the North was to unite Catholic and Protestant workers in the Six Counties
on the basis of a 'democratic and civil rights programme'.[76] Organised workers
in the south were the most progressive force despite the negative influence of
the trade union leadership. There was praise for the role of the IWP and some
politically conscious middle-level leadership in the unions who were associated with the Labour Party. The republican movement had support among
nationally minded small business people, small farmers and skilled and
unskilled workers and was in competition with Labour for the support of
skilled workers in state and semi-state industry. It was claimed that the IWP
had support among workers and was as strong as the republican movement
in Dublin where the *Irish Socialist* was said to sell as many copies as the *United
Irishman*. That analysis sat well with the Communists' own perception of both
their own position as a vanguard working-class party and the republican
movement as the representative of less class conscious and non-proletarian
elements, who in the Marxist schema would naturally take their lead from the
former. It was at the very least a naive view that bore almost no relation to
the political realities in Ireland at that time.

While the IRA would have an undefined 'defensive' role, Johnston did not
envisage a military campaign as outlined in part of the 'Garland Plan'. The
problem was how to weld republicans, Communists and trade unionists
together in one 'progressive' movement. There were two possible strategies:
to wean the labour movement away from middle-class leadership, through a
national liberation front, or to align with the Labour Party for electoral purposes. The second of these was rejected out of hand. Instead, the report recommended the national liberation front as outlined in the 1968 Ard Fheis
motion supporting co-operation with other radical groups. The arguments
on both sides of the debate on abstentionism were given in detail, with the
emphasis on the danger that increased radicalisation would benefit Labour
unless republicans were prepared to take seats.

To implement the new strategy the republican movement needed a single unified leadership preserving the 'historic link with the Republican government, at present vested in the Army Council' constituting a shadow cabinet linked to a shadow state composed of popular organisations when that became credible. This structure would eventually come into confrontation with the existing state in the Republic as envisaged by the 'Garland Plan'. The final report, not published until after the split in January 1970, recommended the ending of abstentionism. The Commission proposals were discussed at meetings of members held in April and May 1969 at which there was a good deal of unease expressed, especially at the report's optimism regarding working-class unity in the North in the face of evidence of growing sectarian tensions. Many were also hostile to the proposed alliance with the Communists. Even those supportive of the general thrust of the proposals believed that Johnston was underestimating the danger, or potential depending on one's perspective, of an outbreak of conflict resulting from the reaction to the civil rights movement. The 1969 document was more realistic than the 'Garland Plan' about building political support through electoral participation and any policy based on the chance of Sinn Féin winning an early majority in Leinster House was abandoned. But even that might not have caused the kind of internal opposition which it did had it not been for the growing crisis in the North which made any project for gradual democratic reform appear misplaced.

The Wolfe Tone Society continued its efforts to organise the type of specialist groups envisaged by the 'Garland Plan' and which were to be part of the putative shadow state structure referred to in Johnston's report. They would have to re-examine how the specialist structure was operating, with the objective of having proposals from the groups accepted as national policy by the organisations in which they were operating. Like Sinn Féin, the WTS appears to have gone into decline in 1968. Although the anti-EEC Defence of the Nation League was still nominally in existence it engaged in little activity. In February the Society decided to hold an educational conference on political and economic issues 'primarily for the benefit of people in the Republican and Labour movements'.[77] Johnston attended the AGM of NICRA as an observer, and Johnston, Máire Comerford and Derry Kelleher were at the IWP conference held on 17 and 18 March. As the crisis in the North developed, a former WTS member, Michael McKeown, worried at 'signs that the extremist element in the Republican Movement which has been quiescent for some time is again in the process of reorganising and recruiting', and might 'launch us once again on the vain merry-go-round of bridge-blowing and anarchy'.[78] There was little sign that the Irish government was overly concerned, and two meetings between Lynch and O'Neill in December 1967 and January 1968 concentrated on trade and combating the spread of foot and mouth disease from Britain.[79] O'Neill informed his Unionist colleagues that 'nothing of a politically embarrassing character' had arisen.[80]

In March 1967 the Northern government banned the Republican Clubs on the grounds that they were simply another name for Sinn Féin. Craig said that there were around forty clubs and that up to half their members were in the IRA.[81] In June 1968 Craig cited RUC reports that the IRA was actively recruiting on both sides of the border and *An t-Óglach* references to preparing for a new campaign. Republicans supported the occupation of the house at Caledon, County Tyrone, where a Catholic family, the Gildernews, had taken possession of a Council house to protest at the discriminatory practises of the Unionist-controlled local authority. This became one of the key events in popularising the civil rights movement. It is also clear that the majority of the republican leadership was content to allow events take their course and its public pronouncements began to sound moderate in comparison to the radical elements whom the Communists and some republicans were describing as ultra-leftists. Johnston described the Peoples Democracy as an 'unstable element' within the civil rights movement.[82] It is also clear that the civil rights movement transformed itself into a popular mass movement on the basis of invigorating Catholic demands to end discrimination rather than as hoped for by the modernisers through building a non-sectarian campaign involving Protestant trade unionists who, apart from CPNI members, were indifferent and even hostile to the campaign. Indeed it was the modernisers' desire to continue to seek such support that led them to oppose the more militant aspects of the civil rights protests.

While the key demand was for a Bill of Rights, it was also clear that republicans were concerned over the increasing intransigence of the Unionists: 'Time is running out. The consequences of failing to budge the Unionists in the North and win definite reforms there during the coming period will be grim for the Irish people all over this island.'[83] The key difference within the movement was between those who believed that the optimum strategy was to pin their faith on political developments that would damage the Unionists and hopefully attract Protestant working-class support, and those who supported the civil rights campaign but who also supported the more militant tactics advocated by Peoples Democracy and believed that the IRA needed to be prepared to intervene when the Northern authorities responded with repression.

Coughlan and Johnston clung to the hope that the civil rights campaign would fulfil its aim of fostering unity between Catholic and Protestant. They urged caution and criticised Peoples Democracy for defying RUC bans, and emphasised that the civil rights movement was based on 'moderate demands'.[84] The IRA Army Council, however, approved the participation of the Tyrone

Command in the Coalisland to Dungannon march that took place in August. Johnston asked Fred Heatley to have a statement prepared by Coughlan read at the meeting in Dungannon on 24 August but Heatley refused, and claims to have torn up the speech in front of Johnston, in the belief that the statement came from the IRA Army Council.[85] Johnston denies that this was the case. Rather, it was Coughlan's own attempt to summarise the situation. It called for a Bill of Rights, a lifting of the ban on the Republican Clubs and the repeal of the Special Powers Act. Following the disturbances that took place in Derry in October the IRA issued a statement denying that it had been involved although republicans as members of the community had taken part. The statement ended on a note of bravado, claiming that, had the IRA been in Derry, the people there would have been protected.[86]

In August, Sinn Féin wrote to Lynch claiming that people in the North had 'at last realised that they have been sold out by successive Dublin Governments and have long ceased to expect any help from you in their efforts to throw off an alien administration and unite themselves with the rest of us'. They called on Lynch to pressure the British to adhere to the European Convention on Human Rights and to concede all the demands of the civil rights movement.[87] Wilson was requested to ensure that during 'the remaining period of your occupation of our country' he should 'allow to the Irish people under your control at least the same basic human rights and standards as you ensure in your own country'.

The week after Derry, petrol bombs were thrown at the British Embassy and a further incident took place on 15 October for which Daniel Greene of Ballymun was sentenced to three months. Lynch met Wilson on 30 October to encourage reform but Robin North of the Home Office said that the IRA would be encouraged if the British government was seen to be putting pressure on the Unionists.[88] Another paper claimed that the Irish government was hoping that the IRA would 'wither away'.[89] There is no record that Lynch and Wilson discussed the IRA although privately Lynch's deputy, Erskine Childers, was concerned that the IRA was 'increasingly dangerous' and he feared that the crisis would be exploited by them in the Republic. He was anxious to know from the British what role the IRA was playing in the North and what information they had about their future plans,[90] an indication perhaps that the southern-based Special Branch agents within the IRA who were supporters of Goulding had little knowledge regarding the northern dissidents. Childers was also no doubt aware that the Department of Justice had first-hand information on decisions taken by the Army Council at this time.[91] Childers's concern may also have reflected the fact that the growing crisis in the North was making the situation and the IRA, and particularly its northern component which was increasingly outside of the control of the leadership, far more unpredictable, as indeed is indicated also by the reactions to events of Goulding and Costello.

The Derry events seem to have surprised the Unionists as much as they did anyone else. The Unionists decided on a firm response but also recognised the need for reform given the pressure that Wilson was under from the Labour left. A long discussion took place at a Northern Cabinet meeting on 29 October at which the consensus was that, although Belfast ought not be seen to be reacting to the threat of disorder, it did need to reform areas such as local government. There was also concern expressed by some Ministers regarding the apparent 'impunity' with which extreme loyalists were able to organise. O'Neill said that, while they had been so far successful in being able to resist pressure for reform, the Derry events had raised the possibility of intervention by Westminster. Proposals for a Unilateral Declaration of Independence were 'absurd'. He also said that while 'anti partition agitators' were at work that they had to recognise the legitimacy of nationalist grievances. They also had to face the dilemma, if they resisted change, of being prepared to rule by 'police power alone' and that in the absence of reform there was a danger of a review of the 1920 constitutional settlement. O'Neill made no reference to any threat of an IRA insurrection.[92]

Wilson and Jim Callaghan met with O'Neill, Faulkner and Craig in Downing Street on 4 November but were disappointed with what they perceived to be the lack of will on the part of the Unionists to address the situation. Craig attempted to convince the British that the IRA was behind the civil rights movement and claimed that the IRA had been infiltrated by Communists and that they had been responsible for a number of incidents in the Republic.[93] The Belfast notes record that Callaghan had accused the Unionists of 'stringing' the government along in the hope of a Tory election victory. In response to Craig's claims regarding an IRA insurrection, based on 'some disquieting news about IRA policy', and that 30 of the 70 known Civil Rights Association members were either IRA members or supporters, Callaghan said that, while there was a risk that the IRA could exploit grievances, that was all the more reason to remove the cause.[94] The consensus in Belfast was that concessions were needed although Faulkner and Craig said they would not accept being dictated to. O'Neill said that the logic of that was to face financial sanctions[95] and he warned them that they would have to face up to their responsibilities or face the consequences both from London and of increased disorder. Interestingly he said that there was a danger they could 'slide into a policy of repression', and could not expect the support which the UK government had given them when they faced 'external threats from the IRA', an indication that no one seriously believed that such a threat did exist. Craig continued to blame nationalist 'extremists' and it is clear that O'Neill failed to convince the Cabinet to go as far as Wilson wanted them to.[96]

Wilson wrote to O'Neill on 19 November to express his concern not over the IRA but about the Unionists' attitude to reform. On 5 November he told parliament that if O'Neill was overthrown then London would have to fundamentally reappraise its relationship with Belfast[97] and much of the letter took the form of veiled threats to take more radical action unless the Northern government acted. Wilson wanted O'Neill to bring the local government franchise into line with that in the rest of the UK[98] and hoped that Northern Ireland would ensure 'proper standards of housing allocation'. The British had 'honoured the conventions that have hitherto governed our relationships. But we should have to have a fundamental re-appraisal of the situation if these things are not dealt with.' It would be preferable if the situation was dealt with by Stormont but if not, 'in view of the very generous financial contribution which we make for Northern Ireland', it would be incumbent on the British government to intervene.

O'Neill's response was far from being as contrite as Wilson, and indeed O'Neill himself, might have hoped. The Northern Ireland government did not accept that abuse of the housing allocation was widespread and noted that reform of allocation was not being introduced anywhere else in 'Britain'.[99] None the less they had taken steps and O'Neill was pleased with the progress being made, but 'if and when the security of Northern Ireland is at risk, you will appreciate the need for measures which are exceptional in the English context'. They had already decided to abolish the company vote for local elections, but it would not be possible within six months to bring the franchise into line with the rest of the UK. In any event he claimed that that was 'primarily an issue appealing to political activists; but it is jobs and houses which most concern the mass of the people'.

O'Neill felt sure that Wilson would agree that the best hope of progress was through the Belfast government and parliament 'and we would regard any fundamental re-appraisal of our constitutional or financial relationship as a most serious step, likely to create more problems than it would solve'. O'Neill also told Gilchrist that the blame for the crisis rested with the IRA which had infiltrated the civil rights movement.[100] Gilchrist was not persuaded of this and told McCann that he felt that the influence of extremists, 'though not non-existent', had to date been of 'little weight'. The danger was that a further turn to the right by the Unionists would provide a stimulus but that the danger had passed.[101] Wilson welcomed the reforms made to date but was 'disappointed that you have not so far felt able to announce a policy of early introduction of universal adult suffrage in local government elections'.[102] However, London remained aloof and Belfast remained intransigent. Indeed the hardliners clearly had the upper hand and discussed a full mobilisation of the B Specials.[103] In December the Cabinet also heard a report from RUC Special Branch on the alleged infiltration by the IRA of the civil rights movement.[104]

Meanwhile the Dublin Embassy, increasingly sensitive to the shifting sands, kept a close eye on tensions within the Fianna Fáil Cabinet. Neil Blaney continued to make militant noises on the North and was depicted by Gilchrist as a 'rough diamond...not to be described as pro-British'.[105] The fact that a number of people were proposing a federal solution in the North was, however, a positive development. He also felt that the Irish government was 'more and more apprehensive' over Sinn Féin and its plans to establish a socialist republic.[106] Again, as with Childers's request for information on the IRA in the North, this probably reflected uncertainty in the face of a crisis rather than any real fear that the IRA was contemplating an armed campaign. The main danger was presented by the possibility that the IRA would be dragged into communal violence in the North or indeed that its members would disregard the apparent opposition of the leadership to a campaign, which in fact was far from apparent to most Volunteers whatever their real intentions might have been.

Notes

1 *This Week*, July 1970.
2 *United Irishman*, February 1967.
3 Mick Ryan, article in Bicentenary Issue of *United Irishman*, 1998.
4 IRA document on Circulation of *United Irishman*, dated 6 February 1967, in private collection in the care of Professor Eunan O'Halpin of TCD.
5 Address by Goulding to TCD Philosophical Society, 16 February 1967, in private collection in the care of Professor Eunan O'Halpin.
6 *An Phoblacht*, no. 8.
7 Wolfe Tone Society Minutes, 24, 25 June 1967.
8 'An Interim Analysis of the Irish Republican Movement', manuscript in private collection in the care of Professor Eunan O'Halpin.
9 Greaves Journal entry for 6 July, 1967, www.iol.ie/~rjtechne/century130703/1960s/greave66.htm, viewed 16 January 2009.
10 *Ibid.*
11 Manuscript in private collection in care of Professor Eunan O'Halpin. The author was clearly living in Britain at the time and refers to 'here' and the role of Clann na hÉireann in any putative campaign.
12 *Irish Times*, 12 February 1967.
13 Interview with Seán Bermingham, 20 April 2005.
14 *United Irishman*, July 1967.
15 *Unity*, 24 June 1967.
16 *Evening Press*, 3 July 1967.
17 Swan (2006), p. 187.
18 *Irish Independent*, 3 July 1967.
19 *Irish Democrat*, August 1967.
20 Interview with Seán Garland, 28 February 2005.
21 Email from Tony Meade, 18 April 2005.

22 *This Week*, 31 July 1970.
23 Interview with Roy Johnston, 19 April 2001.
24 Interview with Johnston, 19 April 2001.
25 Wolfe Tone Society Minutes, 28 November 1967.
26 1967 Sinn Féin Ard Fhéis *Clár.*
27 'Socialism . . . A Definition', Sinn Féin, Dublin, March 1968. Document in possession of Cathal Mac Liam.
28 *An Phoblacht*, no. 14, December 1967.
29 Interview with Jim Lane, 14 May 2005.
30 *Educational Manual*, Part III (Dublin October 1967), p. 1.
31 *Ibid.*
32 Interview with Seán Garland, 28 February 2005.
33 Interview with Roy Johnston, 19 April 2001.
34 Interview with Seán Ó Brádaigh, 21 May 2005.
35 Patterson (1997), p. 91.
36 Private information.
37 Interview with Seán Garland, 28 February 2005.
38 *United Irishman*, July 1968.
39 *United Irishman*, February 1968.
40 Swan (2006), p. 211.
41 Interview with Roy Johnston 19 April 2001 and email of 26 June 2001.
42 Email from Roy Johnston of 26 June 2001.
43 Email from Roy Johnston of 24 July 2001.
44 *Magill*, May 1980, pp. 35–6. McMahon was put on a retainer following his retirement in 1966 in order to maintain contact with his agent.
45 Letter from Jim Savage to Michael Flood, 10 December 1967.
46 Letter from Jim Savage to Michael Flood, 2 May 1968.
47 *Republican News*, July 1968.
48 Hanley Millar (2009), p. 389.
49 C. Andrews and V. Mitrokhin, *The Sword and the Shield: The Mitrokhin Archive and the Secret History of the KGB* (London 2000), p. 384.
50 Interview with Seán Dunne, 20 November 2001.
51 FCO 33/1778, Report by Allinson of 30 October 1968, PRO.
52 *Ibid.*, Gilchrist to FCO, 25 November 1968.
53 *Ibid.*, N. J. Barrington to Wilkinson, 23 October 1968.
54 *Hibernia*, 4–17 December 1970. On 4 December 1970 O'Malley announced that the government had received information that Saor Eire was planning to kidnap leading politicians.
55 FCO 33/1778, report of meeting between Secretary for State and Lynch, 30 October 1968, PRO.
56 *Ibid.*, Record of meeting between Parliamentary Under Secretary and Molloy, 20 November 1968.
57 *This Week*, 5 December 1969.
58 FCO 33/1593, Peck to FCO, 16 February 1971, PRO.
59 Email from Jim Lane, 21 May 2005.

60 Liam O Ruairc, 'A Little Known Republican Military Group: Saor Eire', *The Blanket*, 13 January, 2005, http://lark.phoblacht.net/lor1401051g.html, viewed 5 April 2006.
61 *Irish Socialist*, April 1968.
62 Interview with Ruairí Ó Brádaigh, 22 May 2002.
63 Wolfe Tone Society Minutes, 10 September 1968.
64 *United Irishman*, January 1969.
65 *Irish Democrat*, January 1969.
66 Sinn Féin Ard Fheis 1968, *Clár*, Motion 9.
67 Interview with Seán Ó Brádaigh, 22 May 2005.
68 *United Irishman*, January 1969.
69 Interview with Seán Ó Brádaigh, 22 May 2005.
70 *Irish Socialist*, 21 December, 1968.
71 Interview with Roy Johnston, 19 April 2001.
72 Swan (2006), p. 227.
73 *Ireland Today and Some Questions on the Way Forward* (Dublin 1969), Introduction.
74 Swan (2006), p. 227.
75 Interview with Seán Garland, 28 February 2005.
76 *Ireland Today and Some Questions on the Way Forward*, p. 4.
77 Wolfe Tone Society Minutes, 13 February 1968.
78 'Let Us Prey', *Hibernia*, March 1968.
79 DFA, London Embassy, L116/29; memo sent to foreign missions on 16 February 1968 on meetings between Lynch and O'Neill, 11 December 1967 and 8 January 1968, NAI.
80 CAB/4/1381, Cabinet minutes, 9 January 1968. PRONI.
81 *Hansard*, Commons Debates, Vol. 65, col. 1763, Vol. 66, col. 151.
82 Interview with Roy Johnston, 19 April 2001.
83 *United Irishman*, September 1968.
84 Wolfe Tone Society Minutes, 10 September 1968.
85 Bishop and Mallie (1987), p. 52.
86 *United Irishman*, November 1968.
87 Taoiseach, 99/1/284, letter of 24 August, 1968, NAI.
88 FCO 33/755, Report from Robin North to FCO, 15 October 1968.
89 FCO 33/755.
90 *Ibid.*, telegram from Gilchrist to FCO, 26 October 1968.
91 Department of Justice 2000/36/3, NAI.
92 CAB/4/1406, Cabinet minutes of 29 October and O'Neill memo of 14 October, PRONI.
93 PREM 13/2347, Note of meeting of 4 November 1968, PRO.
94 CAB/4/1413, Memo of Downing Street meeting of 4 November, PRONI.
95 CAB/4/1413, minutes of Cabinet meeting of 7 November 1968, PRONI.
96 CAB/4/1414, PRONI.
97 *Hansard*, Commons Debates, 5 November 1968.
98 PREM 13/284, Wilson to O'Neill, 19 November 1968, PRO.

99 PREM 13/2841, O'Neill to Wilson, 6 December 1968, PRO.
100 FCO 33/762, Gilchrist to London 9 December 1968, PRO.
101 Taoiseach, 2000/6/657, Note from Gilchrist to McCann, 16 December 1968, NAI.
102 PREM 13/2841, Wilson to O'Neill, 23 December 1968, PRO.
103 CAB/4/1422, Cabinet minutes, 2 December 1968, PRONI.
104 CAB/4/1423, Cabinet minutes, 5 December 1968, PRONI.
105 FCO 33/762, Gilchrist to London, 14 November 1968, PRO.
106 FCO 33/762, Gilchrist to London, 12 December 1968, PRO.

7

The Northern crisis and the split

The start of 1969 brought an escalation in tensions in Northern Ireland and there were indications that some Goulding supporters were annoyed at what they regarded as the provocative strategy being pursued by Peoples Democracy and other radical elements in the civil rights movement outside of the control of NICRA. Peoples Democracy was founded in October 1968 in Queen's by students who were involved in the civil rights movement and the university left. They were strongly influenced by black American groups such as the Student Non Violent Coordinating Council (SNCC) and developed in a similar manner towards a more radical position with the PD eventually declaring itself to be a Trotskyist organisation. As Simon Prince has shown, they very much saw themselves as part of a global movement, in particular what had happened in Paris in May 1968, and indeed in Prague prior to the Soviet invasion, whereas older Irish republicans and indeed Communists were suspicious of the 'new left' and its connotations of 'petit-bourgeois' liberalism in relation to sex and drugs, not to mention its open disdain for much of their own values.

While the front page of the January 1969 *United Irishman* supported the continuation of the civil rights marches after Burntollet, where participants were attacked by Paisley supporters, other writers blamed the organisers and demanded that those who took 'individualistic' action should be dealt with in a ruthless manner. 'Northman' attacked Peoples Democracy for threatening to undermine the unity of the civil rights movement by pushing forward demands that were a manifestation of 'ultra-leftism'. Anthony Coughlan still defends that view and regards the Belfast–Derry march as having been a provocation which led to the violence which effectively derailed the modernisers' project.[1]

While opposition to 'ultra-leftism' was part of the lexicon of the modernisers' allies in the Communist parties, many local republicans activists were happy to participate in protests and marches, and IRA members attempted to protect the student marchers along the route of the January march. In contrast the General Secretary of the CPNI, James Stewart, attacked the 'sectarian attitudes' of protestors who were alienating businessmen, intellectuals and farmers and playing into the hands of the Unionists,[2] and the Connolly Association claimed that the issues of civil rights and Irish independence were separate.[3] However, not all of the modernisers shared that view. Seamus Costello was advocating that the IRA could help to bring about a breakdown in the North through selective actions. That ran counter to the line promoted by Johnston and Coughlan who pointed out that that would lead to the abolition of Stormont and thereby impede their plans for Stormont to become the focus of a radical non-sectarian alternative to Unionism. According to Cathal Mac Liam, Greaves met Goulding and Costello in Mac Liam's house around that time and both Costello and Goulding argued in favour of bringing about a breakdown that would lead to the abolition of Stormont and highlight British responsibility.[4]

Goulding's support for this was short-lived and the *United Irishman* continued to counsel moderation. Peoples Democracy was criticised for raising socialist demands on the basis that 'the Civil Rights programme is a reformist one' but that revolutionaries needed to lead such a movement to 'guarantee that reforms will not be betrayed',[5] and quoted Betty Sinclair of the CPNI who denied that seeking short-term reforms was 'reformist'. Advocates of this approach could point as evidence of its success to the tabling by Lord Fenner Brockway of a Bill of Rights for Northern Ireland at Westminster but the Bill did not get on to the Order Paper until 1971. Brockway was the President of the Movement for Colonial Freedom, effectively another CPGB front organisation, which shared offices with the Connolly Association in London.

The year 1969 began with a series of demonstrations in Dublin that seemed to mirror the growing protests in the North. Ironically republicans were again forced into the role of relative moderates and, at a protest at the British Embassy on 11 January, IRA stewards prevented members of the Trotskyist Young Socialist group from attempting to force the Garda lines at the Embassy. Speaking to the crowd at another protest on 14 January, the *United Irishman* editor Seamus Ó Tuathail compared the protests in Dublin to the civil rights campaign in the North.[6] Sinn Féin's disadvantage in the quest for public support was underlined by the fact that in the midst of the housing protests Labour launched its housing policy, including proposals to nationalise all building land, introduce rent control and build ten thousand local authority houses within five years. Sinn Féin could only claim that it was compiling a dossier on Dublin landlords and was not able to compete for the left-wing vote because of its decision not to contest the general election that year.

There were clashes between Gardaí and protestors at a housing protest on 18 January when the Gardaí baton-charged people who sat down on O'Connell Bridge. Seamus Ó Tuathail called on the Gardaí not to allow themselves to be used in a 'class struggle' of which they themselves were part.[7] The protest also led to clashes between stewards and members of the Internationalists who added an exotic Maoist flavour and were described by Meath Labour TD Jim Tully as a 'group of little brats'.[8] They accused Housing Action Committee stewards, who were members of the IRA and the Connolly Youth Movement, of having launched a 'fascist' attack on their members and as 'running dogs of imperialism'.[9]

Gilchrist noted that the Irish media had commented upon the 'Communist' presence at the Embassy protest and that this had created some sympathy for the British dilemma in the North.[10] Gilchrist was perhaps overestimating public anxiety over student radicalism and underestimating the potential political consequences of antagonising public opinion in the Republic through the British response to the civil rights movement. Gilchrist was sent a lengthy report on student unrest by George Dawson, Professor of Genetics at Trinity College Dublin, who dismissed the Maoists as a serious force but claimed that the Republican Club was popular and could be more widely influential if it were 'ruthless' enough in exploiting discontent.[11]

As the general elections approached there was evidence that Fianna Fáil was worried about the electoral threat from Labour, and to a lesser extent somewhat paranoid about the left in general although not specifically about the republican movement. There was also some internal unease in the party and at the Ard Fheis in January some cumainn called for the disbanding of TACA, the fund-raising group which Kevin O'Kelly of Dublin South West described as a 'rich man's club'. There was also criticism of the Criminal Justice Bill and a reference to the sinister influence of a 'cabal' in the Department of Justice who were pushing 'draconian' legislation. That was a reference to the Department Secretary Berry who had been the subject of controversy over his refusal to hand over documents to the Committee for Public Accounts.

In contrast, others demanded a Subversive Activities Board which Des Ryan of Dublin North said was required 'before the Red trickle became a mortal haemorrhage'.[12] A reference to the malign role of the Wolfe Tone Society convinced some of its members of Fianna Fáil's fear of the republican left.[13] While that view is shared by Ed Moloney and Hanley and Millar and partly substantiated by the March 1969 Justice memo,[14] Bishop and Mallie described the modernisers' conception of the threat posed by themselves and of a state plot to remove them from the republican leadership as 'characteristically fanciful and vain' and said that they were no more than a 'minor political nuisance'.[15] In his Ard Fheis speech, Lynch attacked Labour's 'extreme socialist proposals' but made no reference to the republican movement. The government was worried about the Northern crisis impacting on stability and providing an opportunity which the radical and republican left might exploit, and in January McCann had insisted to Gilchrist that the British should intervene directly in the north to prevent any negative effects on the Republic.[16] In March the Ambassador reported that the government was 'seriously concerned' over the impact of strikes and protests but that the IRA organised housing agitation had 'gone off the boil'.[17]

Berry submitted a memo for Minister for Justice O Moráin in which he stressed the influence of Johnston and the Communists within the IRA.[18] Special Branch estimates of membership were unchanged since 1966 at between 1,100 and 1,200 and finances remained poor although boosted by the visit of Goulding to the United States in October 1968 and a contribution of £100 from the Communist Party of Great Britain. The print run of the *United Irishman* had been reduced since 1968 from 60,000 per month to 25,000, which would hardly indicate that the movement was on the cusp of a breakthrough, much less an imminent revolutionary threat. Berry listed incidents involving the IRA, including the EI bus burnings, and the difficulties which they presented in terms of detection and prosecution. However, he did not believe that they warranted the re-establishment of the Special Criminal Court. Instead, IRA members ought to be pursued on 'trivial offences' that could then allow them to be transferred to military custody under Section 45 of the Criminal Justice Bill which was then being considered by the Dáil. He also recommended that the Communist influence within the IRA should be publicised as 'units of the IRA (and Sinn Fein) are uneasy about the new left-wing policy' which could be highlighted through 'an active political campaign' to bring about the 'fragmentation of the organisation'.

That has been cited by Hanley and Millar as evidence of the government's active interest in exploiting divisions within the IRA and could be seen as providing a rationale for the intervention of government agents in the movement. However, there were already Special Branch agents on the IRA Army Council, and Berry, quite likely through one of the latter, was a key actor in exposing the connection between Fianna Fáil Ministers and the IRA, a connection which the modernisers claimed was in furtherance of the split referred to by Berry only weeks before contact was made with a view to passing money and arms to the IRA. Berry, therefore, was clearly not a part of the alleged Haughey/Blaney plot which forms the basis of the modernisers' version of events leading to the split. It is also clear that the motivation for the memo on the part of O Moráin was to use the 'red' smear as part of a generalised attack on the left in the general election. Sinn Féin did not run candidates and, as we have seen, the main focus of the Fianna Fáil campaign was the Labour Party which it claimed was under the same sort of influence as the republican movement.

What Berry proposed was a propaganda offensive to offset what was seen as the undue sympathy and coverage which the IRA and others were receiving from left-wingers in RTE and other sections of the media. Indeed Berry, having made the point that left-wingers in the media were promoting radical change 'without bothering to put such a policy before the people to secure a mandate for it, as a political party has to do',[19] specifically stated that a 'constantly alert propaganda service' could only be conducted by 'political sources [as] it is a need that cannot be filled by any Departmental agency'.[20] It may also have been the case that Berry was far more worried about the IRA than was Fianna Fáil, which was nervous about the electoral threat posed by Labour rather than the threat of revolution from the republican left.

Alongside propaganda attacks on the left, Fianna Fáil trumpeted its own radical heritage. Erskine Childers claimed that the party had a 'radical left of centre approach to all social problems',[21] and Brian Lenihan described the party as closer to Connolly than any other and claimed that it had pioneered a mixture of state and public enterprise in place of a discredited version of old socialism that had been rejected by Lenin in the 1920s. The left-wing posturing did not, however, prevent Fianna Fáil from attacking its opponents as irresponsible extremists. Neil Blaney accused the media of highlighting 'bogus protest demonstrations', while Justice Minister Micheál O Moráin made reference to the 'anarchists and lily-the-pinks on the one side, and the gig actors, Tories, misrepresenters and deluders on the other' who were out to undermine the government.[22] While Gilchrist believed that Neil Blaney was partly motivated by 'deep personae emotion' on the North, he also attributed his 'rabble rousing' to internal tensions within the Fianna Fáil party.[23]

At the Wolfe Tone Society AGM on 8 March Coughlan stressed the importance of the Society's role within the republican movement.[24] Johnston drew up a proposal for a conference involving all elements of the Garland Commission proposal for a National Liberation Front, to include Kadar Asmal, Costello, O'Riordan, Goulding, Johnston and Greaves. The conference did not take place although a similar event was held at the Sheelin Shamrock Hotel in Cavan following the split, organised by the Official Republican Movement and the Communist Party of Ireland. The 1969 conference would have been the effective launch of the National Liberation Front with a view to an early merger but had to be postponed because of the crisis in the North.

The frustration felt by the modernisers over the delays in shifting the republican movement away from abstentionism and towards an alliance with the Communists was heightened by the results of the June 1969 general election. The British Ambassador, Gilchrist, believed that Lynch had set the date despite his concern that the northern crisis might have a negative effect on the government[25] but noted the lack of anti-British sentiment in the campaign.[26] Gilchrist felt that relative calm in the North had deprived Sinn Féin of an issue and referred to its 'apparent quiescence',[27] and that it was focused on 'minor campaigns' which had made no impact on the electorate.[28] The general impression one gets from Gilchrist is that the concerns about the IRA and left-wing radicalism generally, which he had in late 1968, had abated and that influenced London's view to a much greater extent than the jeremiads from Belfast. Gilchrist was asked to address a meeting of the Joint Intelligence Committee in September.[29]

Labour had its best election result since the 1940s, winning 18 seats, ten of them in Dublin where it received over 28 per cent of the votes. In Sinn Féin's absence republican intervention was confined to a tame editorial in the June *United Irishman* which advised readers to choose among the various 'shades of grey'. The Wolfe Tone Society described the election as 'the most important to be held in Ireland since 1932', and its preference was for a government that would abandon the Anglo-Irish Free Trade Agreement, and oppose the take-over of the Irish economy by foreign capital.[30] It urged support for candidates 'whose policies most approximated those considered desirable'.[31]

The limited potential for any group to the left of Labour, and by implication for the alliance proposed by the modernisers, was illustrated by the performance of Sam Nolan of the IWP who took just 242 votes in Dublin Central, where the WTS held a pre-election meeting. The IWP issued *The Irish Way to Independence and Socialism* in April in which it pointed to the common analysis it shared with the republican movement but also stated that the leading force in a radical government would be the Labour movement. Following the election the *United Irishman* claimed that Labour had not done as well as it had hoped because it had not linked national unity to socialism and looked forward to the day when 'Republican-Socialist Ireland will sweep the polls'.[32]

IRA attacks on economic targets continued in the first part of 1969, particularly in the area under Mac Stiofáin's command. In his memoirs Johnston claims that Goulding felt he had to allow such actions in order to keep the militarists happy and that this was a cause of tension between himself and Goulding although most of the attacks were officially claimed through the Irish Republican Publicity Bureau. The first was on the property of Jackobus Holstein at Kilcock. In March, a house on the Ferrans Lock Estate was burnt because it had been bought by a German syndicate. The IRA demanded that it be purchased by the Land Commission and distributed among small farmers. Over 76,000 acres had been sold to non-Irish citizens since 1961, most of it to Germans.[33] The former SS member Otto Skorzeny, who owned 200 acres at Martinstown in County Kildare, was suspected by MI6 of having provided the money for the purchase of seventy estates by Germans from funds belonging to ODESSA,[34] and Irish military intelligence (G2) had been interested in Skorzeny in 1961 in relation to arms deals.[35]

The Irish Consul General in Hamburg reported that the IRA actions had been a 'godsend to those landowners who wanted to work up the German Government to protect their interests'.[36] On 11 June, just a week before polling day, buildings on three farms in Meath and Louth were burned down. One of the farms, at Drakerath Stud, Carlenstown, County Meath, had already been sold by its former owner, Johannes Koln, to the Land Commission although he was still living there at the time of the attack. One of the other farms attacked was also owned by a German but a third, at Oldbridge near Drogheda, was owned by Major D. H. Coddington. That was connected to a dispute concerning fishing rights on the Boyne. An IRA statement of 12 June demanded of Lynch 'what assurance can he give that a "Bay of Pigs" landing will not occur here should any future Irish Government attempt to recover this land now being bought by foreign cartels?'[37]

While the incidents in the Republic were of nuisance value, there were more serious developments north of the border. On 30 March a series of bombs led to power cuts across much of Belfast. The incidents were popularly attributed to the IRA but they had been carried out by loyalists including members of the Paisleyite Ulster Protestant Volunteers. There were further bombings on 4 April, at the waterworks at Dunadry, County Antrim; on 20 April at the Silent Valley reservoir, County Down, and at an electricity pylon at Kilmore, County Armagh; and on 24 and 26 April on the Lough Neagh to Belfast water pipeline. The attacks led to the deployment of British troops to guard key utilities, despite the implications that might have for morale within the RUC. There is no indication as to who Belfast believed had been responsible or that they believed it had been the IRA.[38]

The British chargé d'affaires in Dublin, Peter Piper, informed McCann of the troop deployment,[39] and Gilchrist advised London of Irish sensitivities and the danger that it might provoke a reaction from the IRA.[40] Gilchrist was told that the troops would not be undertaking border patrols and that a Security Liaison and Military Intelligence officer were being seconded to the RUC.[41] London had possibly been led to believe that the bombings were the work of republicans and its reaction was indicative of the realisation that it had taken its 'eye off the ball' and was forced to respond to a rapidly deteriorating situation exacerbated, as it now tacitly acknowledged, by poor and perhaps misleading intelligence from RUC Special Branch.

In response to Aiken's request to meet UN Secretary General U Thant on the crisis, London advised the New York Consul Lord Caradon to state that the problem in Northern Ireland was one of security and stability, not human rights.[42] Aiken assured Caradon that he had not requested a peace-keeping force,[43] although he had told U Thant that the Irish government would make a request if the situation deteriorated.[44] Gilchrist described Aiken's visit as 'shadow boxing for the benefit of their own public opinion' and said that Aiken had said that it was designed to lower tensions, based on the fear of instability spreading to the Republic.[45] On 3 May Lynch told Gilchrist that he was worried about the protests in Dublin and the infiltration of RTE by extremists,[46] something to which Berry had referred in his March memo on the IRA. Gilchrist had come back to a more relaxed view around the time of the Irish general election in June, which influenced the security services' assessment of the level of threat posed by Irish republicans and radicals.[47]

Interestingly Ambassador Gilchrist did not have a particularly high opinion of the Irish government, which he claimed was 'not backward in corruption' and was 'neglectful of its social obligations to its less fortunate citizens'. He was also aware that Fianna Fáil could not repudiate the desire for Irish unity because that would be exploited by the IRA. Fear of the IRA might then force the Irish government to 'appear to intervene' in the North.[48] Universal suffrage for local elections was introduced on 23 April but exacerbated the split within the Unionist Party that forced O'Neill to resign on 28 April. He was replaced by the anti-reformist James Chichester-Clark and the loyalist bombings that had helped to create the crisis that led to his downfall stopped. Lynch requested a meeting with Wilson to discuss the implications of the resignation but the British said that they could not do so until they had first met with the new Prime Minister.[49]

Despite the growing crisis in the North, republican Easter commemorations for the most part were 'disappointingly small'. Speaking in Belfast, Garland cited the 1932 Outdoor Relief riots as the model for working-class unity but also said that the IRA was unequivocally committed to forcing Britain to withdraw, and in Cork Goulding rejected demands that the civil rights movement should moderate its position. The IRA statement, however, attempted to cleave to the modernisers' programme, warning against the dangers of federalism and pledging to agitate around social issues.[50] The Sinn Féin cumann in Sligo was disbanded by the Ard Comhairle on 12 April when it refused to allow members of the Connolly Youth Movement and the Labour Party to take part in its Easter commemoration. Those expelled claimed that a new cumann established to replace it consisted almost entirely of CYM members, which in effect meant that, as in Cork, members of the Communist organisations were joining the republican movement and, as in the case of Jim Savage in Cork, assuming positions of local leadership. Belfast IRA members had also refused to vote for Betty Sinclair of the CPNI in elections to the NICRA executive.

Sinn Féin's dithering over the by-election for the Westminster constituency of Mid Ulster led to resignations of leading members of the movement in Tyrone including Thomas O'Connor, who was an Ard Comhairle member, Brian Quinn, who had been on the Army Council in 1966, and Kevin Mallon, later a leading Provisional. They claimed that abstentionism had no relevance to conditions in 1969 and would ensure the return of the Unionist. A republican meeting in Cookstown selected Kevin Agnew as an abstentionist candidate but he agreed to stand aside if another suitable candidate was found. Austin Currie of the Nationalist Party sought the nomination but he was unacceptable to republicans. Costello and Malachy McGurran met with Bernadette Devlin and pressed her to stand as an agreed, and presumably abstentionist, candidate but she refused to stand on this basis.[51] The republican movement then decided not to participate in the election but most local activists supported Devlin, including, paradoxically, many who were opposed to Sinn Féin taking seats, an illustration of the moralistic view which traditionalist republicans had of the state. Tom Mitchell, who had been proposed as a possible candidate, shared the frustration felt by local republicans who wished to contest and take the seat if it was won, but also felt that the civil rights movement was a means to destabilise the Six Counties leading to a popular uprising.[52] The Mid Ulster by-election was held on 17 April and Devlin was elected as the Unity candidate, defeating Unionist Anna Forrest by 33,648 votes to 29,437. Devlin, at 21, was the youngest woman ever elected to Westminster, where she insisted that a united Ireland was not on the agenda and that raising it would only benefit the 'Green and Orange Tories',[53] a sentiment that was in line with that of the modernisers despite their view of Devlin as an unreliable 'ultra-leftist'. During disturbances in Derry which followed Devlin's election the RUC broke into the house in the Bogside of Samuel Devenny who was badly beaten and later died of his injuries.

The tribunal appointed by O'Neill to investigate the Derry incidents of October 1968 reported in August 1969 and highlighted the diverging assessments of the role played by the IRA made by RUC Special Branch and the British security service. While the Report acknowledged, on the nationalist side, 'a widespread sense of political and social grievance', that was mirrored by Unionist concerns about 'the integrity, and indeed continued existence of the state'.[54] Such communal tensions were exploited by 'political subversive and mischievous elements' and it was noted that 'left-wing extremists' had infiltrated into positions of influence, among whom were Michael Farrell and Eamonn McCann. The latter had tried to prevent violence in Derry and Newry, but they were of the opinion that Devlin would countenance the use of force. The Report said that IRA stewards had exercised a restraining influence on protests, and that there was no evidence that IRA 'are in any sense dominant or in a position to control or direct policy of the CRA [NICRA]'. That contradicted Craig's claim that he had received MI5 intelligence proving that the IRA controlled NICRA, and Merlyn Rees later confirmed that MI5 had not been operating in Northern Ireland at the time.[55] The report placed more onus on the 'infiltration of the CRA both centrally and locally by subversive left-wing and revolutionary elements which were prepared to use the Civil Rights movement to further their own purposes'. To this was added the provocations of the Paisleyites at Burntollet and elsewhere, and 'inept' policing by the RUC. The report's reference to the role of Peoples Democracy and more militant elements illustrates the extent to which they had displaced the more cautious group supported by the republican leadership. It was they who succeeded in provoking the reaction from the state and loyalists that had been anticipated by many republicans and whose tactics commended themselves more to traditionalist IRA members than the quietist approach favoured by the modernisers and their Communist allies.

A report by the British Chief of General Staff Geoffrey Baker on 15 May described the RUC as 'poorly led and ministered'. Special Branch was operating on 'guesswork' rather than intelligence and had no idea who was responsible for the sabotage attacks, which was why the security service had seconded officers. Baker requested that Wilson should also insist that Chichester-Clark should accept assistance from Scotland Yard. While the decision to deploy the army to protect installations was justified, the Northern Ireland government needed to take more responsibility for security, leaving the army 'when required, as its accepted more mobile anti-IRA role'.[56] Despite Baker's report the British security service did not yet appear overly concerned with the threat posed by the IRA. Although it discussed the IRA on 16 June, a report on domestic subversion listed 'disruptive elements' in Northern Ireland only sixth in level of importance, on a par with Scottish and Welsh nationalists, and behind the CPGB, Trotskyists and anarchists, the KGB, fascists and immigrant and alien organisations.[57] The IRA had five hundred members in Northern Ireland and, while finances were low, morale was high. It referred to the development since 1966 'largely under Communist influence' of a strategy based on 'semi constitutional action designed to create a political situation favourable to a military takeover'. Stability was dependent on the IRA leadership's ability to maintain its 'present policy of peaceful penetration' under threat from militants within its own ranks and violence on the part of 'ultra Protestants'. It would find it hard to resist responding to such provocation and there was also the danger that 'the Communist element in the IRA might be tempted to encourage it to resume its traditionally violent role for disruptive purposes'. While aware of the pressure from the traditionalists it clearly misjudged the attitude of the modernising 'Communist element' to violence. It may have been true of some leftists like Costello but certainly not of those from a Communist background like Johnston and those most under their influence within the IRA. It also proves that its real fear was IRA violence rather than a leftist-inspired social revolution.

The security service's traditional enemy, the CPGB, found itself in a similar situation to the IRA leadership, faced by more unpredictable groups spawned by the student movement and the challenge to its hegemony of the trade union left by Trotskyists, something that also impacted upon the Communist Party of France during the 1968 crisis. London was informed by Dublin's belief that the IRA leadership had been won over to the concept of Leninist 'peaceful penetration' rather than the traditional republican project of organising periodic armed uprisings. Of course that view was challenged and overturned by the outbreak of open conflict in August 1969 and the revival of IRA violence, although the main military threat came, as predicted by the security service, from the 'militant' traditionalist element rather than the modernising left.

Gilchrist's comments on his encounters with Irish officials provide evidence of a growing concern about what the IRA might do in reaction to events in the North. Dublin's sources within the IRA were also most likely reporting that Goulding, Garland and Costello were for a time swayed towards a more militant line than advocated by Johnston and others. There was also the danger that general instability would create an environment more conducive to any group wishing to exploit it for politically subversive motives. Again the balance of evidence would suggest that the fact that it was the traditionalist faction that was intent on a military strategy undermines the modernist view that the Irish state perceived it to be its main adversary. The over-dependence on intelligence emanating from the modernist faction also weakened the initial response of the Irish and British authorities to the Provisionals and the upsurge of support for armed action by northern nationalists in which the Goulding IRA also, reluctantly at leadership level at any rate, participated for a time.

The modernisers did make some effort to assuage the suspicions of members and at Bodenstown in June Mac Giolla, while defending the changes that had taken place in the republican movement since1963, stressed that the movement remained 'socialist and separatist' and that Irish socialism was a 'native growth...Those who speak of socialism in a Free State context or in a UK context are fooling no-one but themselves.'[58] A key event that highlighted the growing divisions within the movement was the re-interment of Peter Barnes and James McCormick, who had been executed in 1940 for their part in an IRA bombing in Coventry in August 1939. The ceremony, at Mullingar on 6 July 1969, was one of a series of returns of remains of Irish republicans executed in Britain which Roy Johnston believed were a ploy to distract republicans from political work.[59] Far from pandering to republicans or wishing to 'distract' them, however, the Irish government was concerned that the IRA would use the occasion to mount a display of strength.[60] They had opposed the return of Dunne and Sullivan in 1967 and would have been 'better pleased' had no more taken place after the return of Casement.[61]

In his oration at Mullingar, the Belfast republican Jimmy Steele launched an attack on the modernisers for embracing Marxism and running down the IRA. One of the Dublin IRA firing party, Seán Dunne, recalled being outraged by Steele's speech and wondering whether he ought to shoot him![62] The *United Irishman* described the commemoration as a 'rallying point for the whole movement' but did not refer to Steele's oration,[63] nor did any of the national newspapers, other than a reference by the *Irish Press* to Steele's dubious description of the 1940s as a 'glorious one in Irish history'.[64] Goulding had Steele removed from the panel of republican speakers but attempts by the leadership to discipline dissenters carried little weight as by this time most had already left or begun to defy them openly. Mac Stiofáin played a key role in this as a serving member of the Army Council and the vital link between those in the North who were ready to establish an organisation separate from Dublin, and traditionalists throughout the rest of the country. *Hibernia*, which was generally sympathetic to the modernisers, criticised the event and stated that if the organisers were 'realistically concerned about Ireland they would be looking to the electorate and Leinster House rather than the deep cold well-spring of ultimate oblivion'.[65]

During July and August the Sinn Féin Ard Comhairle considered Johnston's report which recommended the acceptance of the proposals to establish an alliance of radical groups, and abandon abstentionism. The only concession made to opposition to an alliance with the CPNI and IWP was a proposal from Mick Ryan to omit their names. For Seán Ó Brádaigh that was a cynical manoeuvre in the light of the attempt at the 1968 Army Convention to create an actual merger.[66] Mac Stiofáin's attempt to blunt the NLF proposal by reducing it to a 'loose association' was defeated, as was a more explicit resolution from Caoimhín Mac Cathmhaoil to reject the NLF on the grounds that it would leave the republican movement open to being taken over. The proposal was approved by 10 votes to 8, and the recommendation to take seats by 11 to 8. The same proposal was passed by the Army Council in October by 12 votes to 8 and was to be put to an Army Convention and an extraordinary Ard Fheis on 19 October but that was deferred, on the proposal of Mac Stiofáin, because of the crisis in the North.

At GHQ meetings in May and July Ruairí Ó Brádaigh asked Goulding if there were any plans to defend northern nationalists in the event of a loyalist backlash. Goulding said that there were.[67] Goulding later told a meeting of IRA local OCs, however, that the onus, in the event of any crisis, would be on the British government to impose reforms and to disband the B Specials, and that the Irish government ought to be making that demand at international level, which indeed it was according to the British and Irish official papers. Roy Johnston claims that Goulding wanted to leave Belfast undefended as the ensuing situation would have forced the disbandment of the Specials.

There had been rioting following Orange parades, and on 14 July a 76-year-old Catholic, Francis McCloskey, was killed after being hit over the head by a RUC officer during disturbances at Dungiven, County Derry. The Secretary for State for Defence, Denis Healey, advised the Cabinet that withdrawing troops would be ill-advised as it might be seen as abandoning a Unionist government that was 'pursuing liberal policies' but that even if the Unionists reverted to a regressive position that withdrawal would be construed as abandoning the minority. The IRA would be encouraged by such a move and the Irish government might not be able to restrain them. At the time there were 3,420 soldiers in Northern Ireland.[68] The Cabinet Committee on the North attributed the 12 July disturbances to 'hooliganism' and was satisfied that none of the civil rights groups had been responsible.[69]

On 15 July the RUC B Special Constabulary was mobilised and the Unionists appeared intent on facing down the civil rights movement. Chichester-Clark persuaded the Home Secretary James Callaghan to increase the number of soldiers and also to allow the Apprentice Boys to march through Derry on 12 August, the event which precipitated the breakdown and set in train the 'Battle of the Bogside'. Disturbances spread to other nationalist areas across the North in an effort to relieve the Bogside, which in turn led to police and loyalist attacks during which hundreds of Catholic families in Belfast were forced out of their homes. In the midst of the violence, Lynch made a televised broadcast in which he claimed that the Stormont government had lost control of the situation and that the Irish government had asked the British to request that a UN peace-keeping force should be sent to the North. Devlin, who was in the Bogside, asked Austin Bolger of the Irish Department of Defence for Irish Army assistance, 'either officially or unofficially',[70] and the Army set up field hospitals on the Donegal side of the border. Devlin visited the United States the following week where the Irish Consul General in New York expressed concern over Devlin's radical connections. Devlin said that none of the money raised by her would go to the IRA, who she claimed had played no role in the crisis.[71] The Unionist Cabinet affected to be unfazed by what had happened and expressed concern that the crisis would be exploited by 'elements from the Republic'. It authorised the internment of known IRA members although that was not proceeded with.[72]

The Sinn Féin Ard Comhairle, temporarily persuaded of a more traditional response, declared that 'the question now is no longer civil rights but the continuance of British rule in Ireland' and called on the Irish government to demand the immediate withdrawal of British troops and the holding of an All Ireland election under UN supervision. If this was refused then the Irish government needed to deploy all its resources 'including military force if need be'. If it failed to do so then the Irish people needed to organise to take action themselves.[73]

On 14 August British troops were deployed on the streets. The following day the Irish Minister for External Affairs, Patrick Hillary, met with Lord Chalfont of the Foreign Office and Lord Stunham of the Home Office to request that the British should apply to the UN for a peace-keeping force or alternatively agree to a combined British and Irish force. Both requests were rejected. The Irish government succeeded in having the issue discussed by the

UN Security Council on 17 August. The British objected on the grounds that this was a violation of their sovereignty but Hillary was allowed to address the Council where he was supported by the Soviet representative. A decision was deferred on the proposal of Zambia. The British were clearly worried what the Irish response on the ground might be but were reassured by the Irish Army Adjutant General Brigadier McMullen that there was no plan for a general mobilisation[74] and that the Army's actions were designed to persuade the British to agree to a joint peace-keeping force.[75]

In September Childers told the Ambassador that the mobilisation had been to ensure that the IRA did not act.[76] Any hope that the Irish government might have had that the breakdown would persuade the British government to radically reappraise their attitude towards the constitutional position of Northern Ireland was dashed on 19 August in the joint communiqué with Chichester-Clark which affirmed that no change would take place in the position of Northern Ireland without the consent of Stormont. The British also made strong representations to Dublin to take 'all necessary steps' to put an end to IRA infiltration of the North.[77] Stewart was of the opinion that Irish claims that the IRA was weak was simply cover for their fear of taking it on.[78] The British believed that the Cabinet was split on the North and that Lynch was downplaying the importance of the IRA.[79] The Irish Labour Party leadership expressed strong support for the British Army remaining. The Irish government attempted to have the Northern crisis placed on the agenda of the General Assembly of the UN that began on 16 September. The General Committee met to consider this on 17 September where again the British requested Hillary to withdraw in order not to harm efforts at reform. When Devlin spoke with the Irish Consul General in New York, Charles Whelan, on 21 August she told him that she considered the Security Council resolution to be the best thing that the Irish government had ever done. Whelan was impressed with Devlin and her support for unification as the ultimate solution.[80]

The impact of the crisis was convulsive within the republican movement. The IRA was practically non-existent in Derry and had no weapons. In Belfast there were some weapons and local Volunteers played a role in the defence of areas that came under attack. For those who had already been sceptical about the direction in which the movement was going, the August events confirmed their worst fears and sealed the split between the embryonic Provisionals and Dublin GHQ. On 24 August the Belfast dissidents met in Casement Park and decided to use whatever money was available to buy arms with or without the approval of the Command staff.

While the *United Irishman* had looked forward to August with optimism, claiming that the civil rights movement had broken down sectarian barriers to such an extent to have thrown Unionism into a panic, its verdict on the

month's events was to conclude, more sombrely, that ' a tyranny that is maintained by force can ultimately be only overthrown by force'.[81] However, another
piece foresaw that any military clash between the British and/or Unionists and
the Irish army or IRA would be a disaster and that 'on the whole the situation
demands diplomacy rather than force'. The best option remained a reformed
Stormont. All of the demands of the civil rights movement had to be conceded
and northern representatives allowed sit in the Dáil. It was not a revolutionary
situation but it could become a 'training ground' for revolution. Another
article argued the need to avoid 'extremist' demands such as an end to Partition. The contradictions were illustrated by another article which exaggerated
the role of the IRA in defence of Belfast nationalists while Mac Dara looked
forward to the 'final victory'.

The leadership was under severe pressure to do something and set up a
Northern Defence Fund to raise money to buy weapons. Mac Stiofáin clashed
with Goulding over the use of the Defence Fund. Goulding wanted it to go
towards the general support of the movement whereas Mac Stiofáin insisted
that it should all be used to buy weapons. Goulding won the argument and
in turn Mac Stiofáin persuaded several large donors, who he said were unconnected to Fianna Fáil, to withhold their money from the IRA and give it to
the dissidents.[82] The Army Council also issued a statement which claimed that
the IRA had been mobilised along the border and lauded the Volunteers who
had been forced reluctantly to take action and said that the only acceptable
solution was a British withdrawal and the creation of a workers' and farmers'
republic. Goulding needed to reassure IRA militants but Gilchrist believed
that Johnston was exerting his influence to hold back the IRA but that there
was the danger that 'Johnstonism' would be purged and the IRA would embark
on violent actions.[83]

Mac Stiofáin regarded the IRA statement as a fig leaf to conceal the leadership's lack of preparedness and as a ploy to ensure that Stormont was not
abolished, by appearing to confirm the Unionist claim that the violence had
been initiated by republicans.[84] The Officials later justified the statement on
the grounds that it made it 'even harder for Chichester-Clark to accept the
disbandment of the Specials', and that the Downing Street Declaration was
proof that the statement had had 'its desired effect'.[85] Given that Johnston
believed that Goulding was hoping that the B Specials would be disbanded,
it is difficult to know exactly what their strategy was. The Army Council statement also called on the Irish government to deploy the Irish army to defend
nationalists and to raise the issue at the United Nations, which again contra-
dicts Johnston's and Coughlan's claim that they needed to avoid turning the
crisis into an issue of national sovereignty. Lynch responded angrily, stating
that the government would not tolerate the 'usurpation of their powers by
any group whatsoever'.[86] Gardaí baton-charged protestors at the British

Embassy on 16 August, which pleased Gilchrist as he had felt that they had been 'half-hearted' in resisting protestors two days before.[87]

A document for internal IRA distribution admitted that the IRA had been unprepared but that they were now in a strong political position and could use this to push the demand for an all-Ireland solution centred on a constitutional convention. Defence would be addressed through support for local committees. The modernisers, however, when they realised the strength of the demand from the committees for arms, quickly distanced themselves from the defence committees and accused them of being creatures of Fianna Fáil-funded dissidents. A meeting of IRA OCs and Army Council members on 17 August was advised that they should not respond with armed action. Goulding was there and it was assumed that he agreed with Coughlan. Mick Ryan was appointed as Quartermaster General to replace Pat Regan in August in order to intensify arms procurements.

By October the more cautious line again dominated official movement statements and there was less reference to any prospects for Irish unity. The *United Irishman* continued to issue warnings about federalism, and even claimed absurdly that the Irish government was preparing to join NATO because the Army was now using NATO standard paint on its vehicles. Republicans needed to unite with other radicals to oppose Fianna Fáil's 'neo-unionism' and Ó Tuathail warned that a British withdrawal without social change would be meaningless.[88] This further exasperated Ruairí Ó Brádaigh, who saw it as evidence of the leadership's complete lack of understanding of what was going on. As far as he and other traditionalists were concerned, they were responding to the situation with meaningless rhetoric and had opportunistically temporarily adopted a militant stance in the immediate aftermath of the August events in order to capitalise on public anger.[89]

On 16 August a meeting took place in the headquarters of the Communist Party of Great Britain at which Michael O'Riordan represented the IWP, Hughie Moore and James Stewart the CPNI, and John Gollan, George Matthews and R. Palme Dutt were among the CPGB representatives. Greaves and Seán Redmond were present on behalf of the Irish Committee of the CPGB, which in effect was the leadership of the Connolly Association. While the meeting agreed that the events in Derry and Belfast had brought about an unforeseen crisis, they did not believe that this required any radical reassessment of strategy based on non-violence and the hope that stability would lead to a Bill of Rights.[90]

That perspective was given an extended rehearsal in *The Northern Crisis: Which Way Forward* which was written by Coughlan and published soon after the August events by Solidarity for United Political Action on the North, formed to promote the view that the denial of civil rights rather than Partition was the main cause of the crisis. Its sponsors included the Reverend Terence

McCaughey of the Anti-Apartheid Movement, Peadar O'Donnell, and the NICRA and CPNI member Noel Harris. The Department of External Affairs bought 30 copies of Coughlan's pamphlet for £1 but it was not distributed.[91] The Commonwealth Office believed that Coughlan, despite his 'apparent Sinn Féin background', had sought to give a 'constructive and balanced view'.[92] Neither government was seemingly too concerned about Coughlan's claim that they were part of a plan to federate the entire island within the UK. Coughlan conceded that most people agreed with the Irish government's contention that until Partition ended there would be no long-term solution[93] but warned against seeing the crisis as the precursor to achieving a republic, much less a socialist republic. He contrasted the 'disciplined' approach of republicans to that of the younger activists and opposed the demand to abolish Stormont, the alternative to which would not be a united Ireland but direct rule from Westminster.

Although the report of the enquiry into the August 1969 events under the chairmanship of Lord Justice Scarman was not published until 1972, its evidence was mainly compiled in the immediate aftermath of the crisis and again, as with Cameron, contradicted the RUC Special Branch view that the IRA had deliberately engineered the violence. A week before Derry, Special Branch told the Minister for Home Affairs that while it would 'be absurd to say the present situation has been brought about solely by the machinations of the Movement', that 'the tactics employed over the past year are laid down or find a place in their official documents'.[94] The Tribunal, however, concluded that while 'the IRA had, we were assured, a plan for subversion: no doubt it always has had…there was no plot to overthrow the Government or to mount an armed insurrection'.

The RUC claimed that 'Johnston's Connollyite/Communist planning policies' began in autumn 1965,[95] and included a plan to set up and control organisations like NICRA, and that two-thirds of the local NICRA groups and that six of the 14-person executive were members of the movement. In contrast, the British security service concluded that the civil rights movement was not controlled by the IRA and Communists, and that NICRA was an 'uneasy coalition' of republicans, Communists and liberals in which the Communists had made little headway.[96] In any event, the British clearly considered 'Johnstonism' to be a moderating factor. The Minister for Technology, Tony Benn, recorded that on 19 August Callaghan had informed the Cabinet that the Security Service had contradicted the RUC view of the IRA's role in instigating the crisis.[97]

A *Sunday Times* report of 24 August estimated that the IRA had between a thousand and twelve hundred members in the Republic. That information, based on Berry's March memo, had been given to news editors by Lynch at a meeting held in July when Lynch was apparently preparing to move against the organisation as recommended by Berry. *Hibernia* said that the crisis had made it difficult for the government to act.[98] That view was shared by Gilchrist, who felt that Lynch was forced to take a militant line for fear of being outflanked by republicans.[99] Interestingly the Joint Intelligence Committee concluded that Dublin was possibly exaggerating the IRA threat in order to justify its 'unhelpful attitude'.[100]

The events of August 1969 and the approval given by the Ard Comhairle to the report of the Garland Commission made a split in Sinn Féin and the IRA inevitable. An IRA meeting on 17 August at Ballinamore, County Leitrim, held under the cover of an Education Department seminar and chaired by Tom Mitchell, failed to persuade dissidents that there would be an adequate response to any further attacks and a meeting was organised in Lurgan in September at which O Conaill was appointed as the military adviser to the northern defence committees. Jim Lane, who was there, describes the meeting as having been 'a sounding board for what later became the Provo movement'.[101]

The split within the republican movement and the organisation of a new armed group, based initially on the defence committees which were dominated by republican dissidents, was paralleled by the intervention of a number of government Ministers in co-operation with Army Intelligence officers who had made contact with the dissidents. It was those contacts that formed the basis for the April 1970 arms trial and the allegation that either the government or a faction of the Cabinet had deliberately supplied money and weapons to what became the Provisional IRA, as part of a plot to split the republican movement and/or remove Goulding and his supporters. Captain James Kelly, an Irish Army Intelligence Officer, was in the Bogside and reported to the head of Army Intelligence Colonel Michael Hefferon and was ordered to cultivate whatever contacts he had made. On 17 August several people from the North called to Kelly's home in Dublin seeking weapons and he passed them on to the Cabinet sub-committee.[102]

A Cabinet meeting of 16 August had taken a decision to authorise making available money to defend nationalists in Northern Ireland. This became known as the Grant-in-Aid fund. £100,000 was set aside for that purpose and a Cabinet sub-committee was established to deal with the North, comprising Minister for Finance Charles Haughey, Minister for Agriculture Neil Blaney, Minister for Education Padraig Faulkner and Joe Brennan, a TD for Donegal/Leitrim. The government also decided to fund the publication of a newspaper, which became the *Voice of the North*. That money appears to have been made available from the fund until at least January 1970[103] and the newspaper also received money from military intelligence and other sources. The first editor of the *Voice* was Seamus Brady who had worked for the *Irish Press* and was employed by a number of state agencies as a Public Relations Officer.

Following the split, the Official republican movement, as the Goulding wing of the IRA and Sinn Féin was described in the media, claimed that far more than £100,000 had been available, as the sub-committee, or at least Haughey and Blaney, also had access to considerable amounts of money from businessmen who contributed to Fianna Fáil.[104] They cited as proof the fact that a friend of Padraig Faulkner, Naughton, who was a director of the GEC company based in Dunleer, County Louth, had met with a Goulding supporter from Belfast on 17 August and offered to supply him with £150,000. According to the Belfast man, Naughton also sought assurances regarding what the IRA intended to do with the weapons and its position in the Republic. While this became the basis for the Officials' claim that Fianna Fáil was trying to destroy the republican left, the fact that those donating money for arms to the IRA for defence in the North sought assurances that those arms would not be used in the Republic was hardly sinister.

The British knew immediately about the activities of people like Kelly in the North, and on 14 August Gilchrist told London that he suspected that there was 'something more' to the Irish response than the visible activities of the Army along the border[105] and that the Irish government had given the IRA 'liberty of action'.[106] On 9 September Gilchrist reported that several undercover Irish Army officers, including a Lieutenant Dennis Parsons, were in the North.[107] Gilchrist's information was most likely coming from political and Garda contacts in Dublin who were concerned about the links between Ministers, Army Intelligence and the IRA. Apart from their contacts with people who they presumably knew were in the IRA, the Cabinet sub-committee also bizarrely had dealings with the Saor Eire Action Group, which had established a Citizens Committee that was given the use of part of a building in Kildare Street owned by New Ireland Assurance Company. Certainly, leading members of Saor Eire were intimately involved in attempts to import weapons.

Haughey apparently initiated contact with Goulding through his brother Padraig, or Jock, Haughey[108] and also through a priest, Fr Dore, who was based in London. Goulding met Padraig Haughey in London on 18 August where Haughey asked Goulding if the IRA would be able to obtain weapons if they were given money. Goulding told them that they would but that they would require at least £50,000. He was given £1,500. On his return, Goulding told an IRA GHQ meeting that one of the conditions placed on the money by Haughey was the removal of Johnston. Dáithí O Conaill is alleged to have intervened over the objections of others to insist that they should agree to the condition. 'We want guns', he shouted.[109] In his evidence to the Committee of Public Accounts, the head of Special Branch, Chief Superintendent John Fleming, confirmed Goulding's story about the £50,000 requested from Haughey, an indication of the calibre of intelligence emanating from those close to Goulding.[110] Haughey strongly denied having given Goulding any money.

Padraig Haughey also met with Mick Ryan, the IRA Quartermaster General, soon after the fighting in Derry and Belfast. Apparently Goulding told Ryan to accept only rifles and not short arms. Eoin O Murchú who supported Goulding in the split believes now that the Officials' theory that the contacts were part of a plot to derail the republican left was too simplistic and that Haughey and others were reacting both to the pressure of events and to the urgings of republican elements within Fianna Fáil who wanted action taken in defence of the northern nationalists.[111] Jack McCabe, a leftist who supported the Provisionals, shared that view and dismissed the theory that it was motivated by a desire to destroy the left within the IRA.[112] Certainly it would have made little sense for Haughey to have given money to Goulding if the objective was to use Goulding's opponents within the IRA to stage a coup against him. It is also clear that all of the principals in the affair on the government side, and certainly Haughey as a former Justice Minister, would have been well informed regarding the IRA. Indeed one of their main contacts in the IRA was quite possibly a Garda informer although whether that was known to Haughey is more questionable, although he must surely have been aware that Special Branch had excellent intelligence from within the IRA and that therefore any contact he had with the IRA Army Council would be reported to the Gardaí.

Although the Cabinet approved the Grant-in-Aid only in August, the Officials claimed that the first contacts between elements in Fianna Fáil and the IRA were made in early 1969 when a South Derry businessman who was friendly to Neil Blaney allegedly approached the local IRA OC, Francie Donnelly, with an offer of arms and money. Donnelly referred this to Goulding who urged him to maintain the contact but apparently very little came of it.[113] After the August events, the contacts were reactivated when Donnelly and Blaney met twice; at Mallin, County Donegal, in September, and in the Shelbourne Hotel, Dublin, in October. On 22 September Brady and Captain Kelly were said to have called to Donnelly's home and proposed that, if Goulding, Costello and Ryan were removed from the leadership and socialist policies abandoned, a separate Northern Command would be supplied with arms.[114]

It was also later claimed that a meeting between Army Intelligence Officers, accompanied by Padraig Haughey, and members of the IRA Army Council took place in September 1969 in Rathmines where the officers said that they were there with Minister for Defence Jim Gibbons's consent and wanted to know what the IRA's requirements were. According to Prionsias Mac Aonghusa, the IRA rejected the offer of arms but requested money. At a later meeting Army Intelligence was alleged to have requested that Goulding,

Costello and Johnston should be replaced by Garland and that the IRA should move its arms and GHQ north of the border and cease all southern agitations. At this stage the IRA ended negotiations.[115] Why those allegedly attempting to destroy the republican left should have chosen Garland was not explained and did not appear in any Official accounts. Garland was, however, at odds with Goulding and Johnston over IRA strategy and policy for a period after the split when he was said to have been close to American Trotskyist Gerry Foley.[116] Interestingly, Garland was not in Ireland at that time, having fled the country following an IRA armed robbery at Dublin airport in May 1969.[117]

According to a Justice Department report, Haughey met Mick Ryan in September and told him that IRA weapons being moved to the North would not be interfered with by the Gardaí on the condition that the IRA stopped attacking German-owned property.[118] Ironically, Seán Mac Stiofáin was organising those attacks, which were greatly disapproved of by Goulding supporters like Johnston who also regarded Mac Stiofáin as one of the key figures in the alleged plot to split the IRA. In the statement issued by the Meath IRA expressing their support for the Provisionals, they also claimed responsibility for an attack on a German-owned farm on 7 January 1970.

The calibre of the intelligence available to Special Branch and the manner in which it was used to frustrate the arms shipments and to move against Haughey and Blaney raises the interesting question as to where Special Branch was getting its information and the motivation behind the leaking of that information. The Official IRA account of those contacts, as published in the 1971 pamphlet *Fianna Fáil – the IRA Connection*, was based on the transcript of a taped conversation between Goulding, Liam McMillan who was the Belfast OC in 1969, and Malachy McBurney. It sought both to justify their contacts with the Irish state and to rehearse the conspiracy theory regarding the alleged plot to destroy the republican left. The Garda intelligence regarding those contacts – and some of it is similar to that contained in the Official pamphlet but not publicly heard until the Committee of Public Accounts hearings in 1971 – could have come only from some person or persons directly involved. He or they were supportive of the Goulding faction in the IRA and wanted to sabotage the arms supply to the traditionalists, thus serving the interests of both the modernisers and Special Branch.

All of the information given by Goulding to the IRA Army Council regarding the contacts was also couched in a manner designed to encourage them to reject the offer of arms on the basis that it came with the condition of jettisoning himself and socialism. It is quite clear that the state itself and Fianna Fáil were divided between various political and security tendencies with regard to how to deal with the northern crisis and the IRA. It also seems clear that Captain James Kelly believed that he was acting with the authority of the government and Army Intelligence whereas Special Branch was also monitoring the contacts and that intelligence was later used as the basis of charges against Kelly and others in the Arms Trial.[119] It is also curious that Kelly's contacts with Goulding and his supporters continued well after the *de facto* establishment of a separate armed group, through the defence committees, and that money continued to be given to Goulding supporters even at a time when there were open allegations about Fianna Fáil attempting to split or take over the IRA. Fleming claimed that Kelly met Goulding in Virginia, County Cavan, in late September 1969 and agreed to organise the supply of weapons to the IRA in the north as well as training for IRA Volunteers at the Irish Army camp at Gormanstown. On 27 September a meeting to establish a co-ordinating group for the Citizens Defence Committees was held in Lurgan. The Belfast IRA OC Jim Sullivan, who was a Goulding supporter, told the meeting that himself, Paddy Kennedy and Paddy Devlin were going to Dublin to meet with a senior government member and that arms and training would be provided by the Irish army. Jim Lane, who was present, understood them to be referring to Charles Haughey.[120]

Kelly met with IRA people again in early October at Bailieboro and promised £50,000 in a series of instalments. On 7 October Kelly gave Goulding £7,000, a further £1,000 at a meeting in late November and £1,500 in December.[121] This was after the *United Irishman* had revealed what it claimed to be a plot to destroy or capture the republican movement. Kelly said that those he met in Baileboro were members of the northern defence committees. He had been made aware a few weeks after the meeting, by the Head of Military Intelligence, Michael Hefferon, that the Taoiseach had expressed concern over the contacts. Fleming also alleged that Neil Blaney's brother Harry had given the IRA 'quite large sums of money' beginning in September.

Although the Grant-in-Aid account was opened only on 9 October, the first transfer of money to the IRA was made on 7 October. Fleming admitted that he had no idea where this originated but that it may have been from private sources. Fleming said that he became aware of Kelly's contacts with the IRA and of the passing of money from Kelly, Haughey and Blaney to the IRA, from 'reliable sources', which were presumably within the IRA, and that, when this was passed on to his superiors, the Minister for Justice, Micheál O Moráin, had told him to monitor the situation. From his further investigations, Fleming discovered that at least one arms consignment and possibly as many as three came through Dublin airport in early September 1969. Padraig Haughey had arranged the safe landing and transfer of the weapons to the IRA. A later attempt by Padraig Haughey and John Kelly in November to purchase arms was abandoned when they became aware that they were under surveillance and that the person who was to supply the weapons, a Malcolm Randall, was working for British Intelligence.[122]

Fleming said that he had no evidence to suggest that Captain Kelly was attempting to split the IRA. He also stated that, while Kelly might not have known which members of the northern delegations he met were members of the IRA, he ought, as an Intelligence Officer, to have known the southern ones: 'He met Cathal Goulding on umpteen occasions. Surely as a serving Army Intelligence Officer he should know the Chief of Staff of the IRA at that period.'[123] Fleming told the Committee for Public Accounts that most of his information came from an informant, or informants, within the IRA. It is interesting to note that Fleming claimed that Kelly met Goulding so many times, which is not the impression derived from Goulding's own account which refers only to one direct contact.

In his history of the arms crisis O'Brien accepts that the source or sources of the information on the arms shipments were Goulding supporters who hoped to encourage Lynch to take action against Blaney.[124] That raises the interesting scenario that Goulding was wittingly or unwittingly passing on information about his contacts with Kelly to an informer or informers that was being passed on to Special Branch. Roy Johnston believes that he knows the identity of one high-placed informer 'whose motivation I am inclined to think could have been actually political, in furtherance of the Goulding plan'[125] and that there were

> two members of the Army Council exchanging information with two different Government departments during the 60s' and that the Govt [*sic*] actually wanted the IRA to remain in existence as such, because it gave them the excuse to use repression against any emergent left. They made sure it happened from two angles. The 'arms trial' story sort of confirms this, because there is no doubt that the effect was to nip in the bud effectively what the politicisers were trying to do.[126]

However, Johnston's description of one of the informers, and indeed the intelligence assessments of his own role, would suggest that the state was encouraging the IRA to move away from militarism, which would obviously make sense given that its main concern regarding the IRA was the possibility that it would engage in acts of violence in the Republic. With the breakdown of civil order in the North, however, the priority for many within Fianna Fáil, with or without approval from Lynch, was defence of the northern Catholics, and it was this rather than some plot to destroy a mythical leftist threat that underlay their supplying of weapons to the IRA.

On 10 November Gilchrist reported that the Minister for Finance, Haughey, was running a 'trans-border' operation, paid for from Fianna Fáil party funds. It gathered intelligence and distributed money to civil rights people but its main activity was journalistic, obviously a reference to Seamus Brady and the *Voice of the North*. The group was preparing lists of defence committees who would be supplied with weapons in the event of another attack on nationalist communities: 'Numerous weapons have already been supplied, not on the responsibility of the organisation itself but by people who have been given access to the lists.' Gilchrist believed that this was a part of the Irish government's attempt to sideline McAteer and other conservative nationalists and forge contacts with IRA-connected militants. Conor Cruise O'Brien did not believe that Haughey was serious about the plans but wished them to become known to boost his own image. O'Brien told Gilchrist that Lynch had only lately become aware of Haughey's activities and was 'much perturbed'.[127]

Gilchrist had several sources on what was going on including the writer Constantine Fitzgibbon who moved in the same circles as many leading politicians. Fitzgibbon had also undertaken a 'fact finding' tour of the North in late September and asked Gilchrist what line he would like him to put across in his articles. Haughey obviously knew of Fitzgibbon's relationship with the Embassy and asked him to convey to Gilchrist his view that direct British rule was both 'inevitable and necessary'.[128] Gilchrist met Haughey on 4 October at Kinsealy where Haughey apparently told the Ambassador that, if the British were prepared to come to an arrangement with the Irish government on incorporating the North into the Republic, Dublin would be willing to consider rejoining the Commonwealth and allowing the British the use of the old 'Treaty' ports.[129]

Claims by the modernisers about Fianna Fáil infiltration of the republican movement began in October 1969 as the Goulding faction began to foresee the inevitability of a split, effectively drawing attention to the ongoing official contacts with the IRA over money and arms. The *London Evening Standard* of 14 October 1969 published an article which claimed that Fianna Fáil was intervening in the republican movement to support 'right-wing' opponents of the leadership by providing them with arms and training. The timing of the article is interesting as the account to facilitate the transfer of money to the IRA had been opened the previous week and Goulding had personally been given £7,000 on 7 October.[130] It was also at a time when continuing efforts were being made to import weapons so presumably the allegations were at the very least designed to draw attention to that. The article was written by its Defence correspondent, Tom Pocock, who had met Roy Johnston in Dublin. Pocock said that he had been told that three members of the Cabinet as well as Irish Army officers and the 'Donegal Mafia' were supporting the 'right'.[131]

The *United Irishman* held a news conference in the Gresham Hotel on 30 October at which Seamus Ó Tuathail alleged that Fianna Fáil were attempting to destroy the republican movement. Ó Tuathail claimed that the *United Irishman* had spent two months investigating the infiltration and that 'Messrs Blaney, Haughey and Boland are seeking to buy their way into control of Civil

Rights policy in the North so as to ensure that there will be no opposition from Civil Rights while Fianna Fáil concocts the Federalist deal with Britain which is now being planned'. That was at the very least disingenuous given that Goulding supporters had had regular meetings with the 'infiltrators', had received money from them and indeed continued to receive money from them. The federalist 'deal' referred to was alleged to have been agreed, in 1965, under British supervision, between Lemass and O'Neill and would involve the establishment of two regional parliaments in Dublin and Belfast with devolved powers from Westminster.

The *United Irishman* claimed to have evidence for the conspiracy in a speech made by Lynch during a Dáil debate on 22 October in which he said that 'as a practical matter' the government had accepted the existence of Stormont 'exercising certain powers devolved on it by the British Parliament' and suggested that those powers might be retained during a transition to a united Ireland.[132] That proposal had been made by Irish politicians intermittently since the 1920s and resurfaced against the background of the crisis. Neil Blaney had put it forward in April as a staging post to unity if the British were prepared to surrender the requisite powers to a Federal Council. Gilchrist regarded this as political opportunism on Blaney's part but raised it with Hugh McCann who claimed there was 'nothing new' in the proposal and that the Earl of Home when Commonwealth Secretary had discussed it with McCann when he had been the Ambassador in London.[133] H. T. Morgan of the Dublin Embassy described Lynch's proposal as 'vague and impractical'.[134] A Commonwealth Office paper on relations with Dublin stated that federalism might be a useful means of persuading the Irish population to regard unity as a 'distant and peaceful objective'. While it could not be seen to openly support federalism, London should encourage it,[135] which would suggest that the British were not part of any 'plot' to inveigle the Republic back into the UK as alleged by republicans.

The *United Irishman* claimed that the 'spearhead' of the plan to impose federalism was a group around the *Voice of the North* headed by Adrian Corrigan and Seamus Brady, thus tying the theory to accusations that Fianna Fáil was attempting to take over the civil rights movement. Interestingly, the emphasis on NICRA as the target shifted to the republican movement only after the split, and direct attacks on people within NICRA ceased when the Officials and Communists managed to capture control of the organisation. Nor is the *United Irishman's* claim that the *Voice of the North* was designed to impose a Fianna Fáil ideology on the civil rights movement borne out by an analysis of its contents which were not only a range of views from left to right; it also published articles highly critical of Fianna Fáil not only under Lynch but historically.

The first issue of the *Voice of the North* appeared on 12 October, three days after the Grant-in-Aid money became available. It was printed by the *Anglo-Celt* in Cavan. Although Brady claimed to have believed that the paper was funded from money secured by the northerners from sources other than the Grant-in-Aid, he later told the Committee of Public Accounts that he assumed that the *Voice* was 'an official underground operation on behalf of the Government propaganda unit'.[136] He also claimed that Lynch had objected to the content of the third issue because it featured a front-page photograph of the Stormont MP Paddy Devlin, who was close to Goulding supporters in Belfast, and had criticised the Taoiseach. Lynch then ordered the cutting off of all funds to the *Voice*. O'Brien agrees that the decision by Lynch to end funding for the paper and the strongly critical line which the *Voice* had towards Fianna Fáil policy on partition sits uncomfortably with the theory that it was a tool in a government plot to take over the civil rights movement and/or the republican movement.[137]

Despite the claim that Fianna Fáil was trying to 'buy' the civil rights movement and split the IRA, Goulding supporters continued to receive money from the Clones bank account until at least 6 November 1969 and the Belfast Official IRA continued to be given money up to the end of January 1970. A curious sideline to the issue of the IRA's money is that the channelling of money to them from official and officially connected sources took place alongside an unprecedented series of armed robberies which led to the placing of armed Gardaí on Dublin banks. While many of the robberies were carried out by people who were members of the Saor Eire Action Group, Volunteers loyal to Goulding were also involved. That included a major robbery in Dublin airport in 1968 in which £25,000 was stolen. Seán Garland went on the run to Scotland for a period after this.

While the Officials were busy promoting the theory that Fianna Fáil had founded the Provos, the Kelly/Haughey link to the Officials also continued to surface from time to time after the split. When Seamus Dowling of Newry, a member of NICRA, was arrested in possession of weapons at a suspected OIRA training camp near Dundalk on 8 November 1970, Captain Kelly attempted to give evidence in Dowling's defence. The prosecution objected on the grounds that Kelly's evidence would breach the Official Secrets Act but Dowling himself claimed that the arms had been provided by the Irish government. The jury accepted this and returned a verdict of not guilty. Fleming was questioned about Dowling's claim at Committee of Public Accounts where it was suggested that Dowling was a member of the Official IRA but Fleming refused to comment.[138]

By that stage, however, events had developed their own momentum and whatever plans either the Irish government or a faction within that government may have had with regard to exercising influence over the IRA had been undermined by a crisis that was beyond anyone's control. It is also clear that the British security service had abandoned its *laissez faire* attitude which had prevailed through the 1960s. It was forced to do so by the obvious deficiencies of RUC Special Branch and by the fact that the IRA now presented a domestic threat far beyond that of the subversive elements enumerated by the JIC as more serious menaces as recently as June 1969. For both factions within the republican movement the crisis had brought about a situation in which they as much as any other of the actors were caught unprepared and forced to reappraise their strategies radically.

Following the traumatic effect of the August events within the movement, all that remained was for an Army Convention and an Ard Fheis to formalise the split. There was no IRA convention scheduled for 1969 so an extraordinary meeting had to be arranged. Delegates to the convention were selected from local units although there were allegations that Goulding supporters rigged selection conventions. Goulding travelled to the United States in November in an effort to organise support and finance and in San Francisco he told an audience that the IRA was raising money to buy arms for defence and that the eventual solution would come through armed struggle. In Ireland Goulding was receiving public money ostensibly to buy weapons but was retaining it for other purposes.

IRA Volunteers decided between the differing factions for a wide range of reasons. Jim Monaghan, who was on the run following the abduction of Joseph Carey who the IRA believed was an agent provocateur, attended a selection convention in the Laois/Offaly area. He was close to both Garland and Mac Stiofáin and believes that many republicans based their decision on personal contacts and loyalties. He says that he decided to support the dissidents because they seemed to be more committed to organising a military campaign.[139] Seán Dunne believes that there were contradictory elements at work among those who took sides. The split among Dublin Volunteers was not on simple left/right lines. Some of those who opposed the leadership had been key activists in social agitations, while more conservative elements supported Goulding from either organisational or personal loyalty.[140] Seán Garland argues that most of those who supported the Provisionals had been inactive for years or had been opposed on ideological grounds to the new strategy.[141] Seán Ó Brádaigh on the other hand claims that many of those who were alleged to have left the movement had in fact been forced out or sidelined.[142] Journalists like Proinsias Mac Aonghusa who were sympathetic to the modernisers were happy to go along with the 'Fianna Fáil plot' and in *Hibernia* Mac Aonghusa claimed that their objective was to undermine support for the 'left', although he believed the main target was Peoples Democracy rather than Sinn Féin.[143]

While the events in Belfast provided a crucial backdrop to the Army Convention, the Belfast IRA did not send delegates, having decided, as a compromise between Goulding supporters led by the Belfast OC Billy McMillen and dissidents led by Billy McKee, not to participate in the debate on abstentionism. Ruairí Ó Brádaigh and other southern traditionalists tried to persuade the Belfast dissidents to take part in the Convention but they said they would not as that would imply acceptance of the Goulding Army Council. The Convention met at Knockvicar, County Roscommon, on the night of 13 December and continued into the early hours of the 14th. Seamus Costello was in charge of making the arrangements for delegates to be picked up at various locations, and it has been alleged that some of those known to be opposed to the leadership were not collected. One of those sidelined was the former Cork OC Eddie Williams who claimed not to have been informed of either the October Army Council meeting or the Convention.[144]

In his address to delegates Goulding appealed for support on the basis that the Irish government was attempting to destroy the IRA because of its fears over a left-wing republican movement. He linked that to the offers of arms from official sources and said that he had told the Irish Army Intelligence Officer whom he had met that he would accept arms and money only if the government ceased trying to force political changes on the republican movement.[145] The Convention supported the proposals contained in the Garland Report by 39 votes to 12. Goulding later claimed that Mac Stiofáin wanted the abstentionist issue to be dealt with despite Goulding's desire that it be deferred. However, Costello also wanted to force the matter to a conclusion and so a vote was taken. Mac Stiofáin, as spokesperson for the dissidents, then let it be known that they no longer felt themselves under any allegiance to the leadership. Mac Stiofáin also refused to allow himself to be nominated to the Executive. Instead, he later met with Belfast dissidents and they elected a 12-member Executive which selected the first Army Council of the Provisional IRA on 18 December. Its members were Mac Stiofáin, as Chief of Staff, Ruairí Ó Brádaigh, O Conaill, Joe Cahill and Leo Martin from Belfast, Seán Treacy from Laois and Patrick Mulcahy from Limerick. On 28 December the Provisionals issued a statement claiming that the majority of IRA Volunteers supported the dissident Army Council and that the decision of the Convention had been the logical outcome of the 'obsession with parliamentary politics' and the undermining of the IRA which was exposed by the August events.[146]

In an attempt to take some of the wind out of the Provisionals' sails Goulding organised a meeting in Armagh on 7 January 1970 to establish a Northern Command independent of Dublin GHQ, something which his own supporters claimed had been the object being pursued by Fianna Fáil. Goulding supporters, however, maintained that, by conceding the demand for a separate command, the leadership had addressed the stated main concern of the dissidents and thus proved that in leaving anyway they were following a different agenda. A statement from the meeting condemned the Provisionals for having created division and said that 'Fianna Fáil has already succeeded in planting one of its agents in this group'.[147]

In a preview of the Ard Fheis, Dick Walsh of the *Irish Times*, who was sympathetic to the modernisers, referred to the proposal to drop abstentionism as part of a strategy launched in 1966 to win an electoral majority within five years. While that was unlikely he did believe that Sinn Féin might hold the balance of power. He also claimed that Partition would become less of an issue as Sinn Féin concentrated on social and economic policies. The weeks between the Convention and the Ard Fheis witnessed an intense internal battle over cumainn delegates, IRA units and weapons. As this proceeded, many areas issued statements indicating which side they were taking. In late December the North Kerry Sinn Féin Executive condemned what it said was an attempt by the Goulding faction to rig the Ard Fheis and claimed that what was happening was the outcome of 'the deceit and treachery which has been going on in the Republican movement for the past five years'.[148]

The *United Irishman* was adamant that the *Irish Press* was a key element in the Fianna Fáil plot to split the republican movement, and that *Irish Press* Political Correspondent Michael Mills was a conduit for Fianna Fáil money given to the Provisionals. Apparently, Mills had addressed a meeting of dissidents on 14 September and a few days later had set up a meeting between a Goulding loyalist from Belfast and Neil Blaney. Publicly there is no evidence that Mills did favour the dissidents. In fact he praised the outcome of the Convention which he said was a reflection of the strength of the younger members, and said that the civil rights movement had achieved more than any military activity. He also described the IRA as weak with at most two thousand members.[149] In another piece just prior to the Ard Fheis, probably written by Mills, it was claimed that the IRA had up to £100,000 and that some of it had come from armed robberies carried out by members opposed to the leadership, and would be spent on acquiring arms.[150]

The Ard Fheis was held on 10 and 11 January 1970 in the Intercontinental Hotel, Dublin. Mac Giolla's presidential address concentrated on his claim that the Irish government was planning to reintegrate the entire country in the United Kingdom through a federal arrangement and that this was the objective behind the Free Trade Agreement. He also accused Fianna Fáil of attempting to buy control over the civil rights movement. He supported the proposal for a National Liberation Front as the struggle needed an alliance of all radical groups but took no side with regard to abstentionism and called for unity no matter what was decided. Both sides had accepted that a split was inevitable and were hoping either to win the Ard Fheis or to take with them as many members as possible.

The number of delegates who attended, at over 250 which was almost three times the 1968 attendance, was an indication of increased support due to reaction to events in the North but also of the creation of new cumainn comprised of IRA Volunteers to increase the number of delegates available to both sides. The NLF proposal was passed by a large majority but the motion to abandon abstentionism, which required a two-thirds majority, was defeated. The announcement of the vote was followed by a motion proposed by Dennis Cassin and Seamus Costello pledging allegiance to the IRA, which was taken as a tactic to commit Sinn Féin to support the decision of the Convention. That led to the walk-out of around a hundred delegates who made their way to the Kevin Barry Hall in Parnell Square to announce the formation of a group allied to the Provisional Army Council.

In January the Provisionals began to publish *An Phoblacht*, which had no connection other than the name with the Cork paper. An article entitled 'The Attempt to Take Over the Republican Movement' traced what it saw as the Communist infiltration of the movement back to 1963 and described the 1965 special convention and Ard Fheis as key events. Those who had joined the movement from the Communist parties had been facilitated by a few long-standing members who allowed them to adopt the role of 'master minds', Roy Johnston being one of the most important of these in his role as Director of Education. By 1969 the process was near completion with the proposal that the republican movement should amalgamate with the Communist organisations.[151]

While *An Phoblacht* referred to those who had remained loyal to Goulding as 'Free State Party Number 4', its position on the civil rights movement was initially not very different from the Officials' and stressed the need not only for unity but for non-violence which it said had exposed the nature of Unionism. The main difference was the Provisionals' insistence that Stormont should be abolished. It also said that republican and socialist demands had to be secondary. Another common early theme was an emphasis on Fianna Fáil's alleged support for a federal solution, based on the Free Trade Agreement, EEC membership and the takeover of the economy by foreign capital.

An Phoblacht is interesting as proof that initially at least there was very little obvious political difference between the two sides. As in all marginal groups, internal ideological disputes which were magnified into major issues of principle appeared puzzling and irrelevant to most outsiders. Indeed many supporters of both sides must have been confused regarding what exactly divided the two sides. While each attacked the another as being either too left- or right-wing, in reality it was the issues of abstentionism and reaction to events in the North that were paramount, and to a lesser extent, but only for those intimately involved in the organisation itself, allegations of infiltration by Communists on the one hand, and by Fianna Fáil agents on the other.

While the Provisionals rejected 'totalitarian' socialism they were in favour of a Democratic Socialist Republic and nationalisation of industry with the centrality of co-operatives as envisaged in Comhar na gComharsan. Under the scheme, every man had the right to own sufficient property to feed himself and his family but beyond that the state had the right to confiscate any excess. Republicans would divide 'ranches' and facilitate the creation of worker co-operatives. Séamus O Mongáin referred to Tom Doyle, Tomás O Dubhghaill, who had died in 1962, as one of those who had continued to support Comhar na gComharsan in opposition to the new policies being promoted. The fact that Doyle had died in 1962, however, would place the beginnings of the ideo-logical shift earlier than most commentators or participants accept. On 25 January the Executive of Cumann na mBan issued a statement of allegiance to the Provisional Army Council which referred to their rejection of 'an extreme form of socialism'.

The *United Irishman* was equally trenchant in defence of the Officials. The demand for the abolition of Stormont was rejected although the paper still gave out conflicting signals through its use of more militant and traditional slogans. It published a 'Freedom Manifesto' which put the Wolfe Tone Society forward as the model for a network of radical groups. Maximum unity needed to be maintained around the demand for civil rights and that meant that national and social demands had to remain secondary until civil rights were achieved. In the Republic, opposition to EEC and NATO membership was paramount. Ó Tuathail claimed that Fianna Fáil was delighted with the split as it had hoped that Sinn Féin would remain abstentionist rather than effec-tively contesting elections.[152]

The Irish-language monthly *Comhar* allowed Seán Ó Brádaigh and Mac Giolla to put their respective views on the split. Ó Brádaigh emphasised the centrality of abstentionism and that it had been a crucial symbol of the move-ment's opposition to the 'Establishment'. He listed as reasons for the split the undemocratic nature of the socialism being promoted by the leadership, the way in which the people of Derry and Belfast had been let down in August 1969 and the intent of Coughlan, Johnston and Goulding to preserve Stor-mont.[153] Mac Giolla claimed that a combination of parliamentary, extra-parliamentary and military methods was required to achieve a revolution. Interestingly the Irish government response to the split was that it considered the IRA to be weak and that it had already abandoned militarism.[154]

That may have been an honest assessment of the threat presented by the IRA, or alternatively an attempt by Dublin to dampen Unionist fears of an IRA insurrection, and British demands for action against the organisation. There is no doubt, however, that both factions of the IRA became more unpredictable after the split in the context of escalating unrest in the North. The quality of intelligence available to the government from within the movement was possibly also devalued especially given that it seems to have been the case that the main assets were Goulding supporters. That may also have led to an underestimation of the threat posed by the Provisionals.

The *Irish Socialist* report in February on the Sinn Féin Ard Fheis emphasised the Provisionals' reference to an 'extreme form of socialism' and to the alleged attempt by the Connolly Association and the IWP to take over the republican movement. The IWP and CPNI amalgamated in March 1970 to reform the Communist Party of Ireland with the party clearly believing that it was in a good position to make gains. The party press repeated the Official version of the split and claimed that the intervention in the north by Haughey and Blaney had been designed to disrupt the republican movement. Interestingly, Greaves in the *Irish Democrat* blamed the split on 'Fanonism' and the attempt to substitute Sinn Féin for the organisations of the working class.[155] Greaves would obviously have preferred the movement to have remained united prior to any alliance with the Communists, and that project eventually became derailed following the split.

A token, for a time, of the proximity of the Communists and the Officials was the joint 'school' organised by Johnston at the Sheelin Shamrock in March 1970. An IRA Volunteer who attended, while supportive of the National Liberation Front strategy, felt uneasy about the rapidity with which the movement was aligning itself with the Communists. He also felt that the emphasis was shifting far more towards a reformist strategy for the civil rights movement whereas he felt that the situation was opening up prospects for a more revolutionary approach, including the use of armed struggle. He later left the IRA with Seamus Costello when Costello founded the Irish National Liberation Army.[156]

The contradictions between the political direction sought by the Goulding leadership and the movements' militaristic instincts continued to surface within the Officials. Seán Dunne recalls being at a GHQ meeting in the Dominican Priory in Dominick Street in the summer of 1970, the first part of which was taken up with a discussion of Johnston's political proposals. It then went on to approve a decision by the Army Council to retaliate against any loyalist violence on 12 July by killing British soldiers.[157] Tom Mitchell also recalls Johnston being goaded by another Army Council member following an attack by the Official IRA on the British Army as to what Greaves's reaction would be.[158]

The British appeared to be little concerned over the *political* threat posed by either faction. Commenting on the publication of the Provisionals' policy in February 1971, David Blatherwick of the Dublin Embassy described it as comprising 'economic and financial pipe dreams'. He regarded the Officials' National Liberation Front as of little importance and noted that there was still criticism of 'extreme socialists' at their 1971 Ard Fheis. Blatherwick said that the conference must have seemed 'just like home'[159] for Yuri Ustimenko, the Dublin TASS correspondent! Members of the Communist Party were also there and one delegate noted the apparent familiarity displayed by them and some people close to Goulding towards the Russian,[160] who was an exotic presence to most delegates. The new British Ambassador, John Peck, believed that the Officials had close contacts with Communists in other countries and noted that one of Goulding's henchmen was a 'long-standing member of the CP'.[161]

By that stage, however, the politics of the two sides in the republican split were of little importance in contrast to the fact that both were now engaged in armed actions in the North with all the implications which that also had for stability south of the border. It was that, rather than the ideological disputes, which had riven the republican movement between 1962 and 1969, which preoccupied both the British and Irish states, and which led to further radical shifts in republican politics and ideology over the next quarter of a century.

Notes

1 Interview with Anthony Coughlan, 12 December 2001.
2 *Unity*, 26 October 1968.
3 *Irish Democrat*, December 1968.
4 Interview with Cathal Mac Liam, 15 March 2005.
5 *United Irishman*, June 1969.
6 *Irish Times*, 15 January 1969.
7 *Irish Times*, 20 January 1969.
8 *Dáil Debates*, Vol. 238, col. 882.
9 *Irish Student*, January 1968.
10 FCO 33/762, Gilchrist to London 14 January 1969, PRO.
11 FCO 33/762, Report by George Dawson to Gilchrist on 'Student Unrest'.
12 *Irish Times* 29 January 1969.
13 Interview with Roy Johnston, 19 April 2001.
14 See below.
15 Bishop and Mallie (1987), pp. 99–100.
16 FCO 33/752, Gilchrist to London, 31 January 1969, PRO.
17 FCO 762, Gilchrist to London, 11 March 1969.
18 Justice, 2000/36/3, Memo from Berry to O Moráin, 18 March 1969, NAI.
19 *Ibid.*
20 *Ibid.*
21 *Irish Times*, 14 January 1969.
22 *Ibid.*, 24 January 1969.
23 FCO 33/752, Gilchrist to London, 24 February 1969, PRO.
24 Wolfe Tone Society Minutes, 8 March 1969.

25 FCO 33/753, Gilchrist to London, 29 May 1969.

26 *Ibid.*, Gilchrist to London, 20 June 1969.

27 FCO 33/753, Gilchrist to London, 29 May 1969.

28 *Ibid.*, Gilchrist to London, 10 June 1969.

29 O'Halpin, 'Intelligence and Anglo-Irish Relations', in O'Halpin, Armstrong and Ohlmeyer, ed. (2006), pp. 141–2.

30 Press statement by the Wolfe Tone Society, in possession of Cathal Mac Liam.

31 Wolfe Tone Society Minutes, 6 June 1969.

32 *Ibid.*, August 1969.

33 *Der Spiegel*, 2 June 1969, DFA, F 100/11/12, NAI.

34 Stephen Dorril, *Blackshirt: Sir Oswald Mosley and British Fascism* (London 2006), p. 610.

35 O'Halpin (1999), p. 289.

36 DFA, London Embassy, F 100/11/12, 3 June 1969, NAI.

37 *Irish Times*, 13 June 1969.

38 CAB/4/1435, Minutes of Cabinet meeting of 20 April 1969, PRONI.

39 FCO 33/763, Piper to London, 21 April 1969, PRO.

40 *Ibid.*, Gilchrist to Callaghan, 21 April 1969.

41 *Ibid.*, Stewart to Dublin Embassy, 25 April 1969.

42 *Ibid.*, FCO to New York Consulate, 22 April 1969.

43 *Ibid.*, Caradon to FCO, 23 April 1969.

44 *Ibid.*, Report of FCO discussion with U Thant on 25 April 1969, PRO.

45 *Ibid.*, Gilchrist to FCO, 25 April 1969.

46 FCO 33/756, Gilchrist to London, 3 May 1969.

47 FCO 33/753, Gilchrist to London, 29 May 1969 and 10 June 1969.

48 FCO 33/763, Gilchrist to London, 28 April 1969.

49 FCO 33/756, Gilchrist to London, 3 May 1969.

50 *United Irishman*, May 1969.

51 Sinn Féin Coiste Seasta Minutes, 11 March 1969.

52 Interview with Tom Mitchell, 11 January 2002.

53 *Hansard*, Commons Debates, 23 April 1969.

54 *Disturbances in Northern Ireland: Report of the Commission appointed by the Governor of Northern Ireland*, Cmnd. 532 (Belfast 1969), Appendices I and II, Chapter I, para. 6.

55 Peter Rose, *How the Troubles Came to Northern Ireland* (London 2000), p. 129. Kevin McNamara MP told a researcher in England that Craig was constantly citing not only RUC but security service reports on the IRA (information from Dr Kevin Bean).

56 CJ 3/55, Report of Chief of General Staff, 15 May 1969, PRO.

57 CAB 186/3 JIC (A) (69) 27, 16 June 1969.

58 *United Irishman*, July 1969.

59 Interview with Roy Johnston, 19 April 2001. Despite Johnston's feelings the Wolfe Tone Society had requested that all members should attend the re-interment of Volunteers Dunne and O'Sullivan at Deans Grange in July 1967 (Wolfe Tone Society Minutes, 4 July 1967).

60 Taoiseach, 2000/6/162, note from NF to Runai, Dept of Taoiseach, 8 August 1968.
61 HO 282/51, Geoff Collins to Foreign and Commonwealth Office, 22 October 1968, PRO.
62 Interview with Seán Dunne, 20 November 2001.
63 *United Irishman*, August 1969.
64 *Irish Press*, 8 July 1969.
65 *Hibernia*, 18 July–7 August 1969.
66 Interview with Seán Ó Brádaigh, 21 May 2005.
67 Interview with Ruairí Ó Brádaigh, 22 May 2002.
68 FCO 33/777, Report of Secretary of State for Defence, 14 July 1969, PRO.
69 *Ibid.*, MISC 238, 15 July 1969.
70 DFA, 2000/5/42, Memo from M. Forde to Jim Gibbons, Minister for Defence, 13 August 1969, NAI.
71 DFA, 2000/5/42 – report of Consul General Charles Whelan, 22 August 1969.
72 CAB/4/1460, Cabinet minutes of 14 August 1969, PRONI.
73 Sinn Féin Ard Comhairle statement, 13 August 1969.
74 FCO 33/757, Gilchrist to London, 14 August 1969, PRO.
75 *Ibid.*, Gilchrist to London, 16 August 1969.
76 FCO 33/758, Gilchrist to London, 4 September 1969.
77 FCO 33/757, Stewart to Gilchrist, 19 August 1969.
78 *Ibid.*, Stewart to New York Consulate, 20 August 1969.
79 FCO 33/758, Gilchrist to London, 1 September 1969.
80 DFA 2000/5/42, Report of 22 August 1969.
81 *United Irishman*, September 1969.
82 Mac Stiofáin (1975), p. 129.
83 FCO 33/758, Gilchrist to London, 4 November 1969.
84 Mac Stiofáin (1975), pp. 126–7.
85 *Fianna Fáil – The IRA Connection* (Dublin nd but 1971), p. 27.
86 DFA, 2000/5/16 – Statement by Lynch, 19 August 1969 NAI.
87 FCO 33/757, Gilchrist to London, 16 August 1969.
88 *United Irishman*, October 1969.
89 Interview with Ruairí Ó Brádaigh, 22 May 2002.
90 Private information.
91 DFA, 2000/14/185, NAI.
92 FCO 33/758, MacGlashean, 11 November 1969, PRO.
93 *The Northern Crisis: Which Way Forward?* (Dublin 1969), p. 5.
94 *Violence and Civil Disturbances in Northern Ireland in 1969. Report of the Tribunal of Inquiry*. Cmd. 566 Vol. II, Belfast 1972, p. 53.
95 *Ibid.*
96 FCO 33/763, Report prepared by Intelligence Research Department, April 1969, PRO.
97 Tony Benn, *Diaries*, Vol. I (London 2005), 19 August 1969.
98 *Hibernia*, 29 August–11 September 1969.
99 FCO 33/757, Gilchrist to London, 14 August 1969.
100 CAB 185/9, JIC minutes, 18 September 1969.

101 Email from Jim Lane, 21 May 2005.
102 James Kelly, *Orders for the Captain* (Dublin 1971), p. 8.
103 Oireachtas Éireann, *Reports from Committees*, Vol. 19, Part II, p. 17.
104 *Fianna Fáil – The IRA Connection*, p. 17.
105 FCO 33/757, Gilchrist to London, 14 August 1969, PRO.
106 *Ibid.*, Gilchrist to London, 16 August 1969.
107 FCO 33/758, Gilchrist to London, 16 September 1969.
108 *Fianna Fáil – The IRA Connection*, p. 17.
109 Interview with Seán Dunne, 20 November 2001.
110 *Reports from Committees*, Vol. 19, Part II, p. 746.
111 Interview with Eoin O Murchú, 11 June 2001.
112 Cronin (1980), p. 201, note 81.
113 *Fianna Fáil – The IRA Connection*, p. 10.
114 Breasail O Caollai, 'Fianna Fáil and the IRA Connection', *New Hibernia*, December 1986/January 1987.
115 *Hibernia*, 29 May–10 June 1970.
116 Private information.
117 Hanley and Millar (2009), p. 119.
118 Justice, 2001/61/10, Letter from Berry to Lynch, 8 June 1970, NAI.
119 Eunan, O'Halpin 'A Greek Authoritarian Phase? The Irish Army and the Irish Crisis, 1969–70', *Irish Political Studies*, Vol. 23, no. 4, December 2008.
120 Interview with Jim Lane, 14 May 2005.
121 *Report from Committees*, p. 417.
122 Letter from John Kelly, *Irish Times*, 19 March 1998.
123 *Report from Committees*, p. 424.
124 Justin O'Brien, *The Arms Crisis* (Dublin 2000), p. 90.
125 Email from Roy Johnston, 26 June 2001.
126 Email from Roy Johnston, 24 July 2001.
127 FCO 33/758, Gilchrist to London, 10 November 1969, PRO.
128 *Ibid*, Gilchrist to London, 3 October 1969.
129 *Ibid*, Gilchrist to London, 4 October 1969.
130 *Report from Committees*, p. 417.
131 *London Evening Standard*, 14 October 1969.
132 *Sunday Press*, 21 September 1969 and *Dáil Debates*, Vol. 241, col. 1408.
133 FCO 33/763, Gilchrist to London, 15 April 1969.
134 FCO 33/758, Morgan to Peck, 4 September 1969.
135 FCO 33/758 (CC69 43rd Council of Ministers).
136 *Report from Committees*, p. 562.
137 O'Brien (2000), p. 78.
138 *Reports of Committees*, p. 422.
139 Information from Jim Monaghan, 3 March 2005.
140 Interview with Seán Dunne, 20 November 2001.
141 Interview with Seán Garland, 28 February 2005.
142 Interview with Seán Ó Brádaigh, 21 May 2005.
143 *Hibernia*, 7–20 November 1969.

144 Interview with Jim Lane, 14 May 2005.
145 Cronin (1980), p. 202.
146 *An Phoblacht*, February 1970.
147 *Irish Times*, 10 January 1970.
148 *Irish Press*, 29 December 1969.
149 *Irish Press*, 30 December 1969.
150 *Ibid.*, 9 January 1969.
151 *An Phoblacht*, February 1970.
152 *United Irishman*, February 1970.
153 *Comhar*, Feabhra 1970, lth 8–9.
154 Taoiseach, 2001/6/513, transcript of speech by Jack Lynch, NAI.
155 *Irish Democrat*, March 1970.
156 Private information.
157 Interview with Seán Dunne, 20 November 2001.
158 Interview with Tom Mitchell, 11 January 2002.
159 FCO 33/1593, Blatherwick to FCO, 18 January 1971, PRO.
160 Private information.
161 FCO 33/1593, Peck to FCO, 16 February 1971.

Epilogue

The real epilogue to the events and ideological debates described above was not only the armed conflict that lasted until the definitive IRA ceasefire in 1997 but also the political events culminating in the May 2007 agreement between Sinn Féin and the DUP to share power. The enthusiasm engendered by that historic compromise has been since tempered but the structures look destined to survive.

Despite their claim that the Provisionals eventually came to adopt their strategy, the modernising faction gained nothing politically if that was the case, and indeed the only remaining organisational representative of that faction is the Workers Party which has been reduced both in numbers and influence to insignificance. On the other hand former prominent members of the Official movement, including the current party leader Eamon Gilmore, are now in the upper echelons of Labour and the trade union movement, and former members have exercised influence across a wide range of areas in the past thirty years.

Ironically the leading figures in the inheritors of the both leftist and modernising position, the Workers Party and its traditionalist alter ego, Republican Sinn Féin, are Seán Garland and Ruairí Ó Brádaigh, both of whom figure prominently in our narrative. Having begun as marginal figures within radical republicanism they have returned, after a brief period of prominence, to those margins. It is almost as though they were pebbles lifted from the gravel banks of a stream in spate, only to be set down once again after the torrent of history had abated. Of course they do not regard matters in that way and have retained a remarkable consistency over almost half a century.

Central to the internal divisions described in the book was the conflict between those within the IRA and Sinn Féin who clung to the notion that they still represented legitimate governmental authority and those who took a more pragmatic view of the relationship between the movement and the society it sought to change. That continues to separate the contemporary Sinn Féin party from republican 'dissidents'. It is also perhaps worth noting that, at every stage when the faction within the movement which has decided to recognise the existing political and state structure wins the internal struggle, they have begun by justifying the new departure as a pragmatic tactic to further the achievement of traditional republican goals, but have discovered new legitimising rationales as the former are seen to be impractical or at least not achievable in the short to medium term.

Thus Fianna Fáil built an entire new ideology around the defence and development of the state which republicans had rejected violently in 1922. For the Official republican movement, it became socialism within the context of the existing Irish states. Likewise, according to some of its critics, the current republican leadership has privileged the winning of democratic rights for the nationalist minority in Northern Ireland over the bringing about of a 32-county Republic.[1] Patterson notes that, when radical republicanism has attempted to engage in social and economic issues, it risks marginalisation as the state can adopt reformist measures which satisfy the immediate needs of the target constituency.[2] Fianna Fáil did so successfully in the 1930s and ensured the sidelining of radical republicanism, something which the left has periodically sought to address, including during the period under review, without perhaps really understanding the dynamics which have on the one hand led to the marginalisation of the revolutionary element while on the other drawing other elements ultimately into constitutionalism. That perhaps has broader implications for all revolutionary movements in democratic states but is beyond the scope of this book.

The ideological divisions are almost irrelevant now and, while the Workers Party still clings to Marxism, the traditionalist view influenced by Catholic social teaching, and by and large hostile to socialism, is little represented among any republican grouping, although it still has a resonance within the broader society judging by groups such as Cóir which campaigned against the Lisbon Treaty which appeals to republican and Catholic sentiment. And of course the disappearance of the Soviet Union and by and large the discrediting of Marxism make the republican debate of the 1960s appear somewhat anachronistic.

The third major area of dispute in the 1960s centred on the role of the IRA. For the pragmatists, who dominated the post-1962 leadership, the armed campaign of 1956–62 had proved that a similar venture would be doomed to failure. They were determined that if another armed campaign was to be initiated – and at no time during the period under examination did they ever openly say that it would not – it would be viable only in very different political circumstances from those that pertained in the late 1950s. For traditionalists, the task facing the IRA after 1962 was the same as it had always been; to reorganise and prepare itself for an offensive against the British in the north. That same division still exists between Sinn Féin and most of the dissident groups although some of them would not share the RSF attitude towards electoralism, which in any event is irrelevant given the small levels of support which they have attracted in elections.

One of the remaining areas of contention regarding the split in the republican movement in 1969 has been the role of the Irish state in those events. While there are those like Patterson who have given credence to the modernisers' claim that Fianna Fáil or a faction thereof was directly involved,[3] others have dismissed this as fanciful.[4] The recent Hanley and Millar book also appears to support the 'plot' theory on the basis of the March 1969 Berry memo which I argue should be placed in a broader context as evidenced by the available state papers. My own view is that while there was official contact and financial support for the IRA, with or without the knowledge or consent of the Taoiseach Jack Lynch, there is no evidence to suggest that the government or elements within Fianna Fáil were attempting to provoke a split in order to destroy an allegedly menacing republican left.

Indeed it could be argued that, far from the left departure transforming the movement into a new and terrible threat to the Irish state, it may well have been regarded by the Irish authorities as having had a 'diversionary effect' which distracted the IRA from its military role.[5] Roy Johnston's belief that one of the Army Council informers was supportive of Goulding's plans, and that the other high-placed informer also took the Official side in the split, may even point to official encouragement for the 'politicisers'. Those Special Branch contacts were probably also key to exposing the arms imports facilitated by Fianna Fáil Ministers. It is interesting also that the leftist tendency within the Provisional movement in the 1980s was the one which, despite its rhetoric, compromised on the key traditionalist republican values, laying the basis for the current settlement in Northern Ireland. That is an observation not a moral judgement and indeed it could be argued that any revolutionary movement which seeks popular support on the basis of electoral and parliamentary participation is inevitably going to be drawn into acceptance of the constitutional status quo.

It is my contention that the Northern crisis was not the creation of republicans, albeit republicans did play a role in the formation of the civil rights movement. That was largely a seminal influence and republicans were to the greater degree marginal to subsequent developments, reflecting their overall weakness. As Simon Prince has demonstrated, the leftist student element was probably a more destabilising element within the broad civil rights movement. There is little concrete information on the IRA in the North during the 1960s, other than RUC estimates which were probably inaccurate and possibly exaggerated,[6] but Bew, Gibbon and Patterson are probably not greatly overstating their case when they claim that northern republicanism was basically irrelevant before 1969.[7]

Republicans were largely displaced within the broader civil rights movement by moderates who were initially in contact with them through the Wolfe Tone Society, and by the more radical elements associated with left-wing groups such as Peoples Democracy. Whatever the prominence of individual republicans and sympathisers, including CPNI members, in the leadership of NICRA, far from dominating or controlling the movement, by 1968 the IRA was a secondary factor which was highlighted by its marginal formal role in the organisation of the protests and the watershed Mid Ulster election of Bernadette Devlin.

Some of those who have taken the modernisers' project at face value have neglected the extent to which they misjudged the reaction of most Protestants to the civil rights movement and how realistic in contrast were the traditionalists', and indeed the Irish state's, estimation of the dangers of inter-communal violence provoked by loyalist reaction.[8] The prognosis sketched by the modernisers with regard to how the civil rights movement might develop and the prospects for democratic reform and winning over the Protestant working class were proved to be naive. Patterson admits that, while the modernisers had correctly identified the capacity for the civil rights campaign to undermine Unionism, they had grossly overestimated the potential for winning Protestant support.[9] Nor would what has happened since the mid-1990s give grounds for much optimism that those communal divisions will simply disappear because of the lack of armed conflict and a political settlement between what were regarded as the most extreme representatives of the two communities.

While the Irish republican movement had long been weak and isolated, the northern crisis brought about a situation in which the fact that Partition and the status of Catholic nationalists in Northern Ireland were regarded by a large section of the population as matters of real concern meant that its unreconstructed ideology did strike a chord among a much wider audience after August 1969. For many, and not just traditionalist republicans, the northern crisis of 1969 brought with it the opportunity to complete the 'unfinished business' of 1916–22, but ironically not for the modernisers who had sought to make the movement relevant by jettisoning much of its traditional *raison d'être*.

Indeed it was the revival of the 'national question' as a central political issue rather than involvement in 'working-class struggle' that also brought the modernising faction of the movement to brief prominence, and led them to embark on armed actions for several years. They later won several Dáil seats but the increasingly doctrinaire approach of the older leadership alienated the more pragmatic section which split away in 1992 and eventually dissolved itself, leaving the heir to the modernisers' political legacy, the Workers Party, even weaker than the overall movement was in the 1960s.

The same applies to the more dogmatic elements on the traditionalist side. They, in alliance with militant Belfast republicans reacting to the events of August 1969, founded the Provisional movement. For a time that conferred legitimacy on and gained a wider public audience for the unreconstructed republican view of both Irish states based on rejectionism and armed struggle. However, the Provisionals themselves evolved away from that unyielding view, and, just as within the modernist faction, a more pragmatic policy came to dominate their politics and the traditionalist element again split away to form Republican Sinn Féin and the Continuity IRA in 1986.

While most observers regard the Provisionals as representing a radical break from the politics of the civil rights movement, Richard English has been one of the few historians to emphasise the continuity between the Provisionals and the civil rights movement which had radicalised northern nationalists and contributed to the belief that the civil rights movement was preparing the basis for a confrontation that would destroy the Unionist state.[10] That would explain why traditionalists tended to support the more radical elements in the movement who organised the marches, whereas the modernisers attacked Peoples Democracy as 'ultra leftists' and provocateurs.

The history of the movement between 1962 and 1969 is a history of a marginal radical group but one that is important in the overall context of its place in Irish history. It is of interest not only because of the fact that the northern crisis brought it again to the centre of events, as it had been in earlier periods, but also as a study of the internal workings of such a group and the constant striving for political relevance within the context of a rigid ideology that for the period under review appeared to confine the movement to long-term isolation and political weakness. As such it has relevance for the study of radical republicanism before 1962 and indeed in more recent years. That is a theme that has been explored in relation to the IRA in the 1920s and 1930s by Brian Hanley and others.

Radical republicanism has proved to be a resilient strain in Irish society and has been innovative in adapting itself to external forces and broader historical and social change. A consistent phenomenon has been the emergence of moderate trends seeking to accommodate themselves to those forces and this has led to conflict with those resisting change. That is one of the main themes of this book and it is something that was apparent in earlier phases of republican history, particularly in the 1920s and 1930s, but also over the past twenty years as radical republicanism, or the greater part thereof, has come to what has been termed a 'historical compromise' with its traditional adversaries. Such a compromise is not unique, nor of course has the entire radical republican constituency been persuaded of its merits.

Before the IRA ceasefire in 1994 the general consensus was that militant republicanism was a rigid ideology that made it unlikely to compromise. Even as late as 1993 one historian who had met leading Provisionals believed that 'peace in Ireland is unlikely'.[11] While such pessimism was perhaps understandable, it may also have been caused by a misunderstanding of the nature of radical republicanism and a view that failed to take a longer view of the history of the movement which is replete with regular examples of the majority or a significant minority of the movement compromising on both its means and its objectives.

Despite that historical evidence, some historians, even after 1994, clung to an almost mystical view of an IRA dedicated to an esoteric Republic that appeared destined to remain in existence and committed to armed struggle even if temporarily on ceasefire.[12] Bishop and Mallie described violent republicanism as an 'eradicable tradition' immune to political change.[13] While such a view could still be applied to fringe traditionalist groups such as the Continuity IRA, it overlooked the extent to which the main body of radical republicanism was influenced by internal transformation that reflected broader societal and political change. It is not impossible that armed republicanism could once again return as a significant factor but that is unlikely under current circumstances.

The 1969–94 period may have been unique in terms of the longevity and intensity of republican armed struggle but it was still one in which radical internal shifts took place with regard to both the ideology and the tactics of the Provisional movement. Those changes led to further schisms over abstentionism and the use of violence and led to a similar rapprochement with the Irish and British states authored in earlier periods by the leaders of radical republicanism. Ironically the initiators of the new departure in the 1960s gained nothing in the long term even though it has been argued that the Provisionals followed a similar path after 1986.

Notes

1 Anthony McIntyre, *Good Friday: The Death of Irish Republicanism* (New York 2008).
2 Patterson (1997), p. 6.
3 *Ibid.*, p. 111.
4 Bishop and Mallie (1987), p. 99.
5 O'Halpin (1999), p. 303.
6 Billy McMillan, who was the OC of Belfast in 1969, estimated that there were 24 IRA members in the city in 1961 and around 120 in 1969. McMillan (1976), p. 2, p. 10.
7 Bew, Gibbon and Patterson (2002).
8 Molony (2002), p. 59.
9 Patterson (1997), p. 202.
10 English (2003), p. 82.
11 White (1993), p. 175.
12 Bowyer Bell (1998), p. 66.
13 Bishop and Mallie (1987), pp. 4–5.

Glossary

Ailtirí na hAiséirghe – Fascist-inspired nationalist organisation founded in 1942. Included as members and sympathisers a number of significant figures within the republican movement.

Ard Comhairle – Irish term for national executive.

Ard Fheis – Irish term for annual conference.

Cóir – Irish word meaning 'justice', the name of an anti-EU nationalist Catholic organisation.

Coiste Seasta – Standing committee.

Comhairle Ceantair – Literally 'area committee'.

Comhar na gComharsan – 'Co-operation of neighbours'. Republican philosophy of co-operative based economy.

Cumann (plural: cumainn) – Literally 'club'. But used by Sinn Féin, Fianna Fáil and Fine Gael to designate local party branches.

Gardaí Siochana – Literally 'Guardians of the peace.' Irish police force.

Oireachtas – Irish Houses of Parliament.

Select bibliography

PRIMARY SOURCES

Republic of Ireland
National Archives, Dublin
Department of Taoiseach
Department of Foreign Affairs
Department of Justice

National Library, Dublin
NLI Ms. 22,938
NLI Ms. 22,939
NLI Ms. 894 (B) 1, Acc. 4230 (Tighe Papers)

Private possession
Cathal Mac Liam Papers
Roy Johnston Papers
Wolfe Tone Society Minutes 1963–67 (currently in possession of Roy Johnston)
Wolfe Tone Society Minutes 1967–72 (currently in possession of Roy Johnston)
'An Interim Analysis of the Irish Republican Movement', Private collection in the care of Professor Eunan O'Halpin.

Britain
Public Records Office, London
Joint Intelligence Committee
Cabinet Minutes
DEFE
Foreign and Commonwealth Office
Home Office
War Office

Northern Ireland
Public Records Office of Northern Ireland, Belfast
Cabinet Minutes
Ministry of Home Affairs

PARLIAMENTARY AND OFFICIAL PUBLICATIONS

Dáil Debates
Stormont Debates
Violence and Civil Disturbances in Northern Ireland in 1969. Report of the Tribunal of Inquiry. Cmd. 566 Vol. II, Belfast 1972
Disturbances in Northern Ireland: Report of the Commission Appointed by the Governor of Northern Ireland. Cmd 532, Belfast 1969
Tuairiscal 1966/67, Dublin 1967
Reports from Committees, 1971–72, Vol. 19, Part II, Dublin 1972

JOURNALS AND NEWSPAPERS

Build
Canadian Journal of History
Christus Rex
Fianna – The Voice of Young Ireland
Hibernia Irish Statistical Bulletin
Iris an Gharda
Iris Leabhair na bhFiann
Irish Catholic Directory
Irish Historical Studies
Irish Political Studies
Irish Republican Bulletin
Journal of Ecclesiastical History
Magill
Studies
Tuairisc

An Phoblacht (Cork)
An Solas
An t-Óglach
Belfast Telegraph
Campus
Comhar
Cork Evening Echo
Daily Mail
Der Spiegel
Evening Herald
Evening Mail
Farmers Journal
Grille
Irish Communist
Irish Democrat
Irish Independent
Irish Militant

Irish Press
Irish Socialist
Irish Student
Irish Times
Irish Workers News
Irish Workers Voice
Irish Youth
Lia Fáil
Liberty
Limerick Leader
London Evening Standard
Munster Express
People's Voice
Republican News
Rosc Catha
Spectre
Sunday Independent
Sunday Press
Sunday Review
Sunday Times
TCD
TCD Miscellany
The Banner
The Guardian
The People
The Plough
The Promethean
This Week
Tirgrá
Trinity News
United Irishman
Unity
Voice of the Nation
Young Ireland

CORRESPONDENCE AND INTERVIEWS

Seán Bermingham, 20 April 2005
Martin Casey, 18 June 2005
Anthony Coughlan, 12 December 2001
Shay Courtney, 26 November 2001, 21 April 2005
Seán Dunne, 20 November 2001
Seán Garland, 28 February 2005
Roy Johnston, 4 April, 19 April 2001
Noel Kavanagh, 7 March 2005

Jim Lane, 14 May 2005
Cathal Mac Liam, 15 March 2005
Tom Mitchell, 11 January 2002
Jim Monaghan, 3 March 2005
Ruairí Ó Brádaigh, 22 May 2002
Seán Ó Brádaigh, 21 May 2005
Eoin O Murchú, 11 June 2001
Richard Roche, 26 April 2005

Email Correspondence
Roy Johnston, 26 May, 1 June, 26 June, 1 July 2001
Jim Lane, 16 May, 21 May 2005
Tony Meade, 18 April 2005

SECONDARY SOURCES

Adams, Gerry, *Before the Dawn* (London 1996)
Allen, Kieran, *Fianna Fáil and Irish Labour* (London 1997)
Anderson, Brendan, *Joe Cahill* (Dublin 2002)
Andrews, Christopher, and Mitrokhin, Vaily, *The Sword and the Shield: The Mitrokhin Archive and the Secret History of the KGB* (London 2000)
Arthur, Paul, *Government and Politics of Northern Ireland* (London 1984)
Arthur, Paul, *The Peoples Democracy 1968–73* (Belfast 1974)
Beckett, Francis, *Enemy Within: The Rise and Fall of the British Communist Party* (Woodbridge 1998)
Bell, Geoffrey, *The Irish Troubles 1967–92* (Dublin 1993)
Benn, Tony, *Diaries, Volume I* (London 2005)
Beresford, Philip, *The Official IRA and the Rep Clubs in NI 1968–1974* (Ph.D. Exeter 1979)
Berkhofer, Robert F., *Beyond the Great Story: History as Text and Discourse* (Cambridge 1995)
Bew, Peter, Gibbon, Peter, Patterson, Henry, *Northern Ireland 1921–1994* (London 1995)
Bew, P., and Patterson, H., *Seán Lemass and the Making of Modern Ireland 1945–66* (Dublin 1982)
Bishop, Patrick, and Mallie, Eamonn, *The Provisional IRA* (London 1987)
Boland, Kevin, *The Rise and Decline of Fianna Fáil* (Cork 1982)
Bolton, D., *The UVF 1966–73: An Anatomy of Loyalist Rebellion* (Dublin 1973).
Bowyer Bell, J., *The Secret Army* (Dublin 1998) (revised edition)
Boyd, Andrew, *Holy War in Belfast* (Dublin 1969)
Brady, Seamus, *Arms and the Men* (Dublin nd)
Brownell, Josiah, 'The Taint of Communism: the Movement for Colonial Freedom, the Labour Party, and the Communist Party of Great Britain, 1954–70', *Canadian Journal of History*, September 2007
Catholic Truth Society, *Social Justice* (Dublin 1938)

Chubb, Basil, and Lynch, Patrick, ed., *Economic Development and Planning* (Dublin 1969)

Clifford, Brendan, *Connolly Cut Outs* (Belfast 1984)

Coogan, Tim Pat, *The IRA* (London 1984)

Corish, Brendan, *The New Republic* (Dublin 1968)

Corrigan, Aidan, *Eye Witness in Northern Ireland* (Dungannon (?) nd)

Coughlan, Anthony, *C. Desmond Greaves 1913–1986: An Obituary Essay* (Dublin 1990)

Coughlan, Anthony, *The Northern Crisis: Which Way Forward?* (Dublin 1969)

Craddock, Percy, *Know Your Enemy: How the Joint Intelligence Committee Saw the World* (London 2002)

Cronin, Seán, *Irish Nationalism* (Dublin 1980)

Cronin, Seán, *The Ideology of the IRA and the Roots of the Conflict in Northern Ireland* (Ann Arbor Ph.D. 1979)

Daly, Mary E., *Industrial Development and Irish National Identity, 1922–1939* (Syracuse 1992)

Daly, Mary, and O'Callaghan, Margaret, *1916 in 1966: Commemorating the Easter Rising* (Dublin 2007)

Davis, D. J., *The Economics of Welsh Self Government* (Caernarfon 1931)

Delaney, Enda, 'Political Catholicism in Post War Ireland', *Journal of Ecclesiastical History*, Vol. 52, no. 3, July 2001

De Paor, Liam, *Divided Ulster* (Harmondsworth 1970)

Devlin, Bernadette, *The Price of My Soul* (London 1969)

Dixon, Paul, *Northern Ireland: The Politics of War and Peace* (Houndsmills 2001)

Dorril, Stephen, *Blackshirt: Sir Oswald Mosley and British Fascism* (London 2006)

Dunphy, Richard, *Fianna Fáil* (Dublin 1995)

English, Richard, *Armed Struggle* (London 2003)

English, Richard, *Irish Freedom* (London 2006)

Fahey, Fr Denis, *The Tragedy of James Connolly* (Cork 1947)

Fanon, Frantz, *The Wretched of the Earth* (London 1965)

Farrell, Michael, *Northern Ireland, The Orange State* (London 1980)

Feeney, Brian, *Sinn Féin: A Hundred Turbulent Years* (Dublin 2002)

Fennell, Desmond, ed., *The Changing Face of Catholic Ireland* (Dublin 1969)

Flynn, Barry, *Soldiers of Folly: The IRA Border Campaign 1956–1962* (Cork 2009)

Foley, Conor, *Legion of the Rearguard* (London 1992)

Foley, Gerry, *Ireland in Rebellion* (New York 1971)

Foley, Gerry, *Problems of the Irish Revolution* (New York 1972)

Frampton, M., 'Squaring the Circle: The Foreign Policy of Sinn Féin 1983–1989', *Irish Political Studies*, Vol. 19, no. 2, 2004.

Gallagher, Michael, *The Irish Labour Party in Transition, 1957–1982* (Manchester 1982)

Garvin, Tom, 'Priests and Patriots: Irish Separtists and Fear of the Modern, 1890–1914', *Irish Historical Studies*, Vol. 25, no. 97, May 1986

Geraghty, Tony, *The Irish War* (London 2000)

Girvin, Brian, and Murphy, Gary, ed., *The Lemass Era* (Dublin 2005)

Goulding, Cathal, *Inside the IRA: Interviews with Cathal Goulding* (Philadelphia 1974)

Gramsci, Antonio, *Selections from the Prison Notebooks* (London 1991)

Greaves, C. Desmond, *Reminiscences of the Connolly Association* (London nd [1978?])

Greaves, C. Desmond, *The Irish Question and the British People* (typescript)

Hanley, Brian, *The IRA 1926–1936* (Dublin 2002)

Hanley, Brian, and Millar, Scott, *The Lost Revolution* (Dublin 2009)

Hennessy, Thomas, *Northern Ireland: The Origins of the Troubles* (London 2005)

Higgins, Jim, *More Years for the Locust* (London 1997)

Hogan, Gerard, and Walker, Clive, *Political Violence and the Law in Ireland* (Manchester 1989)

John XXIII, *Mater et Magistra*

Johnston, Roy, *Century of Endeavour* (Dublin 2007)

Keating, Michael, *State and Regional Nationalism* (Hemel Hempstead 1988)

Keating, Michael, 'Do the Workers Really Have a Country?' in John Coakley, ed., *The Social Origins of Nationalist Movements* (London 1992)

Kelleher, Derry, *Republicanism, Christianity and Marxism* (Dublin 1970)

Kelleher, Derry, *Irish Republicanism, The Authentic Perspective* (Greystones 2001)

Kelley, Kevin J., *The Longest War* (London 1982)

Kelly, James, *Orders for the Captain* (Dublin 1971)

Kennedy, Michael, *Division and Consensus: The Politics of Cross Border Co-operation* (Dublin 2000)

Keogh, Dermot, and O'Driscoll, Finín, 'Ireland', in John Buchanan and Martin Conway, ed., *Political Catholicism in Europe 1918–1965* (Oxford 1996)

Kerry County Council, *Local Election Results 1899–1991* (Tralee 1999)

Leo XIII, *Graves de Communi Re* (1901)

Leo XIII, *Rerum Novarum* (1891)

Leo XIII, *Saepe Nos* (1888)

Lewis, Saunders, *The Party for Wales* (Caernarfon 1942)

Lloyd, Myrddin, *Plaid Cymru and Its Message* (Cardiff 1949)

Mac an Bheatha, Proinsias, *Tart na Cora* (Baile Atha Cliath 1964)

MacEoin, Uinseann, *Survivors* (Dublin 1980)

Mac Stíofáin, Seán, *Memoirs of a Revolutionary* (London 1975)

Magill, *The Magill Book of Irish Politics* (Dublin 1981)

McCann, Eamonn, *War and an Irish Town* (London 1993)

MacDonagh, Oliver, *States of Mind* (London, 1983)

McGarry, John, O'Leary, Brendan, *Explaining Northern Ireland* (London 1995)

McGuire, Maria, *To Take Arms: A Year in the Provisional IRA* (London 1973)

McKenna, Lambert, *The Social Teachings of James Connolly* (Dublin 1920)

McKeown, Michael, *The Greening of a Nationalist* (Dublin 1986)

McMillan, Liam, *The Role of the IRA 1962–1967* (Dublin 1976)

Maguire, John, 'Internment, the IRA and the Lawless Case in Ireland 1957–61', *Journal of the Oxford University History Society*, Michaelmas 2004

Mahon, Tom, and Gillogly, James, *Decoding the IRA* (Cork 2008)

Medhurst, Ken, 'Basques and Basque Nationalism' in Colin H Williams, ed., *Nationalist Separatism* (Cardiff 1982)

Meenan, James, *The Irish Economy Since 1922* (Liverpool 1970)

Milotte, Mike, *Communism in Ireland: The Pursuit of the Workers Republic* (Dublin 1984)

Moloney, Ed, *A Secret History of the IRA* (London 2002)

Moran, Gerard, ed., *Radical Irish Priests, 1660–1970* (Dublin 1998)

Murphy, Brian, *The Catholic Bulletin and Republican Ireland* (Belfast 2005)

Nairn, Tom, *The Breakup of Britain* (London 1977)

NICRA, *We Shall Overcome* (Belfast 1978)

Nimni, Ephraim, *Marxism and Nationalism* (London 1991)

O'Brien, Justin, *The Arms Crisis* (Dublin 2000)

O'Connor, Emmet, *Reds and the Green: Ireland, Russia and the Communist Internationals 1919–1943* (Dublin 2004)

O'Donnell, Catherine, *Fianna Fáil, Irish Republicanism and the Northern Ireland Troubles 1968–2005* (Dublin 2007)

Official Republican Movement, *The IRA Speaks* (Dublin 1972?)

Official Republican Movement, *Fianna Fáil: The IRA Connection* (Dublin 1971)

Ó Gadhra, Nollaig, *Guth an Phobail* (Baile Átha Cliath 1984)

O'Halpin, Eunan, 'A poor thing but out own: The Joint Intelligence Committee and Ireland, 1965–72', *Intelligence and National Security*, Vol. 23, no. 5, October 2008

O'Halpin, Eunan, *Defending Ireland: The Irish State and Its Enemies Since 1922* (Oxford 1999)

O'Halpin, Eunan, 'Intelligence and Anglo-Irish Relations', in O'Halpin, Armstrong, Ohlmeyer, J., ed. *Intelligence, Statecraft and International Power* (Dublin 2006)

O'Halpin, Eunan, ' "A Greek Authoritarian Phase"? The Irish Army and the Irish Crisis, 1969–70', *Irish Political Studies*, Vol. 23, no. 4, December 2008

O'Leary, Brendan, *The Politics of Antagonism* (London 1993)

O'Malley, Padraig, *Uncivil Wars* (Boston 1993)

Patterson, Henry, *The Politics of Illusion* (London 1997)

Perks, Robert, and Thomson, Alistair, *The Oral History Reader* (London 2006)

Pius X, *Il Fermo Proposito* (1905)

Pius IX, *Quadragesimo Anno* (1931)

Prince, Simon, *Northern Ireland's '68: Civil Rights, Global Revolt and the Origins of the Troubles* (Dublin 2007)

Purdie, Bob, *Politics in the Streets* (Belfast 1990)

Puirséil, Niamh, *The Irish Labour Party, 1922–73* (Dublin 2007)

Quinn, Raymond, *A Rebel Voice: A History of Belfast Republicanism 1925–1972* (Belfast 1998)

Rafter, Kevin, *Sinn Féin 1905–2005* (Dublin 2005)

Redmond, Seán, *Desmond Greaves and the Origins of the Civil Rights Movement in Northern Ireland* (London 1999)

Rogers, Vaughan, 'Brittany', in *Contemporary Minority Nationalisms* (London 1990)

Rose, Peter, *How the Troubles Came to Northern Ireland* (London 2000)

Rose, Richard, *Governing Without Consensus* (London 1971)

Routledge, Paul, *John Hume* (London 1997)

Rumpf, E., and Hepburn, A. C., *Nationalism and Socialism in Twentieth Century Ireland* (Liverpool 1977)

Seoighe, Mainchin, *Maraiodh Seán Sabht Areír* (Baile Átha Cliath 1964)

Sinn Féin, *Nation or Province* (Dublin 1963)

Sinn Féin, *Republican Manual of Education, Part I* (Dublin 1966)

Sinn Féin, *The Separatist* (Dublin 1966)

Sinn Féin, *Imperialism and the Irish Nation* (Dublin 1969)

Sinn Féin, *Ireland Today and Some Questions on the Way Forward* (Dublin 1969)

Sinn Féin, *Republican Manual of Education, Part III* (Dublin 1969)

Smith, M. L. R., *Fighting for Ireland: The Military Strategy of the Irish Republican Movement* (London 1995)

Smyth, Clifford, *Ulster Assailed* (Belfast 1971)

Swan, Seán, *Official Irish Republicanism, 1962 to 1972* (Belfast 2006)

Taylor, Peter, *Provos* (London 1997)

Walsh, Pat, *From Civil Rights to National War* (Belfast 1989)

Walsh, Pat, *Irish Republicanism and Socialism* (Belfast 1994)

Whitaker, T. K., *Economic Development* (Dublin 1958)

White, R. W., *Provisional Irish Republicans* (Westport, 1993)

White, R. W., *Ruairí Ó Brádaigh* (Bloomington 2006)

Wright, Joanne, *Terrorist Propaganda* (London 1991)

Yeo, Stephen, 'Whose Story? An Argument from within Current Historical Practice in Britain', *Journal of Contemporary History*, Vol. 21, April 1996

Index

Agnew, Kevin 105, 159
Aiken, Frank 22–3, 77, 80, 158
Ailtirí na hAiséirighe 4, 33, 36, 38, 40, 69
An Phoblacht 27, 181
An Phoblacht (Cork) 21, 52, 58, 88, 94, 106–9, 120–1, 128–9, 133, 135–6
An Rioghact 31
An t-Óglach 46, 114, 128, 144
Asmal Kadar 60, 156

Baker, Geoffrey 161
Barnes, Peter 162
Barry, Kevin 123
Bateson, Larry 110
Beaumont, Richard 80
Behal, Raymond 23
Behal, Richard 23–4, 92–3, 102, 116, 135
Behan, Brendan 74
Behan, Brian 74
Benn, Tony 168
Bennett, Jack 64, 76–7, 106–7
Bermingham, Seán 11, 63, 69, 107, 124
Berry, Peter 12, 15, 21, 23–4, 52, 57, 63, 101, 133, 154–6, 158, 168–9, 191
Blaney, Harry 173
Blaney, Neil 137, 147, 155–6, 169, 170–2, 175–6, 180, 183
Bolger, Austin 164
Boyce, Eamonn 34

Boyd, Wesley 105
Boyle, Jerry 122
Brady, Seamus 169, 171, 174, 177
Breathnach, Deasún 37, 39, 64–5
Breen, Dan 122
Brennan, Joe 169
Briscoe, Robert 33
Brockway, Fenner 73, 153
Browne, Bishop Michael 35
Browne, Noel 132
Burke, Liam 64
Burke, P.J. 132

Cahill, Joe 179
Callaghan, Jim 146, 164, 168
Callaghan, Paddy 140
Canning, Manus 11, 113
Caradon, Lord 158
Carey, Joseph 135, 178
Carmody, Paddy 77–8
Casey, Martin 135
Cassin, Denis 140, 181
Caughey, Seán 51, 64
Ceitinn, Seamus 48
Chalfont, Lord 164
Chichester-Clark 159, 161, 164–6
Childers, Erskine 32, 145, 148, 156, 165
Christle, Joe 12, 93
Christus Rex 34
Clancy Brothers 56
Clan na Gael 19, 113
Clann na hÉireann 81–4, 133

Clann na Poblachta 9, 33, 36, 76, 95
Clarke, Joe 58, 116
'Claude Gordon' (Jack Bennett) 76
Clifford, Brendan 84
Clutterbuck, Sir Alexander 11
Coddington, D.H. 158
Comerford, Máire 64, 143
Comhar na gComharsan 31, 36, 76, 80, 182
Committee for Democratic Elections 68
Committee for Revolutionary Action 107
Communist Party of France 32, 60, 161
Communist Party of Great Britain 58, 64–5, 69–70, 74–5, 79, 82, 84, 108, 111, 133, 153, 155, 161, 167
Communist Party of Ireland 4, 70, 74, 156, 183
Communist Party of Northern Ireland 64, 67–8, 70, 72, 76–7, 89, 106–7, 121, 124, 129–30, 137–9, 141, 144, 152–3, 159, 163, 167–8, 183, 192
Conlon, Vincent 113
Connolly Association 12, 20, 34, 40, 50, 58, 64–6, 71, 73, 75, 80–4, 91, 123, 133, 139, 153, 167, 183
Connolly Clubs 73–4
Connolly, James 34, 40, 42, 47, 58, 69, 73, 88, 96, 104
Connolly Youth Movement 137–8, 159
Conway, Cardinal Charles 23
Corcoran, Roderick 47
Corish, Brendan 29
Corrigan, Adrian 176
Corriston, Inspector 134
Cosgrave, Liam 94
Costello, Seamus 18, 45, 57–8, 88–91, 96, 109–10, 112, 115–16, 122, 125–7, 131–4, 139–41, 145, 153, 156, 160–2, 171–2, 181, 183
Coughlan, Anthony 19, 52–3, 60, 65, 70, 72–4, 79–80, 82, 105–7, 121–2, 138, 144, 152–3, 156, 166–8, 182

Counihan, Professor 17
Cowan, Peadar 36
Craig, William 21, 102, 109, 141, 146, 160
Crofts, Rev. A.M. 34
Cronin, Seán 10–1, 13, 27, 63–5, 71, 81
Cruise O'Brien, Conor 141, 174
Cumann na mBan 137, 182
Cummins, Liam 140
Currie, Austin 159

Dalton, Liam 136
Daltún, Colm 135
Davitt, Michael 47
Dawson, George 154
De Burca, Mairín 58–9, 115–16, 127, 139
De Chardin, Teilhard 37
De Rossa, Proinsias 104
De Valera, Éamon 11, 35, 39, 83, 95, 98, 101
Devenny, Samuel 160
Devlin, Bernadette 141–2, 160, 164–5, 192
Devlin, Paddy 173, 177
Diamond, Harry 102
Dillon, Joe 136
Doherty, J. 48
Dolley, Michael 67, 106–7
Donnelly, Francie 171
Douglas, C.H. 58
Dowling, Seamus 177
Doyle, Joe 134
Driver, Frank 110
Dublin Housing Action Committee 104, 154
Dunne, James 131
Dunne, Seán 60, 104, 115, 133, 162, 178, 183
Dunne, Seán (TD) 65
Dunphy, Walter 24, 92

Early, Packie 75
Éire Nua 72, 116

Emsav 32
English, Richard 193
EOKA 11, 41, 100
Erskine, Lord 102
ETA 32, 132

Fagan, Niall 116
Fahey, Fr. Denis 33, 42
Fahy, Fr. John 32
Fallon, Richard 136
Farrell, Michael 160
Faulkner, Brian 16, 146
Faulkner, Pádraig 169–70
Feehan, Tadgh 83
Fianna Fáil 10, 12, 32, 35–6, 39, 41,
  66–7, 69, 76–7, 80, 82, 83, 95,
  124–5, 129–30, 154–6, 159, 166–7,
  170–2, 174–81, 189–91
Fianna Uladh 13
Fine Gael 9, 30, 35, 65, 77, 80, 83, 88,
  94, 124–5, 129
Fitt, Gerry 103
Fitzgibbon, Constantine 174
Fitzpatrick, Michael 96
Flanagan, Oliver J. 98
Fleming, John 133, 170, 173–4, 177
Flood, Michael 133
Flynn, Barry 14
Foley, Denis 46–8, 60, 89, 110
Foley, Gerry 172
Forrest, Anna 160
Fouere, Yann 32
Franco, Francisco 32
Fuchs, Klaus 72
Furnival Jones, Martin 99–100, 102

Garland, Seán 10, 15, 22–3, 33–5,
  40, 49, 55–6, 73, 88–90, 95–9,
  110–11, 122, 125, 127, 131, 136,
  139–40, 142, 159, 162, 172, 177–8,
  189
Gibbons, Jim 171
Gilchrist, Andrew 134, 147–8, 154,
  156–9, 162, 166–7, 170, 174–6
Gilmore, Eamon 189

Gleeson, Dan 91
Gollan, John 167
Goulding, Cathal 11, 15, 18–9, 23–4,
  40, 45, 48–9, 51–3, 55, 57–8, 60,
  63–4, 70–3, 80–2, 84, 88, 91, 95, 99,
  106–10, 112, 115–16, 120–2, 124–7,
  130–4, 137, 139–41, 145, 153,
  156–7, 159, 162–3, 166–7, 170–4,
  177–9, 182, 184, 191
Graham, Peter 136
Gramsci, Antonio 81
Greaves, Charles Desmond 6, 20, 65,
  71–83, 91, 122–3, 133, 138–9, 141,
  156, 167, 183
Greene, Daniel 145
Griffith, Arthur 28, 69
Grogan, Larry 46, 110, 116
Grose, Francis 98

Hamilton, Rev. William 34
Harris, Eoghan 105
Harris, Noel 168
Harrison, George 113
Haughey, Charles 13, 15, 21–2, 135,
  155, 169–74, 177, 183
Haughey, Pádraig (Jock) 135, 170–1,
  173
Healy, Denis 163
Heaney, James C 20
Heatley, Fred 64, 106–7, 145
Hefferon, Michael 169, 173
Hillary, Patrick 164–5
HMS *Bloodhound* 23
HMS *Brave Borderer* 92
HMS *Ghurka* 23
HMS *Lofoten* 23–4, 92
HMS *Malcolm* 23
HMS *Relentless* 23
HMS *Virago* 23
Holstein, Jakobus 157
HORSECOPER (RUC informant) 10,
  100
Hume, John 107
Hunter, W.T. 12
Hyde, Douglas 79

Internationalists 154
Irish Communist Group 136
Irish Democrat 19, 40, 70, 73–4, 80,
    83–4, 88, 98, 109, 125–6, 132, 138,
    183
Irish Labour Party 30, 37, 48, 53, 65,
    71, 76, 80, 82, 88, 96, 98, 105,
    107–8, 124–5, 130, 141–2, 154–5,
    157, 165
Irish Republican Veterans of
    America 19
Irish Revolutionary Forces 21
Irish Socialist 30, 137, 142, 183
Irish Workers League 12, 34, 69–71,
    74–7, 80
Irish Workers Party 4, 64, 69, 72, 79,
    82, 88, 90–1, 107–8, 110–11, 121–2,
    124, 126, 129–31, 133, 137–9,
    141–3, 157, 163, 167, 183
Irish Workers Voice 69, 76
Irish Youth 74

Jenkins, Roy 101, 103
John XXIII 30, 36
Johnston, Máirín 65
Johnston, Roy 2, 5, 19, 23, 45, 48,
    51–2, 55, 57, 59, 63, 65–81, 83,
    89–91, 94–5, 103, 107, 110–12,
    114–16, 122, 124–8, 131–4, 136,
    138–9, 141–5, 153, 155–7, 161–3,
    166, 172, 174, 181–3, 191
Joint Intelligence Committee 3, 15,
    99–102, 157, 169, 178

Kavanagh, Noel 17, 34, 63–64, 124
Keane, Frank 136–7
Keating, Justin 65–6
Keating, Michael 41
Keegan, Mairín 136
Kelleher, Derry 37, 140, 143
Kelly, Dalton 126
Kelly, Edward 24
Kelly, James 169–74, 177
Kelly, John 173
Kennedy, Paddy 173

Khrushchev, Nikita 77
Kiernan, Thomas 35
Koln, Johannes 158

Lane, Jim 10, 15, 82, 107–8, 128, 133,
    135–6, 169, 173
Larkin, Denis 88
Larkin, Jim 40
Lawless, Gery 14, 84
Lemass, Seán 12–13, 21–2, 35, 38–9,
    57, 68, 70, 78, 88, 96, 99, 176
Lenihan, Brian 60, 92, 94, 97–8, 105,
    156
Leo XIII 11, 29–3
Leonard, Lorcan 64
Lewis, Saunders 32
Lia Fáil 32–34, 40
Lloyd, Myrddin 39
Lynch, Jack 28, 37, 134, 143, 145, 154,
    156, 158–9, 164–5, 168–9, 174,
    176–7, 191
Lynch, Jack (WTS) 64
Lynch, Patrick 27
Lynch, Walter 59, 116, 127

Mac an Bheatha, Proinsias 42
Mac an Fháili, Ciarán 64
Mac Anna, Tomás 96
Mac Aonghusa, Proinsias 59, 107, 171,
    178
McAteer, Eddie 174
McBurney, Malachy 116, 172
McCabe, Jack 108, 171
McCann, Eamonn 84, 160
McCann, Hugh 22–4, 147, 154, 158,
    176
Mac Cárthaigh, Gearóid 133
Mac Cathmhaoil, Caoimhín 127, 163
McCaughey, Terence 168
McCloskey, Francis 163
McConnell, Robert 100–2
McCormick, James 162
Mac Curtain, Tomás 11
Mac Dara (Richard Roche) 22, 38, 40,
    166

Mac Eoin, Uinseann 63–4, 67, 106–7, 121, 141
Mac Giolla, Tomás 17–8, 20, 45, 57–60, 88, 92, 100, 106, 110, 114–16, 125, 127, 136, 138, 140, 162, 180, 182
McGirl, John Joe 9
McGlade, Frank 116
McGuire, Maria 104
McGurran, Malachy 110, 132, 140–1, 160
McHugh, Roger 64
McInerney, Michael 94
McKee, Billy 179
McKeown, Michael 64, 143
MacLennan, Sir Ian 13, 100
Mac Liam, Cathal 64, 81, 91, 107, 122, 126, 153
McLogan, Patrick 11, 15, 17, 19, 36, 38
McMahon, Philip 9, 21, 133
Macmillan, Harold 38
McMillan, Liam 106, 141, 172, 179
McMullen, Brigadier General 165
McQuaid Archbishop John Charles 17
McQuillan, Jack 13
Mac Stíofáin, Seán 11, 40, 45, 49, 56–7, 75, 95, 107, 110–13, 115–16, 123, 125–6, 131–2, 139–40, 157, 163, 166, 172, 178–9
Mac Thomáis, Éamonn 107, 116, 127, 141
Mac Tiomanaí 47
Magan, Tony 11, 15, 17–18
Maguire, Air Marshal 99
Mallon, Kevin 159
Mandel, Ernest 137
Maria Duce 33
Martin, Leo 179
Matthews, George 167
Meade, Tony 34, 40, 46, 51, 60, 67, 88–9, 93, 97, 107, 109–10, 112, 120–1, 125
Mellows, Liam 73, 122, 128
Mills, Michael 180

Milner, W.H. 33
Milotte, Mike 79
Mitchell, Tom 14–15, 18, 40, 58, 69, 73, 88, 103, 110–12, 116, 127, 141, 160, 169, 183
Molloy, J.G. 134
Monaghan, Jim 178
Moore, Dan 139
Moore, Dr. Edward 12–13
Moore, Hughie 167
Morgan, H.T. 176
Mulcahy, Patrick 179
Murphy, Brian 33
Murphy, Brian (Clann na Poblachta) 67
Murphy, John 10

National Progressive Democrats 13, 69
Nelsons Pillar 93–4, 104
New Books 74
Nkrumah, Kwame 37, 59
Nolan, Liam 110, 113
Nolan, Sam 157
Northern Ireland Civil Rights Association (NICRA) 2, 6, 105, 107, 152, 159–60, 168, 176–7, 192
Northern Ireland Labour Party 67, 77
North, Robert 145

Ó Brádaigh, Ruairí 9, 11–15, 17, 19, 20, 40, 46, 49, 51, 56–8, 73, 94, 107, 110–11, 115, 136, 138, 163, 167, 179, 189
Ó Brádaigh, Seán 15, 17, 29, 45, 47, 52–3, 59, 69, 72–3, 79, 81, 89, 107, 110, 115–16, 125, 127, 131, 138–40, 163, 178, 182
O'Brien, Terry 107
O'Callaghan, Seán 64
O'Casey, Seán 73, 122
Ó Ceallaigh, Pádraig 18
Ó Cionnaith, Seán 84
Ó Conaill, Dáithí 14, 64, 72, 169–70, 179
O'Connell, Emmet 29
O'Connell, John 105

O'Connell, Maisie 65
O'Connor, Donal 114
O'Connor, Thomas 159
O'Donnell, Catherine 103
O'Donnell, Peadar, 27, 35, 40, 66, 76, 122, 168
O'Donoghue, Phil 21, 47, 93
Ó Drisceoil, Ruairí 116
Ó Dubhghaill, Tomás (Tom Doyle) 10, 29, 33–4, 38, 182
O'Dwyer, Pádraig 134–5
Ó Gadhra, Nollaig 22
O'Hanlon Eineachan 9
O'Hanlon, Fergal 9
O'Higgins, Tom 98
O'Kelly, J.J. 35
O'Kelly, Kevin 154
O'Leary, Michael 65–7, 80–1
O'Mahoney, George 136
O'Mahoney, Seán 15, 18
O'Malley, Des 134
O'Malley, Professor 17
Ó Mongáin, Seamus 66, 182
Ó Moráin. Micheal 155–6, 173
Ó Murchú, Eoin 171
O'Neill, Brendan 136
O'Neill, Charlie 134
O'Neill, Fr. Michael 71
O'Neill, Terence 96, 98–9, 103, 106, 109, 143–4, 146–7, 159–60, 176
O'Regan, Jim 64
O'Riordan, Michael 69, 107, 133, 137, 141, 156, 167
O'Sullivan, Redmond 125
O Tuathail, Seamus 120, 153, 167, 174, 182

Paisley, Ian 106, 109, 130
Palme Dutt, R. 167
Parker, K.A.L. 100
Parnell, Charles Stewart 89
Parsons, Denis 170
Peck, John 184
Peoples Democracy 7, 144, 152–3, 160, 178, 191, 193

Peoples Voice 135
Philbin, Bishop William 35
Piper, Peter 158
Pius X 31
Pius XI 31
Plough 65, 75
Pocock, Tom 174
Prince, Simon 132, 152, 191
Princess Margaret 22
Promethean Society 74–5
Puirseál, Niamh 66

Quinn, Brian 110, 116, 159

'Raferty, A' (Paddy Carmody) 77
Randall, Malcolm 173
Redmond Seán 167
Rees, Merlyn 160
Regan, Paddy 167
Republican Congress 60, 73, 92
Republican News (Cork) 133
Republican Review 35
Rice, John Joe 9
Roche, Richard 38, 63, 67–9
Rote Armee Faktion (RAF) 132
Ruane, Tony 116, 127
Ryan, Alphonsus 64
Ryan, Des 154
Ryan, Frank 27, 35, 40
Ryan, Mick 14–15, 88, 122, 127, 132, 137, 167, 171–2
Ryan, Monica 127
Ryan, Richie 94

Saoirse 34
Saor Éire (Cork) 135–6
Saor Éire Action Group 134–7, 170, 177
Saor Uladh 12–14, 70, 93
Savage, Jim 82, 133, 159
Scanlon, Rory 105
Scéim na gCeardcumainn 66
Scullion, John 102
Shannon, Martin 19
Sinclair, Betty 106, 153, 159

Skorzeny, Otto 157
Smith, Chief Inspector 21
Socialist Youth Movement 74
Soskice, Frank 98–9
South, Seán 9, 33
Spence, Gusty 102
Stapleton, Ned 74–5
Steele, Jimmy 162–3
Stewart, Bob 74
Stewart, James 152, 167
Stewart, Michael 134, 165
Stout, William 21, 101
Stunham, Lord 164
Sullivan, Jim 173
Sutcliffe, Phil 93
Swan, Seán 73, 141
Swanton, Desmond 21

The Promethean 75
The Separatist 104–5
Thicknesse, R.N. 93
Timoney, Eamon 34
Tozer, John 69
Traynor, Mick 15, 36
Treacy, Seán 179
Trinity College Republican Club 124,
    154
Troy, Sir Geoffrey 24

Tuairisc 67, 105–6, 108
Tully, Jim 154

UCD Republican Club 124, 137
Ulster Protestant Volunteers 158
Ulster Volunteer Force 102
Union Democratique Bretonne 32
Unity 124, 138
Ustimenko, Yuir 184
U Thant 158

Voice of the North 169, 174, 176–7

Walsh, Dick 180
Walsh, Liam 136
Ward, Peter 102
Whelan, Charles 165
Whitaker, T.K 28
White, Des 124
White, Harry 64
Williams, Eddie 64, 116, 128, 179
Wilson, Harold 99, 101–3, 109, 145–7,
    159, 161
Wolfe Tone Weekly 35

Young Ireland 74
Young Ireland Club 79
Young Socialists 138, 153